GROUNDS FOR UNDERSTANDING

GROUNDS *for* UNDERSTANDING

Ecumenical Resources for Responses to Religious Pluralism

Edited by

S. Mark Heim

WILLIAM B. EERDMANS PUBLISHING COMPANY
GRAND RAPIDS, MICHIGAN / CAMBRIDGE, U.K.

© 1998 Wm. B. Eerdmans Publishing Co.
255 Jefferson Ave. S.E., Grand Rapids, Michigan 49503 /
P.O. Box 163, Cambridge CB3 9PU U.K.

Printed in the United States of America

03 02 01 00 99 98   7 6 5 4 3 2 1

Library of Congress Cataloging-in-Publication Data

Grounds for understanding: ecumenical resources for responses to
    religious pluralism / edited by S. Mark Heim.
        p.   cm.
    Includes bibliographical references.
    ISBN 0-8028-0593-0 (pbk.: alk. paper)
    1. Religious pluralism — Christianity. I. Heim, S. Mark.
BR127.G74 1998
261.2 — dc21   97-35722
                                                    CIP

Contents

CONTENTS

Introduction

THE Fifth World Conference on Faith and Order at Santiago de Compostela in 1993 noted that the churches "are part of a global community marked by religious pluralism" and that varied responses to this situation sometimes cause divisions among Christians: "Christian *koinonia* has been and is diminished by mutual rejection among Christians because of different understandings of dialogue."[1] The experience of the World Council of Churches verifies this statement, for each of its world assemblies since Nairobi in 1975 has seen sharp disagreements among the representatives over the relative roles of evangelism and interreligious dialogue. The same conflicts can be found in most congregations or denominations. Christians do not agree on what to make of other religions or on how practically to relate to adherents of various traditions. In addition to divisions *among* religions, there are divisions nearly as deep *within* religions over how to respond to religious diversity.

The modern Christian ecumenical movement has been a quest for the visible unity of Christian churches, a quest which was deeply rooted in the modern missionary movement. Divisions among Christians were an obvious scandal in witness toward those of other traditions. Unity and mission went together, following Jesus' high priestly prayer in John 17 that "all may be one, in order that the world may

---

1. Subsection IV.C., "Common Witness in Dialogue with People of Other Living Faiths," in Thomas F. Best and Gunther Gassman, eds., *On the Way to Fuller Koinonia: Official Report of the Fifth World Conference on Faith and Order* (Geneva: WCC, 1994), p. 258.

1

believe." The missionary passion motivated many to overcome the traditional animosities between Protestants, Catholics, and Orthodox: they sought to come together, the better to evangelize the world. Today, interestingly, disagreements over mission itself can estrange Christians from each other more sharply than well-worn arguments about justification by faith, sacraments, or authority. Some Christians see the goal of Christian unity superseded by the search for a wider interfaith unity and cooperation.

In short, relations between the churches and relations between Christianity and other religions are increasingly bound together. This book began with the recognition that those who have long labored for Christian unity needed to directly address this major source of renewed division. A group of persons engaged in the Faith and Order movement set out to study the varying Christian responses to other faiths as a church-dividing issue, a conflict of beliefs.

There are many motivations for this study. Christians at all levels — councils of churches, denominations, congregations, individuals — are actively engaged in relationships with adherents of various traditions. These may range from formal dialogues to social or political cooperation to personal friendships to family relationships. If in an earlier age Christians often had theories about other faiths which were rarely tested by actual encounter, today they are as likely to have concrete experiences of religious pluralism for which they rarely find fully satisfying Christian categories. There is a need not just to map out new efforts or ventures, but to reflect on the very real interfaith relations already in place. In the National Council of Churches, for instance, the Working Group on Interfaith Relations maintains long-standing programs of dialogue and cooperation with Jews and Muslims, and is energetically expanding the relationship with other traditions as well. The Secretariat for Ecumenical and Interreligious Affairs of the National Conference of Catholic Bishops maintains an even wider circle of dialogues and cooperative relationships. There are innumerable other examples, local or global; some involving official church bodies, some composed of interested individuals. There is a steadily deepening texture of interfaith interaction. *Whether* this interaction exists or whether it *should* is no longer a question. What it means surely is.

There are important institutional issues faced by Christian leaders in regional or municipal councils of churches across the United States.

Many of these councils, which have been major expressions of the Christian ecumenical movement, are transforming themselves into interfaith organizations. This creates a tension for the Christian members between the desire to build creative and respectful relations with the faith communities in their area and the commitment to the unfinished agenda of Christian unity. Beyond this, local congregations, seminaries, church colleges and schools all face the need to educate and prepare people to respond faithfully to the religiously pluralistic environment in which we live and witness. The challenge to combine authentic Christian commitment and genuine openness to other faiths is a live one in virtually all Christian communities.

For all these reasons, it seems particularly urgent that Christians of all sorts, from varied confessional backgrounds, different denominations, and contrasting theological views, should talk together about this common challenge and the available resources within our Christian heritage to address it. The existing ecumenical movement is the logical, perhaps the providential vehicle for this conversation.

To take up these questions, a study group on responses to religious pluralism was formed in 1992 within the Working Group on Faith and Order of the National Council of Churches. The work of this study group was greatly enriched by a close collaboration with the Interfaith Working Group of the National Council and by consultation with the Ecumenical Networks Working Group.[2] A recent reorganization of the structure of the National Council resulted in all three of these working groups holding their regular meetings simultaneously in the same location. Thus it became possible to have an extended conversation between members of the Faith and Order group and members of the Interfaith Working Group.

As a result of two years of reflection together, a consultation on "Theological Resources for Responses to Religious Pluralism" was planned for the fall of 1994. It met October 13-14 in Newark, New Jersey, and brought together a rich mix of leaders from across the United States:

2. The Interfaith Working Group is that unit of the National Council which coordinates existing programs of Jewish-Christian relations, Muslim-Christian relations, and other initiatives in dialogue and cooperation. The Ecumenical Networks Working Group is composed of representatives from ecumenical or interfaith organizations at the state or regional level (e.g., the Rhode Island Council of Churches or the Washington, D.C., Interfaith Council).

representatives from the Faith and Order Working Group, the Interfaith Working Group, the Ecumenical Networks Working Group, and several Christian communions. Although the primary focus of this consultation was on confessional or denominational diversity within Christianity, a special effort was made to include the perspectives of those working directly at the "grass roots" either in interfaith relations or ecumenical organizations.

It is important to grasp the distinctive aim of this work. Religious pluralism gives rise to a wide variety of issues. There are, for instance, very particular theological, scriptural, and historical questions involved in any serious Jewish-Christian encounter. A quite different, if analogous, set of questions may come to the fore in Hindu-Christian discussion. And all of these will take on a special cultural flavor, according to whether the encounter is between communities in the subcontinent of India or in an industrial city in England. Quite different discussions ensue also, depending upon whether the focus is theological dialogue or resolution of urgent practical conflicts. The work of the Faith and Order study group in no way intended to duplicate these tasks specific to particular dialogues. Such work is already widespread. However, Christians who were deeply involved in such activities made it clear that they felt there was a profound need to explore and articulate the Christian grounding of such efforts. What is it about our faith that encourages and impels us into such relationships, apart from purely prudential or pragmatic motives? Those immersed in interfaith relations confessed that they often wished there were resources that articulated a fuller Christian theological justification for such relations or that more extensive attention was given to the contributions the learnings and insights from such relations might bring to Christian faith. We are aware that many Christian groups regard interfaith dialogue and relations with suspicion or hesitancy. This caution may be rooted in insecurity, a doubt that the traditional categories for interpreting non-Christian religions would retain their plausibility if exposed to too much empirical testing. Or it may be rooted in a conscientious reading of Christian faith which values such concerns primarily as auxiliary aspects of other imperatives: it is important to know enough about other people's religion to be able to care for them in a neighborly way or to evangelize them effectively, for instance. Likewise, enthusiasm for interfaith dialogue can reflect a diminished commitment to distinctively Christian practice, but it can also be rooted in a conscientious realization of that practice. These varying Christian perspectives provide yet another reason to explore the specifically Christian warrants for interfaith relations.

The outline of a distinctive task took shape from such considerations. The focus of this book is not the concrete dialogue between Christianity and another specific tradition, as for instance a discussion of Christian views of incarnation and Hindu conceptions of an avatar. Nor is it the well-trodden field of what is called in theological terms a "theology of religions" or in more secular language a "theory of religion." Such works debate familiar questions such as whether only one religion is true and all others false; whether all religions lead to the same end; whether there are truly contradictions between religious traditions; whether religions are more fundamentally defined as sets of propositional affirmations, social behaviors, or existential attitudes. In fact, Christians often divide among themselves along lines taken up in these discussions. One familiar typology categorizes attitudes toward religious pluralism under three headings.[3] Exclusivists hold that Christianity alone is a fully true and saving faith. Inclusivists affirm the ultimacy of the God revealed in Christ but maintain that the saving power of the Christ-event can also be manifest through or within religious traditions which do not explicitly claim it. Pluralists reject any notion of dependence or priority among the religions and maintain that various religions are independent paths to salvation.

The topic of this book obviously touches on these discussions. But its focus is rather different. It is an internal Christian discussion which seeks to explore the categories and resources that various Christian confessions bring to the interpretation of the realities of religious pluralism. It does not begin with the questions which quickly promulgate division: Is the Koran divine revelation? Can people be saved apart from Christ? Are all religions equally ordained by God? It begins instead one stage earlier in Christian discourse. Even before Christians disagree about the answers to such questions, in what specific Christian terms do they *conceive* the questions? Are they approached primarily in terms of God's purpose and plan in creation? Are they discussed primarily in terms of the work of the Holy Spirit? Are they addressed

3. Taken from Alan Race, *Christianity and Religious Pluralism* (Maryknoll, N.Y.: Orbis, 1982).

primarily with scriptural texts, and if so which ones? Are there voices or creedal authorities from tradition which provide the crucial norms for these issues? Our assumptions are rather basic. The first is that all Christian confessions do have such categories — not necessarily in the form of complex theories or theologies (even traditions which on many points have highly sophisticated and elaborate theological structures may not have such at this point) but rather in terms of theological concepts or scriptural images or community practices which are most readily deployed when issues of religious pluralism arise. Our different communions have theological "instincts," and one of the reasons Christians differ with each other over how to approach religious diversity is that they frame that diversity in contrasting terms. A second assumption is that our various denominations have rarely articulated these terms — and their integral relation to fundamental Christian conviction — in a coherent way.

The consultation from which the contributions in this volume are drawn was framed to address these issues. It is in the nature of an exploratory survey. The first stage in the modern ecumenical movement's search for Christian unity was "comparative ecclesiology." This was a basic dialogue in which the participants suspended for the moment adversarial debate or proposals for agreement. They simply tried to understand, descriptively, each other's actual beliefs and practices, to be certain that both sides were dealing with real and not phantom partners. This process also served to map the most important, substantive conflicts and to weed out those based on polemical distortions, misunderstanding, or contextual differences. The work here serves a similar function. The consultation intended to take a cross section of several Christian traditions, a comparative look at the primary resources they characteristically deploy to understand religious pluralism. We hope that this has some concrete benefits.

First of all, it should help clarify the differences that divide Christians about religious pluralism. At least some of these differences stem from the different ecclesial lenses through which we perceive the question. Precisely the categories that some Christians regard as the key to these issues are unfamiliar or confusing to others. The kind of interchange reflected in this book will hopefully make for better communication and understanding among Christians as they treat these issues. Second, this conversation should help expand the material available for a Christian response to pluralism. When we survey the various theological approaches of the churches to religious diversity, we provide a kind of inventory of resources that already exist for this task. The efforts at formulation and reformulation of understandings of religious pluralism in which we are all involved as individuals and churches can only benefit from this expanded sense of the existing possibilities. Conversations like this one offer hope for the eventual development of a truly ecumenical response to religious diversity — a response which would draw churches closer to each other because it would draw on strengths and insights from them all and which would enable the most authentic engagement with neighbors of other religious traditions. One of the fundamental questions at the heart of the ecumenical movement is whether the unity of Christian churches advances only at the cost of heightened estrangement from those outside that unity. Religious pluralism is the paradigm test of whether, as Christians have professed, unity in Christ is an aim pursued for the sake of the renewal of the whole creation and not as a rejection of the world outside the visible church.

These are large hopes. This book and the consultation from which it comes are only a small and limited step on the way. Even the spectrum of Christian voices heard here is limited, at best only an imperfectly representative sampling of the particular context in the United States. Since this is a beginning and not a conclusion, there is room and need for many more voices to be added. Even so, I trust that this volume will prove helpful to all those in the churches who are struggling to articulate and live an authentic response to religious diversity. It is on the one hand a reference work for understanding each other as we engage in this struggle. On the other hand it is a resource for transformation: we may find elements in the theology and insights of other Christians which might be incorporated in our own vision, enlarging and deepening it, and making it more than ever a shared Christian vision.

Many people played significant roles in bringing this project to completion. Most important are the members of the Responses to Religious Pluralism Study Group of the Faith and Order Working Group of the National Council of Churches. They conceived the plan for this consultation and did all that was necessary to make it a success. Their names are listed below. Dr. Norman Hjelm, director of the Faith and

Order Working Group, provided support for the formation of this study group and invaluable help at each step of the way. Jay Rock and Margaret Thomas from the Interfaith Working Group of the National Council of Churches took the initiative to develop a collaborative relationship which brought the members of our two groups into regular conversation. Representatives from the Ecumenical Networks Working Group of the National Council graciously gave their time to share experiences and challenges of interfaith relations in local contexts. Mr. Charles Van Hof of Wm. B. Eerdmans Publishing Company has provided both encouragement and guidance.

Newton, Massachusetts
March 14, 1995

S. Mark Heim for the Responses to Religious Pluralism Study Group

William Carpe
Mary Ann Donovan
Thomas Finger
Deirdre Good
Elizabeth Mellen
Paul Meyendorff
Lauree Hersch Meyer
Mozella Mitchell
Frederick Norris
Michael Rivas
Nehemiah Thompson

CHAPTER ONE

Accounts of Our Hope: An Overview of Themes in the Presentations

S. MARK HEIM

THIS brief essay offers one map of themes in the essays which follow.[1] I will sketch some of the major theological emphases which are illustrated in our papers: what we might call "confessional instincts" that bear on interfaith relations. The primary focus is on theological resources for responding to religious pluralism. Obviously religious pluralism is not just one thing, and there are many avenues of response to it. "Response" can take place in a dialogue about beliefs and doctrines, in explicit sharing of worship or spiritual practices, in work together on common social projects, or in the simple interactions of neighborliness and love in family, school, or town. We might call these, respectively, a dialogue of views, a dialogue of spirituality, a dialogue of action, and a dialogue of life.[2] Clearly Christian resources for interfaith encounter must encompass a spectrum of elements, some more directly relevant to one kind of encounter than another. This is an additional reason to value the fullest inventory of the spectrum of resources in the various Christian traditions.

If the whole Christian church is to meet the challenges of religious diversity faithfully, it will have to draw deeply upon both its catholicity

---

1. The comments here are mine. But I acknowledge with thanks the suggestions offered by members of the Responses to Religious Pluralism Study Group in response to earlier drafts of this essay.
2. The four are outlined in Samuel Ariarajah, "Pluralism and Harmony," *Current Dialogue* 25 (December 1993): 19.

and its ecumenicity. By catholicity I mean the church's extent across times and cultures. We manifest the church's catholicity when we consult and call upon the experience of Christians who have lived their faith in Christ in the unity of the Spirit in dramatically different circumstances. Catholicity can be very profoundly experienced within a single Christian community. But ecumenicity has to do with extending the scope of this consultation and unity to encompass Christian groups which at some point ceased to include each other as part of the one body, which ceased to practice this catholicity with each other. We need the wisdom of the whole church if we are to give a wholly faithful witness to the whole world.

The papers and — even more clearly — the discussion that flowed from them demonstrated the various theological streams that run through Christian approaches to religious pluralism. Conflicts may often be reduced to the language of exclusivism-inclusivism-pluralism or, even more bluntly, to a forced choice for Christians and churches: evangelism or dialogue. But any significant conversation reveals a more complex network of theological views. Those who share a similar theological approach may yet end up with sharply opposed conclusions. And those who find themselves on the same side of blunter divisions about pluralism may often find, on closer examination, that they arrive there by quite different routes. Divisions over how to react to religious diversity run right through communities that have a common theological tradition. This does not mean that those traditions are irrelevant — only that they are of ample breadth to allow such disagreements to be conducted on shared terrain.

It is clear that Christians mine three general veins of theological resources in approaching issues of religious pluralism. One delves into the implications of trust in God as the sole source of a unitary creation. Here a range of images and ideas comes into play: image of God, general revelation, the light of reason, covenants with Eve and Adam and with Noah. Religious diversity is addressed in terms of a fundamental universal fit between humanity and its Maker, an imprinting of the divine nature in all that is and an endowment of persons with the capacity to perceive that imprint.

A second theological vein runs through the depths of christological confession. Questions about the pluralism of faiths are explored through what we might call preincarnate, incarnate, and postresurrection modalities. An example of the first would be "logos" christological reflections, concerning the ways in which the trinitarian Word of God is already active in the world by virtue of participation in creation and therefore can be known in some measure apart from the gospel. The second involves consideration of the ways in which various faiths might providentially prefigure or reflect the concrete historical reality of Jesus Christ: ways, to use Reinhold Niebuhr's phrase, in which the Messiah is truly expected. The third modality concerns the active presence of the risen and living Christ to those in various religions, perhaps "incognito," on the model of Jesus' resurrection appearances. In all these cases, the touchstone is christological — whether it has to do with Jesus' teachings or with the scope of the benefits of Christ's reconciling work.

The third vein of theological reflection turns to the work of the Spirit and focuses on the continued freedom and providence of God's action. The Spirit blows where it will, and the religions can be viewed through the lens of the possibility of this direct, spontaneous action and presence of God: a possibility which is fulfilled whenever God's creation fulfills some portion of its ordained beauty, justice, and love.

All of the writers are committed to trinitarian faith and therefore none affirms any of the approaches just noted to the exclusion of the others. But the trinitarian themes are enriched and combined in distinctive ways by the various Christian confessions. One prime source for this richness is the diversity of theological sources: Scripture, tradition, reason, experience. Each of the themes can be developed with different patterns of emphasis on these sources, and with varying emphases *within* each source. This variety is wonderfully illustrated in the papers in this book.

Jay Rock's paper, for instance, strikes strongly the classic notes of the Reformed tradition: divine sovereignty and freedom, the centrality of Scripture, the extent of human sin. Because of the limitations of human understanding and pride, we must question any presumption to have control of God's revelation and action. Because of God's sovereign freedom, we must in humility refrain from setting boundaries to the divine providential work with all people. Because of Scripture's unequivocal witness to Christ, we must not suspend our own christological convictions in dialogue. These concerns set a matrix for interfaith issues. Clearly in the past these themes have sometimes been amplified in uncompromising opposition to the religious value of other traditions. God's sovereign freedom and our inherently partial understanding are taken as key reasons to affirm the unique truth of Christian revelation over against all other options. If this conclusion seems difficult or uncomfortable in some ways, we must recognize that God is free to dispose the universe in ways that transcend our comprehension, particularly since our understanding is both finite and darkened by sin. Rock demonstrates that these fundamental themes can be developed in other ways, however, by Protestants no less convinced of their validity. Commitment to the freedom of God, a lively fear of idolatry, and a healthy sense of one's own sinfully distorted judgment — these can all coalesce into a powerful mandate for openness and humility in relation to the religions.

Dan Martensen demonstrates how Lutheranism articulates some similar classical Reformation convictions in a distinctive way. The language and images Lutherans are apt to utilize for interfaith reflection include the hidden God, law and gospel, the paradoxical quality of saving faith (which finds us at the same time sinners and yet justified), God's "left-hand" and "right-hand" kingdoms, and the theology of the cross. Though these are all centered in Christ, they likewise contain powerful cautions against presumptions to bind God's hands or to idolize one's own religious tradition. As with the Reformed tradition, creation is a primary point of reference. Martensen points to the theme of N. F. S. Grundtvig, "first of all human beings, then Christians," as an example of the way in which the natural "folk-life" of members of various cultures, including their religion, might serve as an echo of the Word of God. The resources mentioned tend perhaps toward stressing a negative commonality between Christianity and other traditions, with both sharing the negative aspects of "religion" as a human enterprise. But using the same terms, many Lutherans find grounds for a more positive analysis of world faiths.

Michael Oleksa's paper presents quite a different texture. In continuity with Orthodox views, Oleksa places interfaith questions in a context of creation and eschatological fulfillment. From a deeply sacramental and liturgical sensibility, he stresses the cosmic scope of God's action. All of nature and all history are a manifestation of God's power and a theater for communion with God. In the eschaton this entire creation will be revealed in its transfigured condition, transparent, as it were, to the triune God whose energies sustain and uphold it. There is a universal, inherent longing for God in nature and humanity, which expresses itself in myriad, sometimes confused, ways. "Salvation is an eternal process and everyone is part of it." This outlook combines an unshakeable conviction that the triune God known in Christ is the source and end of all of creation with the confidence that all of nature and all human aspiration find their place in the final consummation.

This cosmic and eschatological perspective in fact can lead to a distinctive practice of mission, of which Oleksa gives some examples. He stresses that the cosmic dimension of many "traditional" or tribal religions is an authentic reflection of the fundamental truth that Christianity confesses. Without following the specific points of his presentation further, we can note here that the theological themes he highlights can also be developed in contrasting ways. The cosmic presence of the triune God in creation can serve as a premise for an argument that various religions authentically express the longing for unity, the many faces of the divine energies within human cultures. Or it can serve as an assumption from which to stress that the unity is incomplete and unrecognized until people know that it coheres in Christ.

The Roman Catholic Church undoubtedly has the most extensive network of interfaith activities of any Christian confession, the largest and most diversified contingent of theologians focusing on these issues. The Vatican II document *Nostra Aetate* provides the modern charter for this work, which is institutionalized in the Vatican Secretariat for Relation with Non-Christians. Mary Ann Donovan suggests that the implication of recent Catholic theology is that "proclamation cannot be the only mode of Christian presence to others." Two fundamental convictions must be upheld: the centrality of Christ in the salvation of the world, and the authentic offer of salvation to all persons. These convictions correlate with a twofold mode of presence: "proclamatory and dialogical, with dialogue the preferred mode in interfaith work."

She suggests three primary resources in contemporary Catholicism for interreligious relations. The first is the experience of Christian ecumenism, which since Vatican II has led to theological reflection on the hierarchy of truth and the possibilities of unity based on less than complete doctrinal agreement. The second is the transformation of mis-

13

sions, in the manner of pioneers like de Nobili and Ricci, to include dialogue with other religions whether at the level of neighborliness, doctrine, social action, or religious experience. The third is attention to popular religion, which often includes cross-cultural and multireligious elements. The emphasis in Catholic tradition on the *sensus fidei* provides a rationale for valuing this symbolic form of pluralistic harmony. The sacramental perspective which she stresses finds God's presence not only in explicit liturgical acts but also in symbols and rituals from other cultures and religions.

Tom Finger's presentation of Mennonite views highlights another set of theological resources. These are centered on Scripture and on the practice of community life and personal ethics. Those Christians descended from the Anabaptist movement place their primary emphasis on the Jesus of the Gospels. The Christian life is preeminently the practice of following after that Christ in concrete discipleship. Interfaith relations, then, tend to be cast in the frame of orthopraxis, not doctrine or ritual. Because of the experience of centuries as a dissenting minority within Western Christendom — often under persecution — Anabaptists are suspicious of authoritative definitions of true Christianity and of any attempts to impose it on others. Their theology is particularly sensitive to the imperialistic possibilities in interreligious relations, whether expressed in military forms or in cultural absolutism. This by no means precludes an evangelical witness to Christ. At the heart of Mennonite life and practice is a conviction that gospel practice is profoundly countercultural. The issues of interfaith relations are more likely cast in the terms of Matthew 25: a test of discipleship as following Christ's teaching, whether the name is known and confessed or not. However, as with all the other Christian groups, this framework does not in itself require only an "exclusivist" or "pluralist" conclusion. One may hold firmly to the Anabaptist Christology with its stress on discipleship and believe that this discipleship is impossible without direct relation to Christ's person in the community of believers. Or one may affirm that wherever the way of the cross is lived, the humble Christ is received.

Peter Slater's contribution to this volume stresses worship and sacrament as the key framework for interfaith questions. Much that has already been said about the Orthodox and Roman Catholic traditions is likewise part of the texture of the Anglicanism he describes. But there is a particular emphasis on spirituality: the interfaith issue is whether we can worship together. Ritual and living spiritual practice, "the ethos of the worshiping communities," are crucial. To know of God doctrinally is less important than to know God in relation in prayer, Eucharist, and experience. If Anabaptism tends to look particularly to a moral, ethical, and social praxis, Anglicanism tends to look particularly to spiritual praxis. From the Anglican perspective dialogue which does not become at some level the attempt to understand and share in each other's worship and ritual practices is likely to seem thin and insufficient.

Slater notes that for Anglicans historically a Logos Christology has been the high road for reflection on religions. This involves the conviction that "Jesus is Christ: but Christ is not only Jesus." A crucial pattern was set by Christian theology's assimilation of Neoplatonism in the early centuries, an assimilation that involved at least a minor "conversion" of theology to the semireligious system it absorbed. But Neoplatonic assumptions about absolute truth and knowledge need not be essential parts of Christian faith. Slater suggests that in a tradition which stresses the development of doctrine as a process integral to the church as an historical communion, other religions can be best seen as candidates for this kind of mutually transformative "syncretism." Conflicts over religious pluralism within the Anglican communion would then most likely take the form of disagreement over how far the non-absolute, prototypical confessions of theology can be "developed" without breaking the continuity and unity of the worshiping life of the church.

The Methodist tradition, stemming from the Anglican, of course shares much with it. John Wesley did not provide any extended treatment of issues of religious diversity. But Nehemiah Thompson speaks in his paper of a "Wesleyan syndrome" or orientation on the subject. Methodists look to Scripture, tradition, reason, and experience as theological sources. But the most distinctive aspects of their use of this "quadrilateral" are shaped by Wesley's own thought on one hand and by the particular place of holiness in Methodist experience on the other. The emphasis on complete sanctification and Wesley's refusal to polarize nature and grace lead to a powerful presumption of prevenient grace. Grace is available to all to move toward perfection, the highest religious experience. The important thing to Wesley, Thompson suggests, is not where we start, but how energetically we make use of the grace available to us to progress toward moral and spiritual transformation. Wesley often affirmed that nominal or immoral Christians were more "pagan" than upright Muslims or Jews.

Thompson outlines an interesting mediating position between the Anglican and Anabaptist views we have already described. Methodism sifts its theological resources with fierce practicality for what most advances the path toward holiness, with holiness understood to encompass both a strong moral element (similar to the Anabaptist emphasis) and a strong spiritual element (similar to the Anglican emphasis). Among Methodists, discussions of the religions are likely then to put special emphasis on the extent to which this fundamental journey toward holiness can be seen as continuous with paths in other traditions. Conflicting answers will often result from varying views of whether personal relation with Christ and confessional commitment to Christ are constitutive foundations of holiness itself as Methodists understand it, or whether it is sufficient to hold that they are integral to the path Christians take toward holiness.

The Christian confessions we have mentioned so far are among those which, as institutions, have been relatively active in formal interfaith dialogue efforts. This does not mean there is always widespread enthusiasm for the efforts in those churches, nor that any fully developed theological rationale is given — or accepted — for them, any consensus that these efforts express the very logic of Christian faith rather than reflect an optional interest. But we turn now to confessions whose voices are, if anything, even more crucial for our purposes: those where religious pluralism may be viewed from a more evangelical perspective. Very significant constituencies and perhaps in some cases majorities in so-called mainline denominations share this perspective as well.

Mozella Mitchell provides an introduction to the theological resources of the African Methodist Episcopal (AME) Zion Church. Many of these are familiar from the legacies of Anglicanism and Methodism which live on in this communion. Like other black Methodist and Baptist bodies, the AME Zion Church was born out of the injustice and oppression African Americans experienced within white communions. This history gave rise to its own unique theological ferment, to distinctive theological views that bear on interreligious issues. Mitchell points out some fundamental characteristics of ecclesiology in her tradition, emphases on "the company of the elect," "the family of God," and "the nation of God." The AME Zion Church is understood as the company of the elect because it came into existence with a special mission: to create a truly free and godly people from those who had been, like Israel, carried into bondage. It understands itself as the family of God because it carried within itself the means of survival for its members. In an often hostile world it was their source of nurture, education, recreation, and support. "Nation of God" characterizes the AME Zion experience as well, indicating the consciousness that it stood for a people, carried a racial and cultural tradition that connected it to all African Americans as well as to African peoples.

The most characteristic theological resources that this tradition brings to the consideration of religious diversity reflect this history and ecclesiology. Scripture is a crucial source, interpreted with special sensitivity to some of its themes that are often muted in other communions. The multicultural character of Scripture, particularly the Hebrew Scriptures, stands out much more strongly here. The struggles for personhood and survival lead to clear priority for action that will meet the urgent needs for employment, legal rights, political dignity, and education. The fundamental conviction that the freedom struggle is God's mission for the church leads to a readiness to see cooperation in that struggle on the part of others, whatever their religious background, as participation in God's mission. In addition, a sense of the multireligious African background from which African Americans came to Christianity is still alive in many parts of the church. The kingdom of God plays a key role as a focal point for understanding how those of various faiths can relate to each other. This is not to say that there are not conflicts over religious pluralism within these churches also. Such conflict is not likely to arise over cooperation and common cause in the struggles mentioned but can come to the fore when issues of salvation and personal faith are raised. A strong theology of the kingdom or reign of God readily answers some interreligious questions, but leaves others still problematic.

James Deotis Roberts made a presentation at the consultation on the outlook of Baptists in a religiously pluralistic age. Unfortunately, the constraints of many other scholarly responsibilities prevented Dr. Roberts from preparing a text for inclusion in this volume. In his talk he noted that Baptists were an extremely diverse group and that unity was not easily achieved even within that family. Baptists are marked by the vigor with which they espouse a free-church, congregational polity; a covenantal structure in all their organizations; and voluntary, personal confession of faith as the key to Christian life and structure. Given their own history as dissenters under established Christian churches, Baptists have been strong advocates of religious liberty and were among the earliest in the United States to extend that liberty to non-Christian religions. However, Baptists have also been deeply committed to personal evangelism and most continue to focus their relations to other religions around a missionary mandate.

Black Baptist denominations have been separated from predominantly white ones by the racism which historically barred African Americans from full participation. This is part of the explanation for a different approach to ecumenism and interfaith relations among black Baptists, similar to that Mozella Mitchell noted for the AME Zion Church. Roberts observed that "biblical fundamentalism and the social gospel existed side by side without any awareness of logical conflict": to black Baptists "both contained the truth of the gospel." This has meant that black Baptists reached out readily to Jewish and Muslim, secular or interfaith alliances in common cause for social change. These alliances are grounded in a profound sense that liberation and deliverance are God's work, to which all people are called. But the relations between this interfaith social gospel and the "biblical fundamentalism" Roberts describes are rarely worked out.

Fred Norris writes out of the tradition of the Christian Churches/Churches of Christ. His paper is a fascinating companion to the Orthodox and Roman Catholic contributions since Norris, a patristics scholar himself, also places great emphasis on the early experience of the church but from the perspective of a modern, North American restorationist movement. The Christian Churches began as a movement eschewing denominational distinctions that was committed to Christian unity for the sake of mission. Three theological pillars of the tradition are the authority of Scripture (more specifically the normative model of the New Testament church), the evangelical imperative, and a strongly congregational polity. Agreement and disagreement about pluralism will be conducted in a nonconnectional ecclesial context, and will revolve principally around biblical models and the continuing practice of missionary outreach.

Consideration of religious pluralism must therefore begin with careful study of scriptural evidence. Norris points out that biblical material itself provides significant grounds to affirm God's providential action in diverse cultures and religions. But even more striking, he reflects on the way in which zealous and serious missionaries generate from their own experience continuing confirmation of these intimations. Because the Christian Churches originated with a passion for unity, Norris suggests there is a particular impetus to seek a *consensus fidelium* across denominations and time. On the subject of religions, this leads him to survey those in many periods of Christian history who combined uncompromising witness to Christ with respect for the divine hand in other traditions. Last of all, he notes that his tradition has been generally hesitant about the assumptions of Enlightenment modernity. This confluence of theological and philosophical views leads to a critical stance toward "pluralist" theologies but also toward the modern forms of exclusivism.

My colleague Sam Solivan, a member of the Assemblies of God, presents a paper which reflects the outlook of many in a wider Pentecostal movement as well. More than any of the other contributors, Solivan states clearly and graciously the views of many who are convinced that the theological resources they bring to issues of pluralism counsel a decidedly reserved attitude toward other religions and toward Christian attempts to "baptize" them or to place a high priority on dialogue. As a movement that is North American in origin, Pentecostalism has a paradoxical relation to the ecumenical movement. To a large extent it has judged mainline churches and their ecumenical alliances and interreligious conversations by the measure of their effect on the growth and vitality of the Christian community. By this standard, the judgment is a largely negative one. But Pentecostalism also understands itself as part of a dramatic and Spirit-led movement toward oneness, a movement which continues to sweep across denominational and cultural boundaries.

Solivan points out that in Pentecostal circles discussion of these questions will have to proceed with reference to scriptural and missiological commitments — similar to those mentioned in other connections above. But in addition the Pentecostal understanding of the Holy Spirit and the Spirit's role in individuals and in community provides a crucial reference point. He notes several of these pneumatological assumptions which he believes are likely avenues for further reflection on interfaith relations. Three primary attributes of the Holy Spirit are its freedom, its role in illuminating truth, and its characteristic work of empowerment. The conviction that the Spirit works in unbeliever and believer alike is at work wherever community is built across human boundaries, and often wells up far from the established sanctuaries of the churches. This is familiar ground for Pentecostals. The central emphasis upon the personal experience of reception of the Spirit also opens up a possible avenue of dialogue around other religious experiences, at least to the extent of "discerning the spirits." As Pentecostals worldwide are drawn largely from the ranks of the poor and marginalized, they also are particularly open to a theological view "from below" which focuses less on doctrine or church structure than concrete transformation and experience.

Floyd Cunningham, a member of the Church of the Nazarene, speaks for a Wesleyan holiness tradition not limited to that single denomination. This tradition has been deeply committed to leading people to Christian conversion, but it has been equally concerned to urge those converts "onward to entire sanctification and Christlikeness." Cunningham points out that there are two sides to the holiness stress on the work of the Holy Spirit. The first is prevenient grace. In good Wesleyan fashion, the Spirit is seen at work with all persons, leading them on toward communion with God in Christ and, specifically, beginning that moral and personal transformation which culminates in true holiness. Part of the universal benefit of Christ's atonement is this extension of moral power to all people. People who willfully reject the light they have, the work of the Spirit in their conscience and heart, may well condemn themselves. But likewise, Cunningham suggests, those who devotedly seek God by the light they are given can be saved, as the faithful fathers and mothers of the Old Testament or (according to Wesley) Socrates was. There is thus a certain freedom and mystery about the Spirit's prevenient work. However, the Spirit is equally the agent of the second blessing, of assurance and full sanctification. The holiness tradition reserves perhaps its most distinctive passion for the transformation of "bare" converts into Spirit-filled and Spirit-empowered, morally transformed Christians. This perspective, Cunningham seems to say, allows him to believe that God works within other religions to achieve in devout persons *prior* to any conversion that transformation which Christian nurture also seeks to realize after conversion. Even apart from the concern for final salvation, there is always good reason to evangelize for the sake of this "second blessing" and assurance.

Alone of our writers, Cunningham introduces the topic of dispensations, which plays such an important role for many Christians in dealing with these issues. The patriarchs before Christ, Christ's disciples before Pentecost: these were each living in their dispensations of grace, one the dispensation of the Father, the other the dispensation of the Son. In both cases their faith was saving faith. But in both cases it anticipated a fullness, assurance, and transforming power which the gift of the Spirit completes. We can understand then how in holiness circles disagreement over the evaluation of religious pluralism will operate with these categories, turning for instance on whether one should stress the Spirit's prevenient, even saving, work in other religions as an analogy to biblical dispensations or whether one should stress that the Spirit testifies always to Christ and that dispensations which fail to realize this fulfillment lose their redemptive power.

This brief summary cannot substitute for the richness of the essays themselves, but it provides a synoptic illustration of our aim in bringing the essays together in this book. What is only sampled here can be expanded and extended by the reader who compares and reflects on the various contributions. We can see that although our denominations may sometimes cast each other onto opposing sides, the "side" of interfaith dialogue or the "side" of evangelism, there is much more at work. Each communion brings its theological framework to the issues. Because our frameworks and language differ, we often miss the extent and manner in which others are seriously addressing the same questions we are, and seeking to do so out of the heart of our Christian faith and tradition. The more clearly and sympathetically we can hear each other, the more of that faith and tradition will be opened to us for the challenges of our pluralistic world.

CHAPTER TWO

Catholics and Interfaith Relations: A Place for Speakers, Listeners, and Intuition

MARY ANN DONOVAN

H UMAN life now requires of every society some kind of cross-cultural engagement; choice is confined to the quality and nature of that engagement. The century now ending has seen the definitive collapse of that geographical isolation which allowed the world religions space and time to develop separately. Roman Catholics formally entered the new era with Vatican II. The whole world was invited to become a conversation partner. Pope John XXIII had addressed his letter on peace[1] to the entire world; the Council summoned by Pope John addressed the world in *Gaudium et Spes*, which begins, "The joys and the hopes, the griefs and the anxieties of the men and women of this age, especially those who are poor or in any way afflicted, these too are the joys and hopes, the griefs and anxieties of the followers of Christ."[2]

1. John XXIII, the encyclical *Pacem in Terris*.
2. *Gaudium et Spes* (The Pastoral Constitution on the Church and the Modern World), no. 1. Other major documents important for ecumenical and interfaith relations include: *Lumen Gentium* (The Dogmatic Constitution on the Church); *Unitatis Redintegratio* (The Decree on Ecumenism); *Orientalium Ecclesiarum* (The Decree on the Catholic Eastern Churches); and *Nostra Aetate* (The Declaration on the Relationship of

---

This chapter was in press before the publication of the International Theological Commissions' document, "Christianity and the World Religions," *Origins* 27 (1997): 150-66.

But the world did not turn an eager ear. For centuries Roman invitations had come weighted with threats for the noncompliant. Catholics had believed and taught that non-Catholics were destined for hell. In 1442 the Council of Florence wrote:

> The Holy Roman Church . . . firmly believes, acknowledges and proclaims that no one outside the Catholic Church can partake of eternal life, and this includes not only pagans but also Jews, heretics and schismatics, but that they will end up in the eternal fire prepared for the devil and his angels, unless they become members of the Church before they die.[3]

It required a breathtaking turnabout for the Catholic Church to acknowledge respect for other Christians, let alone for non-Christian religions. Yet in 1965 Vatican II spoke of degrees of union founded in the one common Christian baptism,[4] and had this to say about the non-Christian religions:

> The Catholic Church rejects nothing which is true and holy in these religions. She has a high regard for the manner of life and conduct, the precepts and doctrines which, although differing in many ways from her own teaching, nevertheless often reflect a ray of that Truth which enlightens all human beings.[5]

The change is even more striking in light of this theologically more significant passage:

> Those [i.e., non-Christians, Jews, and Moslems being named] who, through no fault of their own, do not know the Gospel of Christ or his Church, but who nevertheless seek God with a sincere heart, and, moved by grace, try in their actions to do his will as they know it

---

the Church to Non-Christian Religions). Austin Flannery, O.P., gen. ed., *Vatican II: The Conciliar and Postconciliar Documents,* vol. 1 (Collegeville, Pa.: Liturgical Press, 1980), vol. 2 (Grand Rapids: Wm. B. Eerdmans Publishing Co., 1982), gives the English translation for the conciliar and selected postconciliar documents, and lists in vol. 1 sources for the complete documentation in the original languages, pp. xviii-xix.

3. Denzinger-Schoenmetzer, *Enchiridion Symbolorum,* 36th ed. (Barcelona: Herder, 1973), #1351.

4. *Lumen Gentium* 15.

5. *Nostra Aetate* 2.

through the dictates of their conscience — those too may achieve eternal salvation.[6]

Noting this series of changes, Redmond Fitzmaurice remarks that they reflect "an effort to give due weight to two experiences," one being the Christian experience that the salvation of the world was effected in Jesus Christ. So "in him alone, in whom God has reconciled all things to himself (II Cor 5:18-19), all men and women find the fullness of their religious lives."[7] But the contemporary situation requires that, alongside this theological experience, one must hold "the historical experience of true holiness of life and total God-centredness in the lives of many men and women who are not Christians."[8] So the Roman Catholic position affirms that all saving holiness is somehow a gift of God; yet, "in some way known to God alone, within the structures of their own religions . . . the saving mercy of God, won by Christ on the cross, is offered to non-Christians."[9] The effort is to maintain two insights central to Catholicism: fidelity to the centrality of Christ and conviction that salvation is offered to all.

Not even the more conservative pontificate of John Paul II has reversed this shift of stance. While his encyclical on the missions, *Redemptoris Missio,* affirms the desire and right of Catholics to proclaim the Christian message, it also makes clear that proclamation cannot be the only mode of Christian presence to others. The document should be read in context with other Vatican documents published with the approval of this pope.[10] To proclamation it is necessary to join another

6. *Lumen Gentium* 16.

7. Redmond Fitzmaurice, "What Will the Third Vatican Council Have to Say about Relations between Christians and Men and Women of Other Faiths?" (unpublished lecture delivered in the Ecumenical Summer School at Selly Oak Colleges, Birmingham, England, July 15, 1994), p. 6.

8. Fitzmaurice, p. 6.

9. Fitzmaurice, p. 7, with reference to *Gaudium et Spes* 22: "For since Christ died for all, and since all men and women are in fact called to one and the same destiny, which is divine, we must hold that the Holy Spirit offers to all the possibility of being made partners, in a way known to God, in the paschal mystery."

10. Fitzmaurice summarizes them (pp. 8-11), stressing the importance of the document issued in 1984 by the then Secretariat for non-Christians, *Bulletin* 19/2, where the pontiff in his introduction recalls that the commandment of love (John 15:12-17) is the basic Christian duty, more fundamental than the one to make disciples of all nations (Matt. 28:19).

mode of presence, dialogue. Catholics engaged in direct work with those of other faiths can and do reject the missionary approach in favor of a dialogical one. Thus the two fundamental convictions of the centrality of Christ and the universal offer of salvation correlate with a twofold mode of presence: proclamatory and dialogical, with dialogue the preferred mode in interfaith work.

Through Fitzmaurice's work we have accessed the current Roman Catholic *status quaestionis* on interfaith work. In its light, I will reflect on three topics. (1) What have Roman Catholics learned in the inter-Christian forum that can be of help to interfaith dialogue? Faithful to our insight into the centrality of Jesus Christ and our stress on the importance of doctrine, in dialogue with other Christians we have begun to develop a new reflective process that shapes how we speak to one another, so I name part 1 "The Speakers." (2) What do Catholics bring to interfaith dialogue? Roman Catholics have had long (though seldom happy) experience in interfaith engagement. I raise the possibility that we have something to contibute about listening, so part 2 is called "Listeners." (3) Finally, attending to the sacramental principle so important to Roman Catholicism, I ask how the study of popular religiosity might contribute to interfaith understanding. I am particularly concerned here with the intuitive function of the *sensus fidei*, so I name part 3 "Intuition."

Part 1: The Speakers

Proclamation that God accomplished human salvation in Jesus Christ has involved Christians in teaching, with doctrine serving both to unite and to divide believers from the very beginning. Later, doctrinal issues loomed large during the Reformation, and recently the effort to reach doctrinal agreement among Christian churches marked the entry of the Catholic Church into serious ecumenical discussions in the post–Vatican II era. The discussions, whether bilaterals or multilaterals, centered on theological points controverted since the sixteenth century. The Council's recognition that the truths of the faith are not created equal but rather exist in a hierarchical order "since they vary in their relationship to the foundation of the Christian faith,"[11] facilitated conversation,

11. *Unitatis Redintegratio* 11.

as did the Council's reconsideration of the notion of church itself, which allowed for more or less perfect communion.[12]

Focus on doctrine has led to considerable theological agreement. Catholics and other Christians are talking to one another, and even resolving ancient disagreements, but the fact is that the separate Christian churches remain firmly in place. Speaking together has led to theological understanding but not yet to unity. Yet it remains true that a degree of theological agreement is a prerequisite to unity for Catholics (as for many other Christians). Reflection on the faith-filled discipline governing the formal exercises in speech we know as bilaterals and multilaterals gives insight into a "hermeneutics of unity."

Today a centrist Roman Catholic position, outlined by Avery Dulles, begins with the recognition that a community of proclamation must share common faith, expressed in shared beliefs.[13] "Jesus is Lord" expressed the common belief of the earliest Christians. However, Dulles goes on to say that "complete agreement on all matters of doctrine is unattainable and ought not to be regarded as necessary."[14] Here he refers to a maxim dear to John XXIII: "In essentials unity, in nonessentials liberty, in all things charity." The insight the maxim reflects supports the idea of the hierarchy of truths mentioned above. Fundamental to that hierarchy are the Trinity and the incarnation, belief in which is shared by many if not most Christians. Dulles remarks that "where there is agreement in the basic essentials of the Christian faith, and the practice of valid baptism, a considerable measure of ecclesial communion exists."[15] Likewise, "in the Scriptures and the ancient creeds . . . the mainline churches, whether Orthodox, Roman Catholic, Anglican, or Protestant, already share in common a large fund of doctrinal materials."[16] What does this commonality entail? Most assuredly, "churches sharing such a wealth of common beliefs and the kind of worship and practice that flow from them ought not to regard one another as strangers."[17]

---

12. *Unitatis Redintegratio* 3 and 22.

13. Avery Dulles, "Ecumenism and the Search for Doctrinal Agreement," in *The Reshaping of Catholicism: Current Challenges in the Theology of Church* (San Francisco: Harper and Row, 1988), p. 228.

14. Dulles, p. 228.

15. Dulles, p. 232.

16. Dulles, p. 232.

17. Dulles, p. 232.

When divided Christians come together to speak, what unites them is already significant. If a first step in faith-filled speech is recognition of common belief, the next steps include recognition of the bonds of common worship and practice. Belief, worship, and practice: those who share such bonds are hardly distant associates. (Practice should not be overlooked; Robert F. Taft recently noted that behavior and not doctrine is a major problem between Orthodox and Roman Catholic in the former Soviet bloc.)[18] Thus stage one of a hermeneutics of unity.

Yet, doctrinal differences remain and cannot simply be disregarded if common belief remains important to unity. At this stage Dulles turns to the relationship between distinct doctrines and separate histories. Where such doctrines have been mutually intolerable, he suggests that "the different churches can come into closer communion if they recognize that one another's binding doctrines are, if not true, at least not manifestly repugnant to the revelation given in Christ."[19] To do so is to recognize mutual efforts at holding the same faith, while finding different implications in it. Continuing in the effort to follow the principle of the Council of Jerusalem, so to lay on others "no greater burden than necessary," a second step is to withdraw earlier anathemas. Thus, "the churches should insist only on the doctrinal minimum required for a mature and authentic Christian faith and that doctrines formulated in response to past historical crises should be reviewed carefully to see whether they must be imposed as tests of orthodoxy today."[20] The second stage in the hermeneutics of unity asks that one affirm a partner's effort to hold the faith of the gospel, and that one withdraw earlier condemnations where changed conditions warrant it.

Such steps pave the way for the kind of interpretation which has been employed in many bilaterals, allowing, for example, Lutherans and Roman Catholics in this country to come to mutual understanding on the meaning of justification.[21] For the purposes of this essay, these

18. Robert F. Taft, "The Catholic Church, the Society of Jesus, and the Challenges of Dialogue with the Eastern Churches: Personal Reflections of a Jesuit Orientalist," reported in T. Howland Sanks, "Ecumenical Winter or Spring?" *America* 171 (November 12, 1994): 5.

19. Dulles, p. 236.

20. Dulles, p. 237.

21. H. George Anderson, T. Austin Murphy, and Joseph A. Burgess, eds., *Justification by Faith: Lutherans and Catholics in Dialogue VII* (Minneapolis: Augsburg, 1985).

steps represent stage three of the hermeneutics of unity. What happens is that "through reinterpretation in a broader hermeneutical context, the limitations of controverted doctrinal formulations can often be overcome so that they gain wider acceptability."[22] Where agreement cannot be reached, is there an alternative simply to agreeing to disagree? It may be that "in some cases substantive agreement can be reached between two parties without the imposition of identical doctrinal formulations on each."[23] Dulles recalls an extremely helpful insight of Congar, who applies Niels Bohr's theory of complementarity to the theology of the Trinity:

> My study of the procession of the Holy Spirit in the Greek Fathers on the one hand and in the Latin tradition on the other has led me to recognize that there are two constructions of the mystery, each of which is coherent and complete — although each is unsatisfactory at some point — and which cannot be superimposed. It is a case for applying Bohr's saying, "The opposite of a true statement is a false statement, but the opposite of a profound truth can be another profound truth." The equivalence affirmed by the Council of Florence between *dia tou huiou* and *Filioque* is not really adequate. More than theology is at stake here. As Fr. Dejaifve has noted, it is at the level of dogma that the two constructions are to be found. However, these are two constructions of the mystery experienced by the same faith.[24]

A valid instance of dogmatic pluralism is to acknowledge the mutual complementarity of distinct formulations. This is at the same time a major step in a hermeneutics of unity.

Such a hermeneutics asks the speakers first to examine their common ground, next to acknowledge good intent and to withdraw past condemnations where changed conditions warrant it, then to broaden the hermeneutical context allowing for mutual understanding of controverted points, and finally (where agreement cannot be reached) to investigate whether there can be substantive agreement without identical doctrinal formulation. Respect for teaching, respect for the word

22. Dulles, p. 241.
23. Dulles, p. 242.
24. Yves Congar, *Diversity and Communion* (Mystic, Conn.: Twenty-Third Publications, 1985), p. 76, quoted in Dulles, p. 243.

both spoken and written, and respect for the authority of the word and the authority of the teacher of the word have long been characteristic of Catholicism. That other Christians have the word, that the authority of other Christian teachers deserves respect — this is a new stance for Catholics. If work with other Christians has enabled Catholics to seek first the common ground they hold with others, interfaith dialogue will benefit. In fact, the hermeneutical stages as outlined at the beginning of this paragraph would be useful in such dialogue. Unfortunately the first step appears deceptively simple. To examine common ground among Christians is one thing; it is another when one is engaging a different world religion.

Part 2: Listeners

Roberto de Nobili recognized this when in 1606 the twenty-eight-year-old Jesuit arrived at Madurai, in south India. Through his knowledge of the Tamil language he gained understanding of the caste system and found a way to gain entry into the society as a rajah. He then became a *sannyasi*, a man dedicated to God, learned Sanskrit, and memorized large portions of the Vedas. He studied the religion in its culture to find ways to explain Catholicism to the Indians. He himself dressed in red-ocher cloth, with a caste mark on his forehead. He pondered whether he could permit his Brahmin converts to wear the signs of their caste. His slightly older contemporary and confrere Matteo Ricci was engaged in a similar venture in China. Ricci was a linguist, mathematician, and natural scientist who joined to his mastery of the Chinese language a deep appreciation for the culture. He gained entry to China in 1583, and was granted mandarin status in 1594. He studied the Chinese world to find Catholic parallels for Chinese practices, rituals, and teachings. A major problem he faced was the internal significance of the rituals honoring the ancestors. Both de Nobili and Ricci were missionaries, but they were outstanding in their "conviction that Christianity did not necessitate the extermination of a non-European culture."[25]

25. William V. Bangert, S.J., *A History of the Society of Jesus* (St. Louis: Institute of Jesuit Sources, 1972), p. 159. I am dependent on this source for my information on de Nobili and Ricci.

At Vatican II Catholics heard an invitation to approach the world religions, not as missionaries, but to enter into dialogue and collaboration.[26] The goal has changed, but the project of understanding another religion within its culture remains — and remains challenging. De Nobili became a rajah and Ricci a mandarin in their quest to be all things for all in order to win all for Christ. What does today's quest ask? To enter into dialogue suggests entry into one another's experience. The possibility of entering the religious experience of anyone, much less that of a believer in another world religion, poses a variety of questions, which Jacques Dupuis summarizes: "To what extent is it possible and legitimate for the partners in the dialogue to enter into each other's experience and share a faith different from their own?"[27] He lays out two basic principles: first, one may not bracket one's faith, even provisionally. It is necessary to respect the integrity of one's deepest convictions, or else how can one speak of interreligious dialogue? This principle applies also to refraining from compromise in a syncretistic way, seeking facile compromise. The second principle is complementary: one may not absolutize what is relative out of lack of understanding or simple intransigence. In Dupuis's words: "As the seriousness of the dialogue forbids the relativization of deep convictions on either side, so its openness demands that what is relative not be absolutized, whether by incomprehension or intransigence."[28] What is called for is intelligent discernment; one must assume the posture of a faith-filled listener.

Fidelity to one's own convictions must be matched by respect for the other and the other's commitment. Openness around issues of fidelity as well as areas of ignorance is vital. In such circumstances, shared experience can be mutually revelatory. There is but one Spirit who works through all and in all; where truth is sought with sincerity, the Spirit is present.[29]

Do the requirements make it necessary that interreligious dialogue

26. *Nostra Aetate* 2.
27. Jacques Dupuis, S.J., *Jesus Christ at the Encounter of World Religions*, trans. Robert R. Barr (Maryknoll, N.Y.: Orbis, 1993), p. 232.
28. Dupuis, p. 233.
29. On this point a reading of *Gaudium et Spes* is illuminating; it could be called the Constitution on the Spirit in the Modern World rather than the Constitution on the Church in the Modern World.

be limited to the linguists and theologians, today's descendants of de Nobili and Ricci? Hardly. Contact with members of other religions is a daily happenstance for an increasingly broad number of people. There is a new mosque on the outskirts of Cincinnati; a Sikh residence is around the corner from the building in which this essay is being written; and both Buddhists and Jews run centers which are respected teaching components of the Graduate Theological Union in Berkeley while Islamic studies are accessible at the University of California at Berkeley. Lest this still reek of academe, it helps to recall that the worshipers, residents, and students at these various locations live normal lives, interacting in schools, shops, and neighborhoods with citizens of other denominations — or none at all. So a haircut, a shopping expedition, a visit to the gym, or a neighborhood gathering can be the occasion for discussion of the questions that have always engaged human concern: in one form or another, these remain, Who are we? Where did we come from? Where are we going? Why? And with the fidelity of the tides they recur at times of birth, marriage, and death, and whenever suffering shows one of its myriad faces. What is at issue in interreligious dialogue is the conversation between religiously committed persons on matters of mutual concern:

> In our personal relations with men of other beliefs, dialogue will be truly religious when, however different its object, its partners share a religious concern and an attitude of complete respect for one another's convictions and a fraternal openness of mind and heart. Religious dialogue, therefore, does not necessarily mean that two persons speak about their religious experiences, but rather that they speak as religiously committed persons, with their ultimate commitments and religious outlook, on subjects of common interest.[30]

There is clearly a place for the dialogue of ordinary people. In many cases such dialogue will either lead to or spring from mutual engagement in works of justice and peace, which in itself represents another level of interreligious dialogue. That dialogue itself includes four forms or levels. Again, Dupuis has studied the Vatican documents, and identifies the forms:

30. Dupuis, p. 235, quoting the declaration (no. 24) of the Nagpur, India, conference of 1971 against an elitist notion of interreligious dialogue.

31

> There is the dialogue of life, open and accessible to all. . . . There is the dialogue of a common commitment to the works of justice and human liberation. . . . There is the intellectual dialogue in which scholars engage in an exchange at the level of their respective legacies, with the goal of promoting communion and fellowship. . . . Finally, on the most profound level, there is the sharing of religious experiences of prayer and contemplation, in a common search for the Absolute.[31]

Neighbors, colleagues, scholars have each their role. That partners "share a religious concern" and an "attitude of complete respect for one another's convictions" as well as "fraternal openness of mind and heart" implies the attitude appropriate to discernment of spirits. Such an attitude is essentially one of openness to the movement of the Holy Spirit.[32] Through the active exercise of discernment one comes to the final and most profound level. One caution: the levels are not necessarily sequential; the fourth can intersect with any of the others. One need not move from the dialogue of ordinary life through the dialogue of shared commitment to the task of faith seeking justice, into the dialogue of scholarship and thence into shared religious experience. Any of the levels can lead into shared religious experience. It is that to which all the dialogue is ordered: through mutual prayer across our traditions, and even across our different religions, we hope to come together to the One.

Catholics bring to the quest a history of engagement across cultures (not, I hasten to add, all successful! De Nobili's and Ricci's experiments were sadly quashed), intrachurch encouragement to move in this direction, a sense of the four forms interreligious dialogue takes, and long experience in the traditions of discernment and contemplation. It is these things new and old which we can bring out from the storehouse of our faith. But how does one engage another across cultures? And how does one read the symbols of another culture? In addition to the two fundamental convictions of the centrality of Christ and the univer-

---

31. Dupuis, p. 223.

32. While there is a vast literature on the topic, a handy introduction remains that of Gustave Bardy et al., *Discernment of Spirits,* trans. Sister Innocentia Richards (Collegeville, Pa.: Liturgical Press, 1970). This is the authorized English edition of the article in *Dictionnaire de Spiritualite* 3, 1222-91 (1957).

sal offer of salvation, another conviction also finds its place close to the heart of Catholicism.

Part 3: Intuition

A third conviction at the heart of Catholicism concerns "the sacramental principle"; that is, material creation, blessed by its Maker and further consecrated by the incarnation, continues in this time after the resurrection of Jesus Christ to be touched by the Word of God so that simple things like water and oil, bread, and wine mediate the presence of God's Spirit. The sacramental principle finds expression not only in the formal liturgical actions of the church which include "the seven sacraments" rooted deeply in tradition but also in what rises from the *sensus fidei*, the faith-full intuition of the believing people.[33] The *sensus fidei* is expressed in the language, symbols, and culture of a people, and so in popular religiosity, like that characteristic of Hispanic Catholicism. Orlando O. Espín[34] has reminded us that one cannot study any Hispanic community in the United States without encountering popular religion, whether one regrets or defends the situation.

While popular religion is susceptible to justifiable criticism, it ought not be considered only through its limitations. Espín argues "that

33. John J. Burkhard, "*Sensus Fidei:* Theological Reflection since Vatican II," Part 1: 1965-1984 and Part 2: 1985-1989, *Heythrop Journal* 34 (1993): 52 n. 1, defines the term thus:

> In general, two theological terms have come to express this understanding of the participation of all believers in elaborating Christian truth, *sensus fidei* and *sensus* (or *consensus*) *fidelium.* Sometimes they are used interchangeably; at other times, theologians employ these terms to convey a different nuance. *Sensus fidei* might be used to refer to the Christian's possession of the truths of his or her faith or even of the more fundamental, underlying truth of the Christian belief-system. *Sensus fidelium,* on the other hand, points in the direction of the activity of the subject's belief, i.e., believers or the faithful, in abiding in, or defending, or elaborating the truth of Christianity.

I use *sensus fidei* because that is the expression used in *Lumen Gentium* 12, but like Burkhard I do not wish to be tied to one denotation.

34. Orlando O. Espín, "Tradition and Popular Religion: An Understanding of the *Sensus Fidelium,*" in *Frontiers of Hispanic Theology in the United States,* ed. Allan Figueroa Deck, S.J. (Maryknoll, N.Y.: Orbis, 1992), pp. 62-87.

popular religion can be theologically understood as a cultural expression of the *sensus fidelium*, with all that this understanding would imply for the theology of tradition in the Roman Catholic context."[35] Since the whole church has received and accepted the revelation of God in faith, the entire church (and not solely ordained ministers) is charged with expressing the contents of Scripture and tradition. Because the *sensus fidei* is an intuition, it "is *always* expressed through the symbols, language, and culture of the faithful and, therefore, is in need of intense interpretive processes and methods similar to those called for by the written texts of tradition and scripture."[36] Not only Protestants but many Catholics need to do such interpretation if they are to understand Hispanic Christians. It is most certainly required if Christians of any kind are to understand the symbolic expressions of other world religions. Catholic sensitivity to such expressions can be a particular gift for interfaith relations. Examination of one such expression proper to some Hispanics can serve as an example.

Mary in the person of Our Lady of Guadalupe (or, in the affectionate diminutive, *La Morenita*) is a symbol central to Mexican and Mexican American popular Catholic religiosity. She is herself *la Mestiza;* she has the face and form of the mestizos who first honored her in the sixteenth century. Her iconography reinterprets key symbols of an ancient Amerindian religion within Christianity so as to allow the Mexicans to see themselves as a new people, reborn through Christ.[37] She told the Indians in the person of Juan Diego to go to the bishop (the church); the church, in the person of the bishop, was "to build a temple," what Elizondo calls "a church of compassion." He understands this second command to mean: "Incarnate the gospel among this people, so that Christ will not come as a stranger but as one of them."[38] Come to the church the Indians did, in numbers reaching eight million in the seven years following the event at Guadalupe in 1531.

Those among their twentieth-century descendants who live in this

---

35. Espín, p. 62.
36. Espín, p. 62.
37. See Virgilio Elizondo, *La Morenita, Evangelizer of the Americas* (San Antonio: Mexican-American Cultural Center, 1980).
38. Quoted in Elizondo, *La Morenita*.

country struggle with the problems of assimilation.[39] Juan-Lorenzo Hinojosa distinguishes among them the immigrant, the partially assimilated, the strongly assimilated, and the fully bicultural individual.[40] It is the last group who are claiming the identity of the *mestizaje* in both the racial and the cultural sense.[41] Theologians of all the Christian churches could look to this group, especially to the theologians among them, to learn to understand religious symbols across cultures.[42] Roman Catholic appreciation of the richness of the living resource of the *sensus fidei* in its cross-cultural expression could only benefit by such work, as would the understanding of Hispanic Catholicism on the part of other Christians.

The benefits for interfaith relations should be self-evident. De Nobili and Ricci each entered a second culture, and to all appearances were accepted. Each, however, remained in one sense or another "the foreign rajah," the "outsider mandarin." By contrast, the genuinely bicultural individual is born to both cultures, and so is best situated to assist in mediating understanding across cultures. However, with or without the mediation of bicultural theologians, the practitioners of interfaith dialogue must interpret symbols produced by the intuition of an alien culture. Catholicism can contribute its experience with the symbols of popular religion.

39. Juan-Lorenzo Hinojosa, "Culture, Spirituality, and United States Hispanics," in *Frontiers of Hispanic Theology in the United States,* ed. Allan Figueroa Deck, S.J. (Maryknoll, N.Y.: Orbis, 1992), p. 155, identifies Greeley's recent sociological study, "The Hispanic Catholic in the United States," based on 1,010 interviews with Hispanic Catholics around the country, as confirming a tendency to assimilation among U.S.-born Hispanic Catholics.

40. Hinojosa, pp. 155-58.

41. The seminal study of *mestizaje,* examining both the ethnic and the religious questions involved, is Virgilio Elizondo, *Mestizaje: The Dialectic of Cultural Birth and the Gospel. A Study in the Intercultural Dimension of Evangelization* (Paris: Institut Catholique; San Antonio: Mexican-American Cultural Center, 1978). Elizondo presents some of the elements of his study in the popular synthesis *Galilean Journey: The Mexican-American Promise* (Maryknoll, N.Y.: Orbis, 1993).

42. Espín and Hinojosa, with their colleagues in ACTHUS (The Academy of Catholic Hispanic Theologians of the United States), form a core of such theologians; some of the members comprise the contributors to *Frontiers of Hispanic Theology in the United States.*

MARY ANN DONOVAN

A Closing Word

Our age is not only one in which the cross-cultural element is inescapable, but also one in which ideological confidence has collapsed. People admit not to certainties but to points of view. A review of the last decade's literature on how the world religions relate to each other, Fitzmaurice remarks, indicates that the preference is for relativistic pluralism. Following Knitter,[43] he writes:

> There is now a general feeling that no one religion can lay claim to absolute truth and that even the notion of an abstract distilled essence of what is true religion should be beyond us. The different religions, we are told, reflect experiences and "frameworks which are ultimately incommensurable."[44]

Catholicism precludes a totally relative pluralism; it holds fast to the centrality and uniqueness of Jesus Christ. That very assurance carries with it a tendency to overemphasize doctrinal conformity. The insistence on verbal orthodoxy to the exclusion of all else is a recurring Catholic temptation. The asceticism of exercising a hermeneutics of unity offers an antidote to that disease, an antidote that has become accessible to Catholics through participation in dialogue with other Christians. Through a long history of often unsuccessful interaction with other religions Catholics have begun to learn to listen, most especially when engaging another culture. The posture of a listener is one well suited to the exercise of the discipline of discernment, and to preparation for entering into contemplation. Catholics bring to interfaith dialogue a long experience with both discernment and contemplation. Finally, Catholic experience with the symbols of popular religion, an experience in which the symbols both rise from the depths of intuition and find their interpretation through intuition, is a valuable resource for appreciation of the symbols produced by the intuition of an alien culture.

---

43. Paul Knitter, "Towards a Liberation Theology of Religion," in *The Myth of Christian Uniqueness,* ed. John Hick and Paul Knitter (London: SCM, 1985), p. 184.
44. Fitzmaurice, p. 13.

CHAPTER THREE

Interreligious Dialogue: An Hispanic American Pentecostal Perspective

SAMUEL SOLIVAN

I. American Pentecostalism: A Child of American Religious Pluralism

The story of the birth of North American Pentecostalism emerges from a variety of earlier American religious movements, among which are Methodism, Keswickian Pietism, holiness, the Baptist movement, and Presbyterianism. Yet if one is to understand Pentecostalism properly, one must not only see it against, or in light of, its theological heritage but one must also take into account its socioreligious and political context. Pentecostalism is the child of North American religious pluralism, democracy, and individualism. These three factors were as responsible for the rise of American Pentecostalism as were its theological antecedents.

It was American religious pluralism that made possible the birth and rise of Pentecostalism. Surely it was not the only factor, but an important one. The American democratic experience provided another important element in that it reflected a personalized pneumatology so dear to charismatics in general and Pentecostals in particular. These two elements, religious pluralism and democracy, were incorporated into a Pentecostal polity of congregationalism and the priesthood of all believers. Neither was unique to Pentecostalism, but in the good old American way they where co-opted from earlier religious movements.

Pentecostalism is a truly American religious product. It learned from other traditions, adapting insights and mixing them with its own. Yet the adaptation was selective. Among those things not selected which other denominations had engaged in was ecumenical dialogue. This was due in great part to Pentecostalism's eschatological perspectives on the nature and future of the church and its understanding of the unity of the body of Christ. This antiecumenical bias continues today, with the exception of one or two Pentecostal leaders, such as the late Donald Gee and Dr. Cecil Roebeck. The interreligious dialogue fostered among most mainline Protestants was vehemently rejected by Pentecostals.

Among Pentecostals, religious experience mediated through the theological and philosophical lenses of commonsense realism and American conservatism serves as an hermeneutical tool for assessing any given theological agenda's effectiveness and fidelity to the Scriptures. Ecumenism's historical frame of reference has been the North American mainline church scene. An examination of the history of American Protestantism has led Pentecostal leaders to conclude that ecumenical dialogues, alliances, and interreligious conversations have done little to impact the growth of the Christian community. In fact, the reverse seems to be the case. From this perspective there seems to be enough evidence to indicate that such dialogues and conferences have done little to impact the growth and mission of the church in the world, in light of its Christian mandate in Matthew's Gospel where we are directed to go and make disciples of all people, baptizing them in the name of Jesus.[1]

The long-term trend of lack of growth and vitality in a large percentage of mainline Protestant congregations further exacerbates the criticism made by Pentecostals of ecumenical efforts. The nature and presuppositions of current interreligious dialogue further complicate their position and perspective on this matter. It is from this theological and contextual perspective that I will reflect on the question, What does a Pentecostal theology have to contribute to an interreligious dialogue?

---

1. Matthew 28:18-20.

II. Pentecostals: Observers of the Ecumenical Scene

The ecumenical movement has had a long and rich history of dialogue and critical reflection on those themes and concerns understood to be critical to the well-being of all the churches and consistent with their Christian mandate to be one. Pentecostal involvement in these talks has been, comparatively speaking, of recent date, and their commitment in this area has been at a high price, as history has indicated. Donald Gee was among the earliest — and perhaps most noted — Pentecostals participating in such activity, and it has been only recently, within the past fifteen years, that Gee's ministry has been gratefully recognized and applauded by Pentecostals. It can be said that Pentecostals are among the most recent participants in these dialogues — usually as observers. As such their direct participation at times has neither been sought nor offered, as both parties have had mutual suspicions of each other. This observer status continues today for a variety of reasons which I will not attempt to address in this paper.

Our role as observers is an important prelude to the mutual learning and listening process assumed for healthy dialogue and mutual criticism. As observers of the ecumenical scene and the interreligious dialogues of the past years, our perspective continues to be informed by a set of different assumptions theologically, sociologically, and politically. This is further complicated by the fact that mainstream Pentecostalism has been informed and mediated almost exclusively in these circles by white conservatives. As observers with another worldview, theologically and often politically, Pentecostals provide a point of reference often represented by other conservative Christian communities not represented in these discussions.

III. Possible Contributions a Pentecostal Perspective Can Bring to an Interreligious Dialogue

On the surface some might think the question of what Pentecostal theology can contribute to this dialogue to be an oxymoron. Often Pentecostals have been associated with anti-intellectualism and obscurantism. Yet a closer consideration of the question will prove fruitful. The following perspectives are those of the author and do not officially represent any particular Pentecostal fellowship, yet they do attempt to faithfully represent both a Pentecostal experience and its corresponding theology. It should also be noted that the point of departure of this writer is that of an Hispanic American. As a whole, the perspective shared in this paper will represent a double minority, Pentecostal and Hispanic.

The underlying characteristics of a Pentecostal theological perspective are its pneumatological assumptions. It is from the vantage point of our understanding of the person and ministry of the Holy Spirit that these observations are made. Our understanding and experience of the Holy Spirit should provide us with a genuine openness to differences, that is, to that which is unlike ourselves. The unknown, the questionable, doubt, testing — all are possible for us in light of the fact that we believe the Holy Spirit to be on the one hand the illuminator and, on the other, the one that leads us in all truth.[2]

As illuminator the Spirit provides the necessary light for making the unseen visible. As the one that leads us to all truth, the Spirit not only provides guidance but equips us with the capacity to discern between truth and untruth. The activities of illumination and discernment possess negative as well as positive statements of truth. As noted by Prof. Morse in his recent book *Not Every Spirit*, theology must not only address that which we affirm as Christian truth, it must also disclaim that which is inconsistent with the Christian message.[3] A Pentecostal understanding and trust in the Holy Spirit's ability to illuminate and lead us as we reflect on these issues pertaining to religious pluralism can provide us with a "free space" for inquiry, inquiry that allows for doubt, or new questions, or new answers to old questions. The presence of the Holy Spirit as illuminator and guide can free us to open our hearts and minds to each other and to God.

Another contribution to this dialogue which might be made from this author's perspective is that which Bonhoeffer wrote about in his *Letters from Prison* — a *"view from below."*[4] Pentecostals in general and Hispanic and other Third World Pentecostals in particular represent

2. John 16:13.
3. Christopher Morse, *Not Every Spirit: A Dogmatics of Christian Disbelief* (Valley Forge, Pa.: Trinity Press, 1994).
4. Dietrich Bonhoeffer, *Letters from Prison*, ed. Eberhard Bethge, trans. R. H. Fuller et al., enlarged ed. (New York: Macmillan, 1972).

this view from below in various ways. First, we represent the view of many poor and marginalized people, a minority voice among the cacophony of well-organized, well-financed voices of the mainline churches and the singular voice of the Roman Catholic Church. It is also a view from below in that it represents a theological tradition that places greater weight on experience than on reason, on Scripture than on theology. This view from below represents the suspicion that many have of the established religious institutions that today often find themselves so far from their own constituencies. If in fact one believes, as is often stated in these sophisticated ecumenical circles, that the poor have an epistemological, or hermeneutical, advantage or privilege, heeding their insight, hearing their perspective, may not only be consistent but wise. This is another contribution Pentecostals can make to this dialogue insofar as we are a church of the poor and the unattended.

Another theological perspective Pentecostals assume is that the Holy Spirit is God's gift of grace to unbelievers as well as believers. This we understand to be the prevenient ministry of the Spirit. We believe that the Holy Spirit is at work in the world, convicting it of its sin and estrangement from God and neighbor. This aspect of the Holy Spirit's ministry opens up new possibilities for dialogue with other faiths. This understanding of the Spirit compels us to trust the Spirit's leading in nontraditional circumstances. It should lead us to recognize God's sovereign presence in grace in the world apart from a Christian expression. As creator, God has endowed all of the human family with the *imago Dei*.

This recognition that the Holy Spirit is and has been at work in the world in spite of us, and at times through us, should foster an attitude of true humility before God's gracious love. The belief that the Holy Spirit is at work in the world in those who know not Christ as savior should be a comfort to Christians because we, like our Lord, pray and desire that none be lost but that all might come to repentance. This perspective should not be equated with "cheap grace" or with universal salvation. Rather, this speaks to that paradigm of grace already witnessed to in the Hebrew Bible, as in the case of Abraham, who, without Law or prophets, was a recipient of saving grace. If we really believe and trust the leading of the Spirit, we must believe that the Spirit witnesses and draws unto Christ all who know him not. This pneumatological perspective can free Pentecostals and others to engage in the type of religious dialogue that can afford the Spirit an opportunity to make known its presence in unexpected ways. This approach can also free theology to discover the untold and unexplored world of the Spirit that is not tied to the strictures of rationalism or personal experience. It can free us all to be open to the new and refreshing ways in which the Holy Spirit is and can be at work in the world.

If any theological theme resounds among Pentecostals, it is empowerment. We understand the Scriptures to teach that the Holy Spirit has been given to the church for the purpose, among others, of raising up witnesses of Christ's lordship. The Spirit of Christ empowers for love, justice, and truth. It gives authority and openness to speak and listen to and discern truth wherever it is spoken. The Spirit empowers us to be in community with others who seek after truth, love, peace, and justice. The Holy Spirit's ministry in building community is not limited to the organized church. Wherever there is true community the Spirit has been at work. Dialogue across denominational lines and interfaith lines is an important task of global community building. As Christians, Pentecostals and other people of faith should participate in and contribute to this effort from their theological locus. Empowerment of the Spirit is always a cooperative venture. We do not predetermine where, when, and how the Spirit will choose to work among us, or even in spite of us. Our task is to be open and available, seeking to discern in the light of Scripture, tradition, and the leading of the Spirit. The task of discernment is a critical, risk-taking exercise. We must venture out to test the waters, in this case the waters of dialogue.

Another important insight from our perspective is the culturally inclusive and ethnically diverse character of the church empowered by the Spirit. Even a superficial reading of Acts 2 will demonstrate the Spirit's intent to attend to the global character of Diaspora Judaism. From all the corners of the then-known world they gathered on the Day of Pentecost to witness to the Holy Spirit's invitation to community. The Spirit on that day took most seriously the diversity present, empowering the disciples to speak to the particular ethnic cultural differences present. No single language or culture was raised above the others; the Spirit affirmed the importance of cultural and linguistic diversity. It was not a homogenized or an imposed uniformity. These principles of diversity and inclusion may be helpful in informing our own attitudes and expectancy and those of other communities of faith.

Where the Spirit is at work boundaries of race, gender, class, and language, among others, are overcome.

This principle of diversity can also free us to examine the diverse ways the Holy Spirit is at work among other people of faith. It allows us to explore the variety of ways in which the human community seeks to express its longing and searching after God. A sharing of these expressions of spirituality can be informative and at times even transformative of our own models and modes of spirituality and their accompanying theological assumptions.

A closing observation I would like to make is the import that a pneumatological perspective might have for issues of gender and interfaith dialogue. As we all are aware, an examination of the biblical text will indicate that the third person of the Trinity has been represented in the Hebrew Bible as *ruach,* which is feminine; in the New Testament as *pneumatos,* which is neuter; and later in the Latin Vulgate as *espiritus,* which is masculine. This multigender or androgynous identification of the Holy Spirit can also be helpful as a model of inclusivity in our own deliberations. Canonical, extracanonical, and apocryphal literature makes use of this feminine aspect of the third person of the Trinity. How do our own faith traditions attend to gender inclusion as modeled in the Trinity?

Conclusion

I have chosen to focus the question before us from the vantage point of pneumatology because it seems to me to be central to a Pentecostal perspective as well as providing a theological locus which lends itself more readily to our considerations. There are a number of other Pentecostal theological loci which have been used to argue the case against an interfaith dialogue, but I have chosen not to start there because the logical and immediate conclusion of such an approach would be closure, not dialogue. Because I believe in the Holy Spirit and in the Spirit's ministry of reconciliation, conversion, and community, I have ventured out onto thin ice, trusting the Holy Spirit will sustain, enrich, and use this opportunity to witness to Christ's redemptive love and witness his presence among others. This approach does not deny or diminish the valid theological reservations and even prohibitions that might be raised by other aspects of my Pentecostal tradition regarding interfaith dialogue.

As a Christian of Pentecostal persuasion I affirm along with other Christians the centrality and even uniqueness of the person of Jesus Christ as Savior and Lord. I affirm the central place of the church in the redemptive plan of God for humanity. I affirm the evangelistic character of Christianity and the accompanying mandate to make disciples of all nations, baptizing them in the name of the Father, Son, and Holy Spirit. I also affirm the missionary character of the Christian faith as a logical extension of its evangelistic mandate.

Among the other theological assumptions Pentecostals recognize is the sinful character of human nature. Yet humanity is not totally depraved or without the ability to will for good. I assume the important balance presented in the Scripture between faith and reason as expressed in the Anselmic expression "Faith seeking Understanding."[5] I also assume the central and superior place that the Scriptures have among other important resources. And I recognize our human tendency to treat our theological constructs and assertions at times as if they possessed some divine character. This human tendency to equate theological discourse with divine authority is a reflection of human hubris and results in idolatry. Therefore all our reflections and insights must be carried on in a spirit of humility and repentance, thereby hoping to avoid but not neglect this important and God-given capacity and responsibility to believe and to reflect upon that which we believe.

I would conclude by also sharing four reservations I have regarding our modern notions of dialogue. I would first raise a concern about the theological assumption that newer, innovative positions are somewhat more truthful or better than older ones. Secondly, I would question the assumption that dialogue is the preferred vehicle for insight and getting at truth. Thirdly, I question the assumption that if one studies something long enough one will see the light and change one's mind, the expectation being that if one were to have enough facts about something one would be convinced. Finally, I raise a concern about the presumption that all faith claims are relative and that few if any absolutes exist.

5. Anselm, *Proslogium*, trans. Sidney Norton Deane (La Salle, Ill.: Open Court, 1951), p. 7.

I pray that what I have shared is faithful to the gospel of Jesus Christ, consistent with the Pentecostal tradition that has nurtured me in the faith, and open to the liberating leading and correction of the Holy Spirit. AMEN.

CHAPTER FOUR

Resources in the Reformed Tradition for Responding to Religious Plurality

JAY T. ROCK

Dedicated to Jim and Lucie Hupp,
who love the earth, and heal and nurture people in it

IT may be dangerous to ask an ecclesial bureaucrat like myself to take on a project of theological reflection such as this. In what follows I have found what I think to be life in documents that others might not include among "live theological resources" — not only in the *Book of Confessions* of the Presbyterian Church (USA) but also in other, more recent statements and study papers of the Reformed churches. Moreover, not being by training a theologian but rather a historian of religions, I have addressed my lack of background by spending some time in conversation with a few theologians and colleagues in the hope of presenting here a broader and more representative sample of Reformed thinking than my own. My thanks especially to Margaret O. Thomas and Douglas John Hall for conversational insights which the reader will find cited in written forms for which I bear all responsibility.

1. Two preliminary observations strike me as important. First, the given task, of making clear from a Reformed perspective "the crucial elements" and crucial questions "that would have to figure in a viable theological rationale for interfaith relations," immediately raises ques-

tions of methodology. This was not an inquiry of the early Reformers; with the exception of some, like Calvin, who evidently did language study with Jews, theirs was an experience nearly devoid of religious diversity. We are revisiting the tradition, as we have done in regard to many other concerns, seeking guidance regarding the contemporary questions of religious pluralism. At least as important as the question of a theological *rationale*, then, is the question whether there are any distinctive features of a Reformed *approach* to this theological task.

Secondly, we need to remind ourselves of the obvious: It is difficult to talk about *a* Reformed perspective or approach, let alone *the* Reformed tradition, when the Reformed churches are themselves so diverse. The Reformed tradition has from its inception been multivocal. Its insistence that "God alone is Lord of the conscience" includes the understanding that individuals can and do receive illumination by the Holy Spirit, thus opening the church to continuing and continual reform:

> Protestant traditions of theology insist that God is at work in history, and that the divine Spirit creates, recreates, judges and renews the body of Christ. . . . We are called to participate in the judgement which begins at the household of faith [1 Pet. 4:17], and to participate also in the re-forming of that household. *Semper reformanda!*[1]

We have to remain aware of the plurality and anti-homogenization of the Reformed tradition itself.

2. My task, then, is to bring to a confessional tradition which is itself pluralistic the question of what insights and suggestions of approach it has to offer regarding how we as Christians are to respond to another plurality, that of the many religious communities among whom we now live. We can begin, naturally enough, by asking what the very theological pluralism of the modern Reformed tradition might teach us regarding Christian relations with people of other faiths.

A look at the recent Presbyterian Church (USA) response to the crisis sparked by the 1993 "Reimagining" Conference is suggestive of one Reformed approach to the issues of theological plurality: The resolution of the 1994 General Assembly affirms on the one hand "con-

---

1. Douglas John Hall, *An Awkward Church*, Theology and Worship Occasional Paper, no. 5, Presbyterian Church (USA), 1993, pp. 11-12.

fessional standards," including "the one triune God," the "uniqueness of God's incarnation in Jesus Christ," the "death and resurrection of Jesus Christ for our salvation," the "authority of Scriptures," and the tradition of the apostolic faith. It then goes on to say:

> We affirm that the task of the church is to express the truth of Jesus Christ in every age, effectively, clearly, imaginatively. . . . We affirm that our task as a church is to confront and converse with our culture from the perspective of our theological tradition. . . . This will not be the last opportunity for ecumenical, cross-cultural and interfaith conversation. We affirm the importance of women's voices and work in the church and the important task of developing and articulating our theology.

This document reflects a consensus in one Reformed denomination; it suggests that the continuing affirmation of theological pluralism rests on a basis which is *christological* and *conversational*.

The first lesson to draw from this example is that for pluralism to be viable it must be based on a commitment to the essential affirmations of the community. Neither the theological pluralism of a particular confession nor a broader interreligious pluralism will be granted any guiding authority in the community's life if it amounts to mere relativism.

This suspicion of relativism is raised even by sophisticated observers in regard to the contemporary theological pluralism of the Reformed tradition. For example, in their major study of Presbyterianism, Coalter, Mulder, and Weeks comment that

> Diversity, understood as equal participation, became a key way of understanding the nature of the church itself for American Presbyterians and mainstream Protestants. Theological pluralism, understood as the equal validity [sic] of different visions of the Christian tradition, emerged as a basic theological principle. . . . The PC(USA)'s adoption of "A Brief Statement of Faith" in 1991, plus a *Book of Confessions*, may mean that the church has not rejected its confessional character or its Reformed legacy.[2]

2. Milton J. Coalter, John M. Mulder, and Louis B. Weeks, *The Re-forming Tradition: Presbyterians and Mainstream Protestantism* (Louisville, KY: Westminster/ John Knox Press, 1992).

But theological pluralism is not relativism. It does not give up its essential legacy, but "assumes real commitment"[3] to it. Nor does it operate without discernment; it does not in fact grant "equal validity" but an equal hearing to the variety of voices which takes part in the "task of developing and articulating our theology." It is engaged in "expressing the truth of Jesus Christ" through the ongoing, committed theological *conversation* of the community.

What *must* then be in any theological response from the Reformed tradition to the questions raised by interreligious plurality? Such a response must include the commitment to wrestle with — and not circumvent — the essential Reformed affirmations of the gospel of Jesus Christ in this new context of religious diversity. It will avoid "theologies that only legitimate" dialogue, and that are based on relativist understandings of religious truth which "provide little or no help in dealing with problems of mutually exclusive absolute claims."[4] Moreover, it will be rooted in an approach which is itself dialogical.

3. "Through a cynical intellectual sleight of hand some critics have linked pluralism with a valueless relativism. . . . Relativism, like pluralism, is an interpretation of diversity. . . . On the whole, relativism simply means that what we know of the world and of truth we can only know through a particular framework. . . . A thoughtful relativist is able to point out the many ways in which our cognitive and moral understandings are relative to our historical, cultural, and ideological contexts. So far, the pluralist would be a close cousin. But there are two shades of relativism that are antithetical to pluralism. The first is nihilistic relativism, which denies the very heart of religious truth. . . . The second shade of relativism that must clearly be distinguished from pluralism is a relativism that lacks commitment. . . . The pluralist, on the other hand, stands in a particular community and is willing to be committed to the struggles of that community. . . . The theological task, and the task of a pluralist society is to create the space and the means for the encounter of commitments, not to neutralize all commitment." Diana L. Eck, *Encountering God* (Boston: Beacon Press, 1993), pp. 193-95. Her entire discussion of pluralism, pp. 190-99, is helpful.

4. George Lindbeck, "Are There Limits to Religious Pluralism? If So, Why?" in the proceedings of a Christian-Jewish consultation entitled *The Limits of Religious Pluralism*, ed. Allen Brockway et al. (Geneva: World Council of Churches, 1987). Nor will such a response find any adequate basis in an approach such as that adopted by the panel of the World Alliance of Reformed Churches that drafted the 1986 statement on Reformed theology and the Jewish people: to skip over an understanding of "Jesus Christ — his Life, cross and resurrection . . . and belief in the trinity of God," even though they are "main points which separate Christian from Jewish belief," since those theological essentials "are not exclusive to . . . the Reformed tradition." Ellen Flesseman-van Leer and panel, "Aspects of Historical Reformed

Thus one of the major building blocks of a Reformed *approach* to interreligious issues is this affirmation by the tradition of the essential need for multivocal community when it comes to understanding how God is relating to us, and how we ought to relate to God.[5] Community is central to God's will:

> In sovereign love God created the world good and makes everyone equally in God's image, male and female, of every race and people, to live as one community.[6]

> God wills unity for the church, for humanity and for creation, because God is a *koinonia* of love. . . . The deeper *koinonia* which is our goal is for the glory of God and for the sake of the world. The church is called to be a sign and instrument of this all-encompassing will of God, the summing up of all things in Christ.[7]

> Koinonia . . . will help us experience and look forward to the fullness of the reign of God with its promise of salvation, reconciliation and renewal for the whole of humanity and creation. . . . [It] will be marked by a lifestyle of dialogue, including that with neighbours of living faiths. . . . Christian *koinonia* can be enriched by interfaith encounter. In dialogue, Christians learn to present their faith with humility and experience the wondrous variety of God's presence in creation.[8]

We live our faith in community. Moreover, as Margaret O. Thomas reminded me, "God speaks to the community, and therefore we test

---

Theology Which Are Pertinent to the Relations between the Reformed Churches and the Jewish People," in *Reformed Theology and the Jewish People,* study 9, ed. Alan P. F. Sell (Geneva: World Alliance of Reformed Churches, 1986).

5. "It is typical of the Reformed ethos that there is a readiness to build upon earlier formulations and to confess the faith in ways pertinent to changed situations. Moreover, churches belonging to this tradition are to be found in all parts of the world. These churches have each had their own specific development. Consequently, the Reformed tradition today is very variegated indeed." Flesseman-van Leer, pp. 4-5.

6. "Brief Statement of Faith," Presbyterian Church (USA), 1991.

7. From the "Message to the Churches" from the Fifth World Conference on Faith and Order, World Council of Churches, 1994.

8. "Report of Section IV: Called to Common Witness for a Renewed World," in *On the Way to Fuller Koinonia,* ed. Thomas F. Best and Gunther Gassmann, the official report of the Fifth World Conference on Faith and Order, Faith and Order Paper, no. 166 (World Council of Churches, 1994), pp. 254-55.

new insights through the discipline of community." Our Christian life in community, and this "principle of testing theological insight by community, lead us into an ecumenical, and perhaps into an interfaith, search for truth. The same ability to discern God's will in the midst of diversity which characterizes interchurch ecumenism will be the force which impels us in interfaith ecumenism."[9]

3. Three contemporary statements expressive of the Reformed tradition may provide further insight into its distinctive theological resources for engaging religious plurality. The first is a study paper of the Presbyterian Church (USA), adopted along with documents on Christian-Jewish and Christian-Muslim relations by its General Assembly in 1987. *The Nature of Revelation in the Christian Tradition from a Reformed Perspective,* as it is called, includes a section (IX) on "Revelation and the Mission of the Church in a Pluralistic World."[10] This document identifies aspects of a Reformed understanding of revelation that provide "theological reasons for a more positive view of other religions," while also noting a number of "open questions about Revelation and other religions." Permit me a summary citation:

> The first and clearest thing to be said . . . is that the church has a mission to bear witness to the revelation it has received in Jesus Christ and through the Scriptures. The Gospel of Christ is good news for all peoples, and his disciples are called to share it in dialogue with others. The legitimate motive for this mission and this evangelistic witness is God's love for all people. . . . Christians . . . are impelled by faith to relate to all aspects of God's creation with love and respect and with expectation of seeing the Creator's hand in what we meet. . . . In this witness our approach can only be confessional. That is, we can only express and share what we have experienced and what we have learned . . . through the historical particularity of God's self-revelation in Jesus, in whom the Christian community has found the way, the truth and the life. . . .
>
> The beliefs and practices of other faiths are strikingly similar in various ways to our own . . . this makes it hard to dismiss the teaching and practice of other religions as entirely wrong. . . .

9. Margaret Orr Thomas, in conversation.

10. The document was prepared by the Advisory Council on Discipleship and Worship, Presbyterian Church (USA), Louisville, Kentucky.

Adherence to other faiths is grounded largely in an experience of religious life in which people feel themselves to be in touch with an ultimate reality, just as our acceptance of Christianity is largely grounded in our experience of God's gifts in Christ. Knowing this, can we maintain that our religion is an at least substantially true apprehension of God's self-revelation but theirs is only a tissue of superstition, idolatry, and error? . . .

From a Christian point of view, the reality of relationship between God and people is what matters most . . . and all people must be presumed to stand in relationship to God. . . . God, "who desires all human beings to be saved and come to knowledge of truth" (1 Tim. 2:4) has surely been at work in the lives of all people, seeking to establish fellowship with them. . . .

Another reason for being concerned to treat other religious traditions with respect is that they are a part of the cultures that make us who we are. . . . All Christians have a continuing need to understand the mingling of religious traditions in their own lives so that they can bring their entire selves to the obedience of Christ. . . .

The Confession of 1967 . . . [draws] a sharp contrast between revelation and religion. . . . Revelation is the act of God (for instance, in becoming incarnate in Jesus); religion is a human activity. . . . The Christian religion in particular . . . is not on the same level as the Gospel, or God's self-revelation in Christ, but is as subject to God's judgment as any other religion. . . . In principle there is certainly a difference between divine acts of self-disclosure and human response to them. . . . Nevertheless . . . every proclamation and every acceptance of the Gospel of Christ is an expression of Christian religion. . . . We never meet revelation, as divine action, in separation from human (and religious) phenomena. [The] risk in overemphasizing the distinctness of all religion, including Christian religion, from the action of God . . . is that faith in the reality of our experience of God's presence and action in our lives will be undermined.

Could we go so far as to affirm that some of the insights of other religions could assist us Christians in a better understanding of God's self-revelation in Jesus Christ and in the Scriptures? . . . Can we acknowledge a possibility that there is revelation in other religions . . . in [the] narrower sense in which it signifies divine self-disclosure in which God has entered into personal communication with human beings in particular events?

We must not bend or trim our faith in God's revelation in Jesus Christ in order to achieve an artificial agreement [in interfaith dialogue]. . . . We may learn from non-Christian religions insofar as what we learn can be incorporated into, and enrich, our personal and corporate relationship with the God of Israel who is revealed in Jesus Christ. . . . Entering into interfaith dialogue in no way diminishes our calling to share the good news of Jesus Christ with all people, with all due respect for every good thing that God has given them in their religions. . . .

There are at least three emphases that are helpful to our discussion in this exploration of revelation: the relation of revelation to religion; the role in it of experience; and the fact of its particularity. But before we turn to these, it is worth noting that this view of revelation is rooted in a vision of God lovingly "at work in the lives of all people," who "must," then, "be presumed to stand in relation to God." The drafters of this document are among those in the Reformed tradition who would "argue that God has indeed been present in the cultures [of those who have not heard the gospel proclaimed], [in the] divine gifts and divine goodness revealed, even before missionaries arrived with formal teaching and preaching."[11] This is one understanding of the sovereignty of God: "God is the creator of the whole universe and . . . he has not left himself without witnesses at any time or any place. The Spirit of God is constantly at work in ways that pass human understanding and in places that to us are least expected. In entering into a relationship of dialogue with others, therefore, Christians seek to discern the unsearchable riches of God and the way he deals with humanity."[12] We will return to this central affirmation of sovereignty, but note here that this understanding of revelation affirms that we can learn from people of other faiths.

One of the more interesting features of this study paper is its critique of the neo-orthodox distinction of Barth and others, between

---

11. From "Report of Section IV." The report continues, "To take this claim seriously is not only potentially to rethink our theological methodology, but also to rethink the meaning and nature of the tasks of mission and evangelism."

12. *Mission and Evangelism: An Ecumenical Affirmation*, 7.43. A document approved by the World Council of Churches' Central Committee, July 1982, and adopted by the General Assembly of the Presbyterian Church (USA) in 1983, as a "faithful expression" of its commitment to mission and evangelism.

divine self-disclosure and the human response of religion. The drafters do not affirm the radical discontinuity which Barth articulated between (Christian) revelation and all other belief systems. Rather, they insist on the inseparability of revelation from the human, religious forms which allow it to be received. In terms of theological approaches to religious plurality, there is something to be said on both sides of this critique.

On the one hand, distinguishing revelation over against religion, including Christianity, emphasizes the limitedness of human understandings and institutions, and reminds us that God's activity is an essential mystery. "What Paul Tillich called 'the Protestant principle' — the insistence that nothing is ultimate except God . . . — . . . the sovereignty of God . . . and the affirmation that 'God alone is Lord of the conscience' all underscore the time-bound and relative character of any formulation of the mystery of God's grace in Jesus Christ."[13] This understanding requires a humility regarding our own faith, and an openness to that of others.[14] "As our Christian affirmation meets the faith of others, we are not called to respond in judgment but in awareness of the limitless, saving presence, power, and grace of God."[15] At the same time, it reminds us that we stand in relationship to none other than God alone.[16]

13. Coalter, Mulder, and Weeks, pp. 274-75.

14. This view is reflected in the Presbyterian Confession of 1967: "The church in its mission encounters the religions of men and in that encounter becomes conscious of its own human character as a religion. . . . The Christian religion, as distinct from God's revelation of himself, has been shaped throughout its history by the cultural forms of its environment. . . . The Christian finds parallels between other religions and his own and must approach all religion with openness and respect. Repeatedly God has used the insights of non-Christians to challenge the church to renewal. But the reconciling word of the gospel is God's judgment upon all forms of religion, including the Christian. The gift of God in Christ is for all men. The church, therefore, is commissioned to carry the gospel to all men whatever their religion may be and even when they profess none" (II.3.). It is precisely this elevation of the gospel above the judgment on religious forms that our document critiques.

15. "Turn to the Living God: A Call to Evangelism in Jesus Christ's Way," a resolution adopted by the General Assembly of the Presbyterian Church (USA) in 1991, III.A.2.

16. As the Barmen Declaration declares, there are no other sources of revelation, no other lords, to which we can give authority: "Jesus Christ is the one Word of God we have to hear."

"Truth lives: it is incarnate. The Bible bears a special witness to it. We cannot possess the Word of God, because it is not possessable. It is not possible to *have* the truth; but it is possible to feel its presence and attest to it. We do not have authority, but stand under it. Truth transcends all theological formulations; it transcends the Scriptures, the creeds, tradition. In its essence, it is mystery."[17]

On the other hand, the insistence that "we never meet revelation, as divine action, in separation from human (and religious) phenomena" is an affirmation that upholds "the reality of our experience of God's presence and action in our lives." This affirmation of the role of experience in revelation is echoed strongly in the various strands of contextual theology in current Reformed thinking. In fact, one of the major influences of feminist, African American, and other theologies of particular communities on Reformed consideration of interfaith questions is their gift of a hermeneutic clearly related to experience.[18] Granting a clear role to experience in the receiving of God's revelation in Christ, as this document does,[19] opens up the possibility that the experience of others might also be a vehicle for authentic revelation. This bears greater discussion as part of an approach to religious pluralism.

We should also note the related emphasis of this study paper on the "historical particularity of God's self-revelation in Jesus," the Christ. For our discussion it is important to notice that this particularity is not only a "scandal," but also a door to God. "This is, after all, the only way God could act with humanity," Douglas Hall noted to me. We only

---

17. Douglas John Hall, in conversation.

18. "The rise of Black theology marked the first of several movements that highlighted justice as the primary agenda for theology and the church. . . . By the 1980s feminist theologians became perhaps the most prominent new theological voices espousing the call to justice. . . . The common theme of justice runs through the affirmations of diverse thinkers from Third World, feminist, racial ethnic, liberationist, and gay rights groups. Because the theme of justice was and is prominent in the biblical account, justice has become for many the key for determining the central message of the scriptures. . . . [But is] justice itself . . . adequate as the single interpretive lens for understanding the gospel of Jesus Christ[?]" Coalter, Mulder, and Weeks, pp. 137, 228. The point in our connection is that justice is a category of experience.

19. This kind of understanding is already present in the Second Helvetic Confession, for example, which affirms that "God can illumine who and when he will, even without the external ministry [of the preached Word]" (chap. I).

meet particular people, particular dogs, etc.; but it is the relationship with a particular man or woman or dog that allows me to understand something about the life of men, women, or dogs. Similarly, relationship with Jesus doesn't cut us off from a broader knowledge of God; in fact it opens our horizons in relation to God.[20] The particular Jesus becomes the door to God. "And doors," Hall reminded me, "are to go through." This kind of Reformed Christology is a resource in regard to religious pluralism, in that Jesus functions not to cut us off, or limit us, but to move us into deeper and other relationship — with God and with other people. "We Christians can never dispense with Jesus. This is our one particular. But Jesus opens us to the universal God and the wider world, including the wider household of faith."

4. I cannot resist referring next to an essay by the Lutheran theologian George Lindbeck in which he outlines a somewhat "idiosyncratic" theological "legitimation" for religious pluralism. Its elements do not strike me as at all antithetical to much of Reformed thought, for his argument is based on the "biblical themes of election, witness, service, unfaithfulness, and pilgrimage."[21]

"Construing the Christian situation as closely analogous to that of Israel," Lindbeck points to biblical texts (such as Amos 9:7) which challenge

> the easy assumptions of Israel and the church that they alone have been guided and chosen by God to fulfill his purposes in the world. They may believe that they are the only peoples elected to testify to the proper identity of the one true God . . . for Christians, supremely of Jesus Christ, but this does not exclude the possibility that other nations, other religions, have also been appointed to their particular though quite different God-given missions. . . . No universally valid generalizations can be made in this biblical outlook regarding the nature and the role of other religions and quasi-religions except that God in his . . . providence uses them for his own purposes. . . .
>
> Christians . . . have a commission to witness to all, but not to convert all. It is for God to choose whom he will add to the company of witnesses, and clearly not all are elected for that purpose. He has

20. Similarly, Tillich speaks about Jesus as a concrete particular which opens us to the universal without negating its particularity.

21. Lindbeck, "Are There Limits?" p. 28.

other purposes and other missions for the vast majority which they (like Christians) fulfill with varying degrees of faithfulness and un-faithfulness. . . . The need for modesty on the part of God's peoples is reinforced when one considers the gap between their calling and their response, their election and their faithfulness. . . . To be elect is to stand in special measure under God's judgment. . . .

[Based on] the scriptural emphasis on the servant role . . . the witness of the church must take the form of selfless and sacrificial concern for the needs of all human beings whether they are outside or inside the community of faith. Only thus can authentic testimony be given to the one who died that others might live. . . . The primary motive of mission on this view cannot be to win converts. . . . If conversions take place, this must be a by-product of efforts to help human beings be better human beings. . . .

The 1500 years of Constantinian Christendom were an anomalous interlude which, while not excluded by the logic of faith, is also not integral to it. Unlike Jews, furthermore, Christians have no promised land within history, and are thus authorized by their scriptures to think of themselves even more than do Jews as pilgrims and wan-derers who have here no abiding city. In Constantinian situations this emphasis has normally been interpreted in individualistic and there-fore other-worldly terms, but once freed of the incubus of social, cultural, or political establishment, an essentially diaspora under-standing of Christianity seems bound to re-assert itself . . . [and] strangers in foreign lands are naturally inclined to favor . . . plural-ism. . . . (Pp. 25-28)

There is strong resonance in some Reformed thinking to Lind-beck's construction. For example, many Reformed people can readily embrace the idea of the humble openness to God and others that comes with an awareness of our human potential for sin. The possible role of repentance in an affirmation of religious pluralism was expressed in Santiago de Compostela: "Through repentance, people open them-selves freely and completely to the work and presence of God in their lives and, in humility, become aware of their own failures. The history of the Church makes clear that such lives of repentance and spiritual depth have been the source of Christianity's real missionary power."[22]

22. "Report of Section IV," par. 11.

Understanding the *metanoia*, the radical opening and turning to God, that is required to walk in the Christian way, can allow us a clearer vision of the power of God at work in all lives.[23] This kind of perspective can also lead to affirmation of a more eschatological dimension of pilgrimage:

> As Christians we live always with something before us, something still promised to us, which as yet we do not possess. "For now we see in a mirror dimly, but then face to face: Now I know in part, then face to face . . ." (1 Cor 13:12). Christians expect . . . an *Eschatos,* an appearance in the end time of . . . the very ground of our being. . . . Everything about our present understanding and perception is temporary and time-bound, and will in due course be transcended by greater truth. Christianity is for those who think like this by its nature eschatological, a principle of hope. As Christians we are always *in via*, always on the way, always travelling towards the future of God which will almost wholly surprise us.[24]

Such insights into sin and pilgrimage militate against triumphalism, and open us to pluralism.

Similarly, Lindbeck's understanding of election as the choosing of a people by God for a particular mission is familiar and suggestive for Reformed thinking. For the early Reformers the category of election

---

23. "Sin is not our nature but its derangement. Redeeming grace regenerates, restores, and redirects fallen humanity; it does not destroy or replace created human nature [which] constitutes a gift from God that may be taken as an indication of God's purposes. . . . The way that comes to us in Jesus Christ is a particular pattern that qualifies and redirects human affect and action. It does not spontaneously grow or develop . . . there is no evolutionary inevitability about it. Instead, it is both articulated and called forth by the particularities of a specific history and preeminently by a particular figure in that history. . . . There is little reason to expect either smooth or untroubled transitions among people from the skewed devotions and misdirected ways that historically entrap them to the way, the truth, and the life in Christ. To walk in the Christian way requires a change in ourselves." Douglas F. Ottati, *Jesus Christ and Christian Vision* (Minneapolis: Fortress Press, 1989), pp. 125-26. To understand the personal and communal conversion to God it requires is to "comprehend what the centrality of Jesus Christ finally means" (p. 136).

24. Kenneth Cracknell, "The Theology of Religious Plurality" (paper delivered at the WCC's Consultation on the Theological Significance of Other Faiths, held in Baar, Switzerland, September 3-8, 1993, and printed in *Current Dialogue* 26 [June 1994], published by WCC Office on Inter-Religious Relations).

was, at least in part, a critique or redefinition of Christendom. It asserted that God alone knows the true Christian. An important distinction of Reformed thinking in this regard, e.g., for Barth, Tillich, Bonhoeffer, and the Niebuhrs, is that between the idea of *election* and the idea of an *elite*. What the ideas have in common is the affirmation that there will be but a few — "in theological terms, the realistic recognition that not everyone will see and respond to the holy. The distinguishing factor is their *telos:* the purpose inherent in an elite is precisely to produce a small and distinct group; but the purpose inherent in election, is that a few are chosen to do something for the many. The elect are not an end in themselves, but are a means to an infinitely greater end. The Kingdom is infinitely greater than the church." Reformed thinking on election seems to have a double angle of vision. One focus is on the present, and then the question is, Who is saved? But this is always held in relation to a focus on the ultimate future fulfillment of God's will, and the question of *telos.* "What will such a fulfillment look like? How does it affect us now? The future fulfillment includes all people in potential, in some kind of community that is beyond our imagination. This vision of God's [inclusive] will in creation and re-creation meets me as hope in the present."[25] Exploration of how God's choice of a people is related to God's ultimate purposes in creation and redemption — whether it be along the lines Lindbeck suggests or otherwise — is bound to enlarge our theological approach to interfaith relations.

5. A further development of the theological understanding that relates the themes of servant church, sovereign God, and reconciliation is found in a study document presently circulating in the United Church of Canada. This working paper, *Toward a Renewed Understanding of Ecumenism,* was drafted by the Inter-Church Inter-Faith Committee of that church and has been sent out widely "for discussion and response" in order to prepare a statement for adoption which will "redefine the ecumenical agenda of The United Church of Canada." Its vision flows out of the conviction that "the chief ecumenical scandal of our time is not the disunity of the Christian church [but] the institutional preoccupation of the church in the face of the suffering in the world." Its affirmations explore some important theological tenets for engaging religious plurality. Please bear with another lengthy quotation:

25. Hall, in conversation.

"The Church should recognize that God is creatively and redemptively at work in the religious life of all mankind." . . .

There has been a continuous tradition in the United Church . . . of seeking to trust in, and respond to, the presence and power of God's Spirit in our lives and in the world. This presence and power is called the Reign, or Kingdom, of God. . . . From beginning to end, the Bible speaks of God as Creator of the whole world, including all its creatures and all its people. . . . Jesus adopts this biblical vision and proclaims the Reign of God . . . fulfilled. . . . Jesus preaches, teaches, heals, lives, dies and is raised for the Reign of God. . . . For Jesus, God's healing and fulfilling purposes are directed towards the whole world, including the sparrows, the lilies, the outcast, the oppressed, the sick, the sinners, and holy people, regardless of race or religion. . . .

The presence and power of God's Spirit . . . is not restricted to Jesus or to his followers or to the Church . . . but extends to people of other faith communities. Jesus instructs the community of his followers to seek and celebrate the presence of this Spirit wherever it may be found. . . . How well we live with compassion, how well we build communities of peace with justice, and how well we act with others to restore the world to wholeness are measures . . . of our faithfulness to this biblical vision. . . .

For Christians . . . all people have unity under God by virtue of the fact that Christ has "reconciled the world" to God. Christians are given this vision of the oneness of humankind and are called to act upon it, not only in witnessing to Christ, but in practicing all the implications of being in one family with all other human beings. . . .

Human life is intimately and inextricably interrelated with everything else in creation. . . . Human beings belong to nature, and serve as stewards of nature under God. . . . No one religious community or group can accomplish the task [of the stewardship of creation] alone. . . .

This understanding of whole-world ecumenism, then, flows out of the biblical picture of the Reign of God, the unity of the human family, the interrelatedness of creation, and the reconciling activity of Christ. . . .

A United Church operating out of this understanding will continue to bear faithful Christian witness. It will testify to the truth it believes, but in a spirit of humility, with . . . sincere openness to the insight, wisdom and grace that God's unpredictable Spirit has brought into view through people of other religious traditions and those of none. . . . A United Church operating out of this understanding will no longer embrace ideas that, for instance, equate the Church with the Reign of God, or present the Church as the only vessel of salvation, or identify Christians as the only children of God. . . . The Westminster Catechism declares that the chief end of human beings is to glorify God and enjoy God forever. An understanding of ecumenism that affirms the freedom of God, the reconciling work of Christ, and the presence of the Spirit's "fingerprint" in people of every religious tradition will encourage Christians to see and enjoy the glory of God reflected in the faith and lives of people of other religions and ideologies. . . . [And] "Those who are truly oriented towards God . . . will simultaneously be oriented towards God's world" (D. J. Hall, 1991). For it is "the world" God loves and intends to save, to heal, to liberate. . . .

All that God is doing in the world . . . is not accomplished only, or even primarily, through the Church. The Church advances God's work through the modest yet significant task of being a sign and sacrament of God's presence and power for the world. The unity of the Church . . . is a sign of the promise of God for the unity of the whole world. . . . If the church is to be an able servant of God in the work of the world's fulfillment . . . it must be firmly grounded in the remembrance and love of Jesus, "the church's one foundation," and constantly engage the living Word of God in the scriptures. . . . The demands of whole-world ecumenism call for a deepening commitment to Jesus and a closer following in the way of his servanthood. . . .

The mission of God is larger than the Church, but the Church has its part to play. . . . The Church is to bear witness to God's Reign and seek to understand others, to attend to their needs, and to discover allies among them in the common work of healing the Earth. . . . What is new is the . . . setting above all else of God's mission to and with all peoples to heal and fulfill the creation. . . .

For some Christians, the idea that "God is creatively and redemptively at work in the religious life of all people" (Report of the Commission on World Mission, 1966) will be a questionable one. . . . There has been a long tradition in some churches of claiming that Jesus is the only one through whom the saving knowledge and power of God has been revealed. . . . Can it not be affirmed that [Jesus'] way was the way of love with justice . . . that his life was "full of the Holy

Spirit" . . . and that his truth was the truth of God's Reign that extends over the whole creation? Jesus' way and truth and life are indeed God's way and truth and life. But God's way and truth and life are not limited to Jesus and his followers. . . . Salvation always entails having the same Spirit as that which was in Jesus. Salvation, life in the Reign of God, always and everywhere is the result of being born of the Spirit "from above" (John 3:3). However, that Spirit, which was the Spirit of Jesus, "blows where it wills." It would not be true to Jesus' own faith to exclude everyone but himself and his followers from the saving activity of God. . . .

One of the central assertions of this document, that " 'God is creatively and redemptively at work in the religious life of all mankind,' " offers one theological understanding of how God's redemptive activity in Christ is related to God's wider redemptive aim: the "way and the truth and the life" are not reserved for those in Christ; rather, salvation, life in the reign of God, is available as a gift through the uncontainable action of the one Spirit. I find this argument reminiscent of the statement in the WCC's "Guidelines on Dialogue" (I.B.11), that "The Gospel cannot be limited to any particular culture, but through the inspiration of the Holy Spirit sheds its light in them all and upon them all"; or to Panikkar's thesis that Christ, the "universal redeemer," is "present in one form or another in every human being as he journeys towards God."[26] All such arguments may be "an unwelcome intrusion into the integrity of other religions,"[27] and may lead to a loss of Christ though a devaluing of the real humanity of Jesus.[28] However, there may be wider acceptance of this document's idea of the universal and redemptive Spirit.[29] As clearly as it has

26. Raimundo Panikkar, *The Unknown Christ of Hinduism* (Maryknoll, N.Y.: Orbis, 1981), p. 67.

27. Nehemiah Thompson, "Toward a Christological Approach to Interfaith Dialogue," *Ecumenical Trends* 23, no. 4 (April 1994): 12.

28. Jane Smith points out this aspect of Stanley Samartha's thought in her excellent survey of theological positions regarding salvation, in "Understanding and Witnessing to Christ in a Pluralistic World," report from the Baar Consultation on the Theological Significance of Other Faiths, in *Current Dialogue* 26 (June 1994).

29. I think Jane Smith is right when she says that "Most mainline Protestants probably hold to some version of this position [salvation is available to non-Christians but is mediated through their own religions by the grace of God through

insisted on the role of Christ in redemption, Reformed thinking has also insisted that God requires no particular forms of mediation — no system of priestly mediation — but calls individuals into the reconciled community directly, by the Spirit. More persuasive altogether is the paper's articulation of God's reign, of God's intention in relation to the whole world, and of the role for the church and for people of other faiths in this wider work of redemption.

Among the generative questions that they answered, the early Reformers addressed that of God's will for creation and found that the redemptive purposes of God depended on the salvation of all the elect in and through Jesus Christ. It is clear in all the confessions that this saving activity, however, is part of God's larger design for all creation: life is headed toward a specific goal. Later Reformed theology has formulated this divine aim in creation in other language. The former Presbyterian Church in the United States, for example, in a paper entitled "The Nature of the Unity We Seek,"[30] affirms that "it is God's creative intention that the world live as one. . . . We proclaim that God wills all humanity to be one, that the Church is called to embody that unity in its own life, that the church's unity is a sign and means of the unity of humankind." Similar ideas find sharper expression in the Confession of 1967:

> God has created the peoples of the earth to be one universal family. In his reconciling love he overcomes the barriers based on racial or ethnic difference. . . . The church is called to bring all men to receive and uphold one another as persons in all relationships of life. . . . Biblical visions and images of the rule of Christ . . . culminate in the image of the Kingdom. The Kingdom represents the triumph of God over all that resists his will and disrupts his creation. Already God's reign is present as a ferment in the world, stirring hope in men and preparing the world to receive its ultimate judgment and redemp-

---

Christ]. They don't agree that there is no salvation possible in other religions, but in general they do agree with the Reformation position that salvation is through Christ alone" ("Understanding and Witnessing"). Explorations of the role of the Spirit in redemption may be accessible to those of a slightly wider range of theological viewpoints.

30. Adopted by the 118th General Assembly of the Presbyterian Church in the United States.

tion. . . . In steadfast hope the church looks beyond all partial achievement to the final triumph of God.[31]

The document before us continues this emphasis on the redemption of all creation, but sees God's reign as a reality that is very much present if not yet complete.[32] The kingdom "extends over the whole creation," and already gives people the gift of unity "by virtue of the fact that Christ has 'reconciled the world' to God." The *telos* of the creative and redemptive work of God, in either formulation, is the redemption of all and the establishment of God's reign in all its fullness.

At the heart of this vision of God's ultimate purposes in creation, for Reformed people, is an understanding of God's sovereignty:

Every mobile has a plumbline, whether visible or invisible, that runs through its gravitational center. So too any . . . Christian community must have a plumbline. That center in the Reformed tradition is a radical devotion to a sovereign God. . . . We join with all Protestants in acknowledging the authority of scripture and justification by grace through faith. But we [of the Reformed tradition] also affirm that the fullness of Christ's good news is not made completely transparent in disciples unless they take with utter seriousness "the majesty, holiness, and providence of God who creates, sustains, rules and redeems the world in the freedom of sovereign righteousness and love."[33]

31. Confession of 1967, II.A.4, and III.

32. This is consonant with such expressions as that in the Second Helvetic Confession: "Our Fathers had the Gospel in this way in the writings of the prophets by which they attained salvation in Christ through faith, yet the Gospel is properly called glad and joyous news, in which . . . is preached to us in the world that God *has now performed* what he promised from the beginning of the world . . ." (chap. XIII, my emphasis). Note, however, that "for the Reformers [the hope of God's kingdom] occupied only a very minor place. In the first place, the Kingdom of God was not primarily used as future eschatological symbol, but was rather understood as God's actual reign, present in the Church. . . . The thought of the transformation and fulfillment of the whole of creation, if mentioned at all, holds, surprisingly, a relatively minor place, attention being directed towards eternal life and the resurrection of the individual. . . ." Flesseman-van Leer, pp. 18-19.

33. Coalter, Mulder, and Weeks, pp. 244, 284. "There is but one only living and true God . . . all sufficient . . . alone fountain of all being, of whom, through whom, and to whom, are all things; and [God] hath most sovereign dominion over them, to do by them, for them, and upon them, whatsoever himself pleaseth. . . ." Westminster Confession, chap. II.

The power of sovereignty is the power to transform. "God's sovereign love is a mystery beyond the reach of man's mind. . . . But God reveals his love in Jesus Christ by showing power in the form of a servant, wisdom in the folly of the cross, and goodness in receiving sinful men. The power of God's love in Christ to transform the world discloses that the Redeemer is the Lord and Creator who made all things to serve the purpose of his love."[34] This document challenges us to take the sovereignty of God especially seriously, not only in terms of what it might mean regarding what God is already doing in the lives of people of other faiths and what we might find of wisdom and partnership among them, but also in terms of understanding the whole world as the proper object of God's love and our service. If God is sovereign, is not discernment a better response to the truth and activity of people of other faiths, than responses of exclusion, inclusion, or fear? The sovereign love of God revealed to us in Jesus Christ challenges us to ever fuller understanding of God's presence and purpose in all creation, and to taking up our human part in the transformative work of God's redemption of it.

The church, again in this view, is not coterminous with God's kingdom or reign.[35] Instead it is a sign and a means to the end of human unity. "As Christians we are conscious of a tension between the Christian community as we experience it to be in the world of human communities, and as we believe it in essence to be in the promise of God. . . . In the heart of this tension we discover the character of the Christian Church as a sign at once of people's need for fuller and deeper community, and of God's promise of a restored human community in Christ."[36] Likewise, understanding mission as modeled in the life and passion of Christ, and its proper scope to be as wide as God's love for creation, suggests an undeniable connectedness with the world and

34. Confession of 1967, I.B.

35. Such thinking both radically alters, and echoes, early Reformed understandings of the "invisible church": "Outside the church of God there is no salvation. . . . Nevertheless . . . we do not so narrowly restrict the church as to teach that all those are outside the church . . . in whom faith sometimes fails . . . or in whom imperfection and errors due to weakness are found. For we know that God had some friends outside the commonwealth of Israel. . . ." Second Helvetic Confession, chap. XVII.

36. "Guidelines on Dialogue," World Council of Churches, par. 14.

with other people, not a setting apart from the world. The church has a role to play which is at once humble — as a sign, and giver of testimony — and powerful, taking part as a means in bringing about the unity and justice of God's kingdom. It is with such an end in mind, if unstated, that cooperation with people of other religions is actually mandated by the Book of Order of the PCUSA: "The Presbyterian Church (USA) will seek new opportunities for conversation and understanding with non-Christian religious bodies in order that interests and concerns may be shared and common action undertaken where compatible means and aims exist" (G-15.0104). Relations with people of other faiths will necessarily be understood differently as this kind of nontriumphalistic theology of the church is further developed.

6. A few brief remarks to conclude. The first is to at least make recognition of the fact that I have not made use of the theological affirmations and studies of the past years dealing with Christian-Jewish relations. The Presbyterian Church (USA) study paper (1987) on the theological understanding of Christian-Jewish relations, and related statements from the United Church of Christ and the Reformed Church, make covenant a central focus. "We affirm that the living God whom Christians worship is the same God who is worshipped and served by Jews. We bear witness that the God revealed in Jesus, a Jew, to be the Triune Lord of all, is the same one disclosed in the life and worship of Israel."[37] All of these statements agree in affirming that the covenant between God and the Jewish people, or Israel, has not been abrogated, or superseded. These affirmations offer surprisingly little help to us regarding religious pluralism, however, because their focus is on a correct theological understanding of the specific intrafamily relationship between Christians and Jews. Calvin and the early Reformers saw Israel within the context of the *ecclesia aeterna,* as a part of salvation history. God's faithfulness to the covenant is the foundation of salvation. In fact, it would "be an absurdity if man's unfaithfulness could shake the Covenant." The covenant relationship is

> not built on man, but upon God alone, [and] must stand fast and immovable even if man's disloyalty revolts against it. . . . Calvin states repeatedly that God's faithfulness to the Covenant is without

37. "Study Paper on Christian-Jewish Relations," Presbyterian Church (USA).

end. Israel is and remains chosen by God. To contradict this destroys the foundations of salvation, which rest upon God's mercy and cannot be destroyed. The reformatory *sola gratia*, by mercy alone, is rooted and established in Israel.[38]

Christianity's relationship with the Jewish people is intimately intertwined in its understanding of its own identity, and of God's redemptive activity, but with historical and hermeneutical dimensions that repeatedly make it a special case rather than a model for insights regarding the relationship to religious plurality in general.

More than from any exploration of covenant, or of salvation, instructive theological insights for religious pluralism are likely to come through further consideration of God's sovereignty in creation; the meaning of incarnation and reconciliation; the role of the Holy Spirit; and "post-Constantinian, diaspora"[39] understanding of the church. A new theological understanding of the church, especially vis-à-vis God's kingdom, will be especially relevant to this discussion. "As we move out of Christianity's monarchical phase, and into a more beggarly phase, dialogue will be more possible. We will need not a triumphal theology but another, humble theology. As we're kicked out of the emperor's house, we will discover others who have lived there for a long time. We may develop a theology for the diaspora with others."[40]

Finally, a renewed exploration of Scripture and of revelation in regard to religious pluralism will be essential to any further Reformed approach to religious pluralism. "God speaks in the questions that come out of experience. The questions send you back to Scripture and the tradition. Staying with the questions can in turn raise questions about the tradition of how the text is read, [until] you find the tradition and the text speaking again."[41] The experience of many Christians is making them aware as never before of God speaking to them through people of other faiths. What does this mean? What might it mean theologically to be one faith among many? "We do not yet have a Schüssler Fiorenza to do such a wrestling with the text from the viewpoint of interfaith

38. Hans-Joachim Kraus, *Israel in the Theology of Calvin*, Occasional Paper, no. 1, Office of Ecumenical and Interfaith Relations, Presbyterian Church (USA).

39. Hall, in conversation.

40. Hall, in conversation.

41. Thomas, in conversation.

relations and religious pluralism."[42] A serious wrestling with the biblical text and our hermeneutical traditions from such a viewpoint is needed to nourish the further development of theological questions and resources for religious pluralism.

42. Thomas, in conversation.

CHAPTER FIVE

A Mennonite Theology for Interfaith Relations

THOMAS FINGER

I. Religious Normativity and Cultural Normativity

Christianity's traditional assumption about its normativity among the world's religions has been much critiqued in recent years. A chief reason is the charge that religious absolutism leads to cultural and economic imperialism and oppression. For instance, in the well-known volume *The Myth of Christian Uniqueness,* John Hick complains that "Christian absolutism, in collaboration with acquisitive and violent human nature, has done much to poison the relationships between the Christian minority and the non-Christian majority of the world's population by sanctifying exploitation and oppression on a gigantic scale."[1] Marjorie Suchocki adds that "Absolutizing one religion, such that it becomes normative for all others, is a dynamic with clear parallels to sexism, whereby one gender is established as the norm for human existence. Therefore the critique of sexism can be extended as a critique of religious imperialism."[2] Tom Driver agrees that "both sexism and racism are supported by the doctrine of a single, unique, unsurpassable Christ who has appeared 'once for all' in the past."[3] Many similar quotations could be cited.

1. John Hick and Paul Knitter, eds., *The Myth of Christian Uniqueness* (Maryknoll, N.Y.: Orbis, 1987), p. 17.
2. Hick and Knitter, p. 150.
3. Hick and Knitter, p. 216.

One might wonder whether such sentiments emerge chiefly among academic scholars prone to exaggerate Christianity's negative side. While this may sometimes be true, it is noteworthy that ecumenical mission efforts themselves, as recently as the 1960s, often linked Christ's superiority with that of certain Western trends. Konrad Raiser, current general secretary of the World Council of Churches (WCC), argues that from about 1950 to 1970 the ecumenical movement was guided by a paradigm of *christocentric universalism*. This term was coined by Willem Visser 't Hooft, for many years the mission-minded WCC general secretary, in his book *No Other Name*[4] — whose title Paul Knitter's influential *No Other Name?* surely recalls.[5]

This paradigm stressed Christ as "Cosmocrator," the cosmic Lord whose effective rule operates everywhere.[6] This seemed to imply *universalism:* that history as a whole is "salvation history," is God's salvific work. God was thought to be active chiefly through *secularization:* the freeing of social, cultural, and economic forces from religious limitations to reshape all reality through their historicizing sweep. This movement seemed most visible in international economic trends, which, originating from the West, were apparently directing all nations toward greater interdependence and prosperity.[7] Christocentric universalism's proponents were especially impressed by Arend Th. van Leeuwen's *Christianity in World History: The Meeting of Faiths in East and West.*[8] Van Leeuwen argued that all ancient civilizations — Chinese, Indian, Middle Eastern, Near Eastern, and Mediterranean — were "ontocratic": rooted in an unvarying cosmic order and ruled through sacral kingship. Only through the biblical traditions — *and* Greek rationalism — was this ontocracy challenged and a God who works through historical change to destroy ontocratic structures brought to light.

In the foreword to van Leeuwen's volume, Hendrik Kraemer, probably christocentric mission's foremost ecumenical proponent from the 1930s to the 1950s, praised it for its "analysis of Western civilization

4. Visser 't Hooft, *No Other Name* (Philadelphia: Westminster, 1963), pp. 103-13.
5. Knitter, *No Other Name?* (Maryknoll, N.Y.: Orbis, 1985).
6. Konrad Raiser, *Ecumenism in Transition* (Geneva, Switzerland: WCC Publications, 1991), p. 43.
7. Raiser, pp. 49, 65-66.
8. Van Leeuwen, *Christianity in World History: The Meeting of Faiths in East and West* (Edinburgh: House Press, 1964).

as a unique phenomenon, in contradistinction with the great ontocratic civilizations — a uniqueness which can only be accounted for by the biblical-prophetic and Greek rational strains in it."[9] Lesslie Newbigin affirmed that "A truly biblical understanding of the process of secularization will lead the Church out to the frontiers where that process is most vigorously at work, to be the interpreter of the offer of freedom and the threat of bondage which are hidden within the movement of secularization."[10]

As the reference to "the threat of bondage" shows, christocentric universalism's proponents also critiqued many aspects of secularization, and of Western civilization's broader impact on other cultures. (Since the 1970s, Newbigin seems to have dropped positive references to secularization altogether.) And even though they vigorously opposed all syncretism,[11] their approach to other religions was not sharply *exclusive* — restricting salvation to all who confessed Christ — but usually *inclusive* — allowing for salvation through other religions, although its ultimate agent was Christ.[12] Nonetheless, this relatively recent linking of Christ's normativity with certain Western trends in ecumenical circles helps explain why the connections between religious and cultural absolutism are being so rigorously scrutinized in those same circles today. For, as Raiser notes, it soon became evident that Western technocracy's spread was spawning not unity but divisions: between rich and poor, north and south, humankind and its environment. This dominating force, indeed, increasingly appeared to constitute a closed, materialistic system, based on violence, devastating its own biological foundations, and driven by the logic of profit and power.[13]

The connection between religious normativity and cultural normativity provides an illuminating vantage point for sketching a Mennonite approach to interfaith relations. For at the heart of the Anabaptist

9. Van Leeuwen, p. x.

10. Newbigin, *Honest Religion for Secular Man* (Philadelphia: Westminster, 1966), p. 137.

11. E.g., Visser 't Hooft, pp. 113-25; for his perspective on interfaith dialogue, see pp. 117-20.

12. Cf. Hick and Knitter, p. viii; a third position, which the authors of this volume share, is the *pluralist*, briefly defined as "a move away from insistence on the superiority or finality of Christ and Christianity toward a recognition of the independent validity of other ways" (p. viii).

13. Raiser, pp. 63-64.

impulse one finds a radical critique of cultural normativity — yet one which is not opposed to, but is actually rooted in, an understanding of religious normativity.

II. Basic Themes for a Mennonite Approach

Mennonites have been a practical and ethical more than a reflective and theological people. This has been partly due to historical factors. Since Reformation times we have often been denied access to education and to the culture in which higher education moves. It also stems from our insistence that affirmations of faith and theologies (or worship or church structures, for that matter) are empty, and often blasphemous, unless the faith which they express is lived. Accordingly, in articulating a Mennonite theological perspective on most topics, the problem lies not in selecting from an abundance of written resources, but in finding any at all.

Consequently, I will draw largely on generalizations, chiefly about Anabaptism, on which scholars generally agree, but whose implications for interfaith relations have seldom been unfolded. (I will be emphasizing Mennonite ideals which, let me be honest, have not always been matched in practice.) Fortunately, the first-ever Mennonite conference on religious pluralism took place during the summer of 1994, providing some papers (as yet unpublished) and discussion — some of it different from my perspective — which I will include. I will also use statements from Mennonite mission agencies collected for our National Council of Churches of Christ study process.[14]

Anabaptism arose at a time when Christian absoluteness had long been connected with imperialism (against Germanic tribes, Slavic tribes, Moslems, etc.) and used to buttress the church's superior social status (ownership of land, predominance of church officials from higher classes, etc.). The entire Reformation involved significant protests

14. See Thomas Finger, "What Are Mennonites Saying about Religious Pluralism?" *Mission Focus* 1 (1993): 33-38. In the same volume, see also Ashish Chrispal, "Confessing Jesus Christ as the Lord in the Context of Religious Pluralism" (pp. 25-31), and David Shenk, "Muslims and Christians: Finding Doors through the Walls" (pp. 39-44). The address for this periodical is 3003 Benham Ave., Elkhart, IN, 46517.

against church collusion with social power. (Through the centuries, of course, the church had challenged as well as cooperated with current powers in various ways.) But rather than opposing the church's role in oppression by rejecting all normative Christian claims, the Reformers sought to reduce and revise these claims — such as papal authority — by others they deemed more fundamental — such as biblical authority. The Anabaptists followed this general strategy of criticizing Christianity's perversions by what they considered its core. More than other contemporary groups, they regarded Jesus' entire life — including his teaching, example, suffering, and cross — as the ultimate norm for all human activity, and for critiquing all its flaws.

In what follows, I will first develop from the general Anabaptist perspective four themes for a Mennonite interfaith theology. Then, with input from the recent Mennonite interfaith conference, I will sketch three more. After considering a pluralistic approach[15] authored by a Mennonite (Gordon Kaufman), I will discuss, in dialogue with it, two points especially relevant to our current situation.

A. General Anabaptist Affirmations

1. *Jesus Christ, including his specific teachings, example, and way of life, provides the ultimate norm for all human living.*[16] Unlike their contemporaries, Anabaptists made no two-level anthropological distinction: between one way of life with its accompanying norms which all humans could follow, and another for Christians alone. Gone were Catholic distinctions between nature and grace, and Protestant ones between civil and religious righteousness and between the worldly kingdom and Christ's. Anabaptists proposed only one norm for Chris-

15. For a definition of pluralistic, see note 12 above.

16. This was affirmed by three of the four major papers at the Mennonite interfaith conference: John Toews, "Toward a Biblical Perspective on People of Other Faiths," esp. pp. 7, 19; J. Denny Weaver, "Christus Victor and Other Religions," who attributes any recent uneasiness about this to our "newfound position and respect earned in the public order" (p. 19); and Gayle Gerber Koontz, "Evangelical Peace Theology and Religious Pluralism: Particularity in Perspective," who affirms this repeatedly in explicating John Howard Yoder's theology. For the fourth paper, Gordon Kaufman's, see section C below.

tian — and thus for any truly human — life: Jesus Christ in his historical specificity. Though such a standard had been considered normative by many monastic groups,[17] Anabaptists applied it to the entire church.

Anabaptists rejected arguments that Jesus' commands should be adjusted to current social realities or postponed until society was more ready, or that they could be realized only at history's end. Against objections that literal adherence to Jesus' way was not yet possible, they insisted that God's kingdom was already present and practicable in just this sense. One should not assume, however, that because they stressed Jesus' concrete humanity Anabaptists placed correspondingly less emphasis on his deity, even though some contemporary Mennonites might imply this.[18] If anything, the extremities Anabaptists experienced caused them to rely more than others on Jesus' divine presence and power. It has been convincingly argued that divinization — transformation by participation in his divine nature — formed Anabaptism's soteriological heart.[19] In other words, Jesus Christ himself, in his divine

17. Groups such as the Franciscan Tertiaries and Brethren of the Common Life, originating from monastic impulses but consisting of married persons who often remained in secular occupations, grew rapidly during the fifteenth century. Kenneth Davis traces Anabaptism's main lineage through these to ascetic movements back to the desert fathers, rather than to heretical medieval movements or Protestantism (*Anabaptism and Asceticism* [Scottdale, Pa.: Herald, 1974]). This, along with the rejection of two-level anthropologies and salvation as divinization (see n. 19), suggests striking similarities between Anabaptism and Eastern Orthodoxy, though significant historical connections have not been demonstrated (see Finger, "Anabaptism and Eastern Orthodoxy: Some Unexpected Similarities?" *Journal of Ecumenical Studies* 31, nos. 1 and 2 [winter-spring 1994]: 67-91).

18. Modern Mennonites have been deeply influenced by Harold Bender's *The Anabaptist Vision* (Scottdale, Pa.: Herald, 1944), which listed Anabaptism's main features as: "the essence of Christianity as discipleship," "a new conception of the Church as a brotherhood," and "the ethic of love and nonresistance as applied to all human relationships" (pp. 20, 33). All three points, along with Jesus' teaching and example, could be, and have been, understood very largely in social-ethical terms, though this was far from Bender's purpose. Underlying such reductionism is often the assumption that Anabaptism can be adequately defined by emphasizing its *distinctives* — e.g., its stress on Jesus' humanity — while its *commonalities* with other Christian traditions — e.g., confession of Christ's deity — were relatively unimportant. In my view, this results in a very incomplete, one-sided, and ahistorical account of Anabaptism.

19. See Alvin Beachy, *The Concept of Grace in the Radical Reformation* (Nieuwkoop, The Netherlands: B. DeGraf, 1977); cf. Finger, "Anabaptism and Eastern Orthodoxy." Though Anabaptists often spoke of Christ's divine "nature" as that in which Christians participate, this term was not technically equivalent to divine "essence."

and human reality, and not simply a teaching abstractable from his living presence, provided the ultimate[20] by which Anabaptism sought to revise all other ultimate Christian and cultural claims.

2. *Peace, sharing, and justice are at the heart of this normative way.* Jesus' teaching and example against resisting evil by force seem most contrary to what individuals and societies apparently must do for self-preservation. Accordingly, the Anabaptists' commitment to follow him often became most visible at this point, especially in their refusal of military involvement.[21] However, Jesus' overall vision of peace *(shalom)* included sharing material goods and harmony among social, ethnic, and gender groups.[22] Consequently, Anabaptists sharply criticized many injustices of their time. They shared material goods among themselves (sometimes in total communal fashion) and aided other needy persons whenever they could. This social vision contradicted all oppressive, imperialistic structures. They were willing, on the contrary, to suffer horribly at the hands of imperialistic structures and authorities. Since these authorities were commonly thought to exercise a divine, absolute power, Anabaptists withstood their terrors only through firm belief in a yet more ultimate one.

3. *Jesus' way generally appeals more to the oppressed, marginalized, and poor than to others.* Anabaptism's greater stress on Jesus' way, with its critique of social oppression and his suffering and cross, may explain why it appealed mainly to peasants and simple artisans.[23] And Ana-

---

20. Finding the best term for this dimension of Christ is difficult. "Absolute" seems adequate insofar as it indicates the opposite of something merely relative; yet "absolute" can connote the complete totality of something, and we do not maintain that Christ comprises the complete totality of revelation, or of God (insofar as God is trinitarian [see point 9 below]). "Normative" is adequate insofar as it denotes a standard, but inadequate for conveying a living reality. "Ultimate" seems the best term for what we want to say about the fullness of Jesus Christ.

21. A small minority of Anabaptists believed that they could take up the sword in God's final, apocalyptic judgment. Historians long treated these, such as the fanatics leading the occupation of Munster, as representatives of the entire movement, despite the fact that most Anabaptists were persecuted for the opposite reason (their pacifism).

22. See Finger, *Christian Theology: An Eschatological Approach,* vol. 1 (Scottdale, Pa.: Herald, 1985), pp. 282-91.

23. Lutheran and Reformed approaches attracted many princes and rising bourgeoisie, whose treatment of lower classes often approximated that of former ruling elites.

baptists who were not from the lower classes usually joined them, for deprivation of goods, property, and civil rights often followed their conversion. I do not mean that Anabaptists — or Jesus — wholly favored the poor, as an entire social class, and wholly condemned the rich, considered simply as an opposed class. This would equate Jesus' way with another human social scheme. Jesus' way is open to all, demands repentance from all, and critiques all social systems. Nevertheless, since the poor are often more open to the reversals it demands, and accept it more gladly and more often, while the rich are far more often closed to it, "the poor" are favored or "preferred" in this sense.[24]

4. *The greatest opposition to Jesus' normative way comes not from non-Christian religions but from perverted forms of Christianity.* In Reformation times the "Turks," who nearly broke through Vienna, greatly threatened European civilization. Anabaptists, because they rejected military service, and because their formation of separate churches was thought to weaken the political unity necessary for resisting such opponents, were usually tried for treason (not simply for heresy). Moreover, since some Anabaptists predicted that God's judgment on Europe would come through the Turks, Anabaptists were often regarded as favoring this enemy.

At his trial, Michael Sattler was asked whether he would fight for the Turks. He replied that he would never fight — but that if he did,

> I would rather take the field against the so-called Christians who persecute, take captive, and kill true Christians . . . for the following reason: the Turk is a genuine Turk and knows nothing of the Christian faith. He is a Turk according to the flesh. But you claim to be Christians, boast of Christ, and still persecute the faithful witnesses of Christ.

24. Aruna Gnanadason (a non-Mennonite) of the WCC's Justice, Peace and Creation Unit prepared a paper for the Mennonite interfaith conference. She described "the liberative emphasis of the gospel" in a way that privileged the poor (p. 11). Since she was unfortunately unable to attend, this paper could not be discussed as intended. Paul Knitter recommends that "The fundamental option for the poor and nonpersons" provide the starting point for interfaith relations (in Hick and Knitter, p. 186 [see point 8 below]). For fuller discussion of how the "poor" are favored, see Finger, *Christian Theology*, vol. 1, pp. 284-88, 301.

This response probably increased the barbarity of Sattler's penalty.[25]

Sattler did not affirm positive values in Islam — about which he likely knew little. But he suggested that for Anabaptists, authentic Christianity had no special links with Europe. European civilization, rather than enjoying God's favor because it was "Christian," was more fully under God's judgment than other civilizations precisely because it resisted and falsified Christ's message, which it knew better than others. Today many ask: how can Christianity be normative when it is so Western? Anabaptists might well respond that the West, as a whole, is probably further from Christ's true way, and more opposed to it, than other civilizations. Persons in other cultures, and thus often in other religions, will likely be more open to Jesus' real message than Westerners.[26]

B. Current Mennonite Affirmations

Informed by the foregoing themes, Mennonite theologians propose guidelines like those below for today's interfaith relations.

5. *Approach other religions with openness and willingness to learn.* While Mennonites generally believe that ultimate truth has been revealed in Christ, most do not assume that other religions know nothing at all about it. John Howard Yoder cautions against making general claims about particular religions, first, because the Bible doesn't, and second, because such judgments should be based on actual contacts.[27]

---

25. Quotation is from John Howard Yoder, ed., *The Legacy of Michael Sattler* (Scottdale, Pa.: Herald, 1973), pp. 72-73. The verdict prescribed that Sattler be given to the hangman, " 'who shall lead him to the square and cut off his tongue, then chain him to a wagon, there tear his body twice with red hot tongs, and again when he is brought before the gate, five times more.' When this is done to be burned to powder as a heretic" (p. 75).

26. Such an assertion disagrees with Rosemary Ruether's skepticism as to whether Christianity "can be disincarnated from its Greco-Roman flesh" (in Hick and Knitter, p. 139).

27. Gerber Koontz, p. 11; Toews argues that texts affirming Jesus as the only way to salvation (Acts 4:12; 1 Cor. 3:11; 1 Tim. 3:5) are addressed to Christians, not others. Yet that Jesus is the only way to salvation for all is an implication of his lordship (pp. 7, 20-21). Even the most conservative Mennonite mission boards officially affirm positive values in non-Christian religions (Finger, "What Are Mennonites Saying?").

No a priori reason exists for assuming that another religion is responding to another god (or the same God, as John Hick assumes).[28] Yet the major motives for this openness are christological. For Yoder, the ultimacy of Christ, in whom "Light and truth have taken on the vulnerability of the particular," directs us to be radically vulnerable in relations with others.[29] Love of adversaries; the dignity of lowly, continual repentance; servanthood — all are central to Jesus' story. Coercion should never infiltrate interfaith contacts because noncoercion in all affairs, as exemplified in Jesus, is itself part of the gospel.[30] In all such relationships, Yoder underlines the importance of patience.[31]

Expecting to learn more about God from such openness, Mennonites need not think of Jesus as God's sole revelation, but rather as revelation's norm. Earl Martin, as Mennonite Central Committee's co-secretary for Asia, affirmed that before entering a culture, "God is present there. Hence we walk on Holy Ground." We should thus "be attentive if God should want to speak to us through the persons of faith and life traditions different from our own."[32] From his New Testament studies, John Toews concludes that God is present in the religious histories of all people. This approach may sound like the *inclusive* position, for it often seems to attribute saving truth in other religions to Christ.[33] Yet with their emphasis on concrete relationships in particular settings, Mennonites usually resist broad inclusivist affirmations like "all religions are pathways to God" and resist identifying points where positive parallels among religions exist.[34] J. Denny Weaver sug-

---

28. Hick, *An Interpretation of Religion* (London: MacMillan, 1989), pp. 245-46.

29. Yoder, "The Hermeneutics of Peoplehood," *Journal of Religious Ethics* 10 (spring 1982): 65; cf. Gerber Koontz, pp. 14, 28.

30. Gerber Koontz, pp. 13, 15.

31. Yoder describes pedagogical, pastoral, and ecumenical patience, and the patience of the minority, of repentance, and of modesty (Gerber Koontz, p. 21).

32. In Finger, "What Are Mennonites Saying?" p. 36.

33. Toews bases his case especially on Acts (pp. 12, 24). He claims that in the New Testament "The religious history of various peoples is a kind of pre-history for God's new revelation and complete salvation in Christ," although Christ judges as well as fulfills other faiths (pp. 19-20). Yoder affirms that whatever good anyone does, it is not apart from Christ (Gerber Koontz, p. 10). These statements seem inclusivistic.

34. Cf. Finger, *Christian Theology: An Eschatological Approach,* vol. 2 (Scottdale, Pa.: Herald, 1989), pp. 308-17.

gests that trajectories — arcs through the same general field which intersect at various points but need have no similar shape, origin, goal, or length — better express the relationships among religions.

6. *Emphasize and embody chiefly Jesus' story and his way.* Mennonite "dialogue" is above all interpersonal involvement; verbal discussion will likely be artificial if not embedded in living relationships. And though verbal activity may include theological affirmations, Mennonites generally fear that these will be too abstract, or even distortive, unless frequently illuminated by Jesus' story, to which they refer. There is no good news about Jesus' lordship or normativity which is not more concretely defined and exemplified by his servanthood and self-giving way.

Above all, the Mennonite task is *embodiment* of this way.[35] Yet this is costly. Yoder suggests that the major obstacle to emphasizing Jesus' normativity "is the unwillingness of many people to pay the price required for genuine reconciliation and greater social justice to take place on earth."[36]

The problem with much missionary activity was not that it was "tied to Jesus but that it denied him, precisely in its power, and its disrespect for the neighbor. . . . Its error was not that it propagated Christianity around the world, but that what it propagated was not Christian enough." The real task therefore is not "to talk less about Jesus and more about religion, but the contrary."[37] Further, if this message will more likely be received at society's margins, and by comparatively few, it seems unlikely that religious truth will be arrived at through consensus among majorities, especially if their spokespersons come from hyper-educated classes. Whereas much interfaith dialogue seeks to correct self-righteousness by emphasizing our epistemological limitations, such a Christocentrism seeks to correct it "by following

35. For Yoder, according to Gerber Koontz, "proclamation of the gospel is foremost a matter of embodiment and only secondarily a verbal or intellectual message" (p. 14). Some at the interfaith conference, such as William Klassen, recommended focusing interfaith dialogue around the issue of "the Good" rather than "the True." I emphasized, however, that Christian affirmations must also include at least some cognitive claims, and many participants apparently agreed.

36. Gerber Koontz, p. 13.

37. Gerber Koontz, p. 14, quoting Yoder, "The Disavowal of Constantine," *Annals 1975/76* (Tantur: Ecumenical Institute for Advanced Theological Studies, 1979), p. 57.

more fully the Jesus who condemned self-righteousness and exemplified inclusive attitudes towards those defined as social and religious outcasts."[38]

7. *Place the main emphasis on witness and respectful, open relationships in particular settings, not on discerning and hastening history's overall course.* Pluralistic approaches often claim that recent changes have shaken the interreligious world, and that new relations among religions are required to save humankind and the earth from catastrophe.[39] Anabaptists and Mennonites have often felt nearly overwhelmed by evil; few groups have as great reason to take human destructiveness seriously. Yet Mennonites generally believe that evil has already been decisively defeated (though not all its manifestations destroyed) on the cross, and that its final destruction is up to the God of resurrection.[40] Accordingly, while we seek to discern the signs of the times as perceptively as possible, we have difficulty believing that saving our race and the earth is ultimately a human task.[41] Assuming total responsibility for this seems like a tacit confession to the absence of a living God.

Rather than deciphering history's overall course and outcome, Mennonites emphasize faithful listening and witness in local situations, which are more than sufficiently challenging in today's complicated world. Gayle Gerber Koontz suggests that interfaith dialogue rooted in such settings will emphasize (1) quality of relationships rather than apparent "inclusiveness" or "exclusiveness" of faith artic-

---

38. Gerber Koontz, p. 20.

39. E.g., Hick, p. 17, and Gordon Kaufman, p. 13, in Hick and Knitter, eds., *The Myth of Christian Uniqueness.*

40. This is a major emphasis of the so-called *Christus Victor* motif, which is being widely appreciated among Mennonites as an interpretation of Jesus' work. It was a key theme of J. Denny Weaver's paper at the interfaith conference. See also John Driver, *Understanding the Atonement for the Mission of the Church* (Scottdale, Pa.: Herald, 1986), and my *Christian Theology,* vol. 1, pp. 317-59.

41. Gordon Kaufman, a "pluralistic" Mennonite theologian (see section C below), disagrees somewhat, arguing that the nuclear threat has placed humankind in "a radically new religious situation, one completely unanticipated in Christian tradition" (*Theology for a Nuclear Age* [Philadelphia: Westminster, 1985], p. viii), in which simply leaving things in God's hands can be "an ultimate evasion of our responsibility as human beings" (p. 8). This can indeed happen, but only if this trusting in God is divorced from active following of Christ in all of life. Kaufman seems to be significantly more skeptical about "traditional claims about God's providential care and power" (p. x) than most Mennonites would be.

ulations, (2) genuine vulnerability, and (3) openness not so much toward one's convictions as toward the open future of the relationship.[42] Further, since Christian faith is most fully embodied in communal form — the church — dialogue should never be pursued by experts alone, but only within broader interactions among communities and individuals.[43]

C. Gordon Kaufman's Approach

Kaufman, a contributor to *The Myth of Christian Uniqueness*, presented one of four main papers at the Mennonite interfaith conference. Though Gordon has long been a Mennonite pastor, most Mennonites have considered his theology significantly to the left of theirs.[44] Only in recent years has he become more involved in Mennonite discussion. While it seemed to me that the majority of conference participants differed from Kaufman, some appreciated certain of his emphases, and all were challenged by him. In describing the Mennonite perspective, then, I will include his. It will help us assess the relationship between a pluralistic theology of religions and the one I have been elaborating (see also notes 41, 51, 56, 62, 63, and 79).

I have claimed that, for Mennonites, Jesus Christ himself, as Lord, comes first, and that his teaching and example are normative because they are his. Kaufman, however, began with the more general claim that for Mennonites ethics comes first, before doctrine. This should lead Mennonite theology, he argued, to focus on our present situation, rather than being a "hermeneutic" endeavor, largely of scriptural interpretation, as it usually has been. If Mennonites do this, they will see that while some Christian doctrines can illuminate current issues, others

---

42. Gerber Koontz, pp. 27-28.

43. Mennonites might well concur with Jürgen Moltmann's advice that formal dialogue be undertaken not as a universal practice but only when merited by particular common concerns (in Gavin D'Costa, ed., *Christian Uniqueness Reconsidered: The Myth of a Pluralistic Theology of Religions* [Maryknoll, N.Y.: Orbis, 1990], p. 153).

44. See, e.g., H. Victor Froese's critique, "Gordon Kaufman's Theology 'Within the Limits of Reason Alone': A Review," *Conrad Grebel Review* 6, no. 1 (winter 1988): 1-26, with a response by Kaufman (pp. 26-28).

will have to be reconstructed, some radically, to help us confront today's enormous problems.[45]

Kaufman reported that he was raised with high Mennonite ideals. But after these were exposed to theological education, holding on to them as privileged truth seemed "much too simplistic" and at least partly motivated by "stubborn, prideful self-defensiveness and self-assertion" (p. 3). He came to regard existence as intrinsically pluralistic, and humans as only capable of insight into "partial and relative truths" (p. 4). Theology, then, could only be viewed as a product of imaginative human construction (p. 6). Kaufman stressed "the thoroughly human character of all our assertions" so that Christian claims are essentially no different than any other religion's or philosophy's (p. 14).

This means that no one possesses "final truth, truth adequate to orient humankind in face of the enormous problems we confront in today's world."[46] Kaufman insists, however, that this pluralism does not downgrade unusual viewpoints — like the Mennonite one — but makes a place for the importance of each. Moreover, since no one religion is adequate, we must learn to appreciate the importance of all of them, to gather as many resources as possible to avert planetary catastrophe. Kaufman insists that Christians must enter interfaith dialogue "on equal terms" with others; if we assume that our affirmations are more than "simply ours," we will likely be authoritarian and arrogant (p. 15). Claiming absolute truth for our beliefs is sinful (p. 20), much as treating theology as hermeneutic is an "idolatry of ancient texts" (p. 24).

Kaufman endeavors, however, to develop a pluralistic outlook that does not spawn sheer relativism. He seeks to reconstruct Christian theology according to certain values which emerge through his reading of "bio-history"; these can be confirmed (or debated) by anyone who considers the same data.[47] Chief among these is humankind's historic-

---

45. Kaufman, "Mennonite Peace Theology in a Religiously Pluralistic World," p. 5. The following page numbers in the main text refer to this paper. (Kaufman makes many of the same points in Hick and Knitter, pp. 3-15.)

46. Hick and Knitter, p. 13.

47. The main theme of Kaufman, *In Face of Mystery* (Cambridge: Harvard, 1993); at the interfaith conference, Weaver took a contrasting nonfoundationalist approach (p. 20), though some were uncomfortable with it.

ity: our capacity to imaginatively reconstruct our environment in light of future goals. Most fundamentally, whatever promotes historicity has normative value. These other values prove to be "responsibility, self-understanding, well-ordered freedom, and concern for the organic and physical world to which we belong."[48]

At the end of his task, after elaborating these values, Kaufman seeks to illumine them by turning to the traditional symbols, "God" and "Christ." "Christ" becomes "the appearance of a new communal ethos in history, rather than a metaphysically unique individual." The symbol can be extended beyond the church "to all communities of genuine healing, love, and justice."[49]

Though Kaufman feels that his bio-historical perspective "is quite different from anything found in traditional Christian reflection" (p. 19), it nevertheless provides "an excellent . . . framework for situating, and interpreting . . . the radical New Testament imperatives . . . of such great importance to Mennonites" (p. 18). Anabaptism's "emphasis on the fundamentally historical significance of the Christ-event," in contrast to traditional theology's concern with its metaphysics, "constitutes an important step toward" Kaufman's interpretation of "Christ" as "that point *in human history* where radical self-giving love comes into sharp focus" and becomes central to a communal self-understanding.[50]

---

48. Kaufman, *In Face of Mystery*, p. 130; these are elaborated on pp. 125-209; cf. Kaufman, "Mennonite Peace Theology," pp. 15-18.

49. Kaufman, *In Face of Mystery*, pp. 396-97. Yet Kaufman adds that what constitutes such "profoundly humane patterns of life" is taken to be "paradigmatically epitomized in the Christ-images of [the] seminal period" (p. 397). For my response, see note 79 below.

50. Kaufman, "Mennonite Peace Theology," p. 23 (cf. n. 79 below). In his response to Kaufman, Scott Holland affirmed his trends toward imagination over mimetic memory, translucent world pictures over narrative closure, embodied ethics over a disembodied church, Christomorphism over Christocentrism, and a poetics of obligation over a metaphysics of morals. By the latter terms, Holland meant to indicate the more common Mennonite approach, especially Yoder's (cf. Holland's "How Do Stories Save Us?" *Conrad Grebel Review* 12, no. 2 [spring 1994]: 131-53). General discussion of Kaufman's and Holland's themes was lengthy and varied, including some agreement and significant disagreement.

D. Some Current Considerations

Having presented several historic Anabaptist and current Mennonite affirmations, I close with my own responses to two contemporary issues, hopefully in continuity with points 1-7, and in dialogue with the pluralistic theology represented, among others, by Gordon Kaufman.[51] Because the first issue is too complex to be fully elaborated here, I phrase it as a question.

8. *Can one seriously participate in interfaith relations without deep normative commitments?* Pluralists usually insist, as Kaufman does, that for all participants to have equal voice and really hear each other, all "preestablished absolutist or definitive positions" must be renounced.[52] Yet they also acknowledge that if significant consensus is to be attained and sheer relativism avoided, some common way of assessing beliefs and practices must be found. Many recommend that ethical criteria, instead of doctrinal beliefs, assume this role. Paul Knitter proposes liberating praxis: "the fundamental option for the poor and nonpersons." This, he insists, is no "'foundation' . . . or sure-fire criterion of judgment, but . . . an approach, a context, a starting-point that will be further clarified as it clarifies and creates new common ground."[53] Knitter claims that correct beliefs about Christ are unnecessary for such involvement.[54]

Yet can one commit oneself even praxiologically without some normative beliefs as to how things really are or ought to be? Who, for instance, are "the poor"? Can we identify "nonpersons" without some notion of what constitutes a person? Can we agree on who is "oppressed" without some positive vision of "liberation"? I am not suggesting that participants need clear conceptual definitions of such terms before dialogue or action begins. Admittedly, precise *definitions* usually emerge through such involvement. But I am asking whether one can undertake meaningful action without strong implicit *convictions* and *commitments* that reality is and ought to be a certain way, and that

---

51. Kaufman should perhaps not be so easily classified as "pluralist" as some others to whom I will refer, since he makes an explicit attempt to formulate normative claims.

52. Knitter, in Hick and Knitter, p. 181.

53. Knitter, in Hick and Knitter, p. 186.

54. Knitter, in Hick and Knitter, pp. 192-93, 196-97.

these contradict other such convictions and commitments, and are thus potentially articulable as distinct affirmations about the universe.

Pluralists don't deny that we begin with some convictions. Yet they often speak as if these were easily revisable or dispensable. I am asking whether the deepest of these are not in fact "conditions of possibility" for any truly committed action; whether they are not so essential for our sense of meaning and purpose that our praxis would be undermined or radically altered were they seriously challenged or changed. If so, I am not sure that such normative commitments would function much differently than normative theological beliefs about, say, Jesus Christ which entailed significant ethical implications.

I am not yet persuaded that pluralistic theologians can dispense with such norms, for at least three kinds appear in many of their writings. First, ethical approaches, like Knitter's, cannot be stated without criteria like "salvation," the *"basileia,"* "human welfare," "liberation," etc.[55] Second, some pluralisms, like John Hick's, are rooted in normative claims about the religions' relationship to reality. Hick asserts that all religions are culturally shaped ways of apprehending "the Real," the saving reality which lies beyond them all but which, like Kant's *noumenon,* is unknowable in itself, and manifested only through such *phenomena.*[56]

Third, and most significant for the crucial relationships among absolutism, imperialism, and oppression, some pluralistic theologies affirm norms developed in Western history. Hick acknowledges that modern science, technology, and the ideals of equality, freedom, and democracy arose in the West through "the rebirth, in the European Renaissance and then in the Enlightenment, of the Greek spirit of free enquiry."[57] Yet he argues that they could have emerged anywhere. Unlike van Leeuwen, he insists that these forces — whose effect every-

55. Knitter, in Hick and Knitter, p. 187.

56. Hick, pp. 245-46. Kaufman has critiqued this approach as a form of monism, not pluralism ("Religious Diversity and Religious Truth," in *God, Truth, and Reality: Essays in Honour of John Hick,* ed. Arvind Sharma [New York: St. Martin's Press, 1993]). Ruether makes a claim similar to Hick's: "the Divine Being that generates, upholds, and renews the world is truly universal, and is the father and mother of all peoples without discrimination. This means that true revelation and true relationship to the divine is to be found in all religions" (Hick and Knitter, p. 141).

57. Hick, in Hick and Knitter, p. 25.

where "must be . . . progressive secularization both of thought and of society"[58] — had no intrinsic connection with Christianity. Though Christianity happens to have been the first religion significantly transformed by modernity, this process, with its great potentialities and perils, now moves on to reshape all religions and cultures. Today we can see that such worldwide transformations are "part of a universal soteriological process" available through all religions and offering "the possibility of a limitlessly better existence . . . [which] can begin to be realised in each present moment."[59]

This process accelerated after World War II. According to Langdon Gilkey, "Europe disappeared as a major power. . . . The West no longer ruled the world" and "rough parity" among cultures emerged.[60] Hick finds that a roughly concurrent "modern explosion" of knowledge about non-Western religions became "perhaps the most important factor" revising Christian absolutism.[61] In any case, this movement, which now allegedly sweeps the globe, originated in the West. Gordon Kaufman acknowledges that his way of establishing bio-historical norms also "grows out of western historical thinking" and is in this respect "particular, relative, and limited."[62] Yet he clearly recommends these norms as criteria for evaluating the particularities of all religions and cultures.[63]

58. Hick, in Hick and Knitter, p. 26.

59. Hick, p. 380. In this emerging global reality we can recognize "a contemporary illumination of the Spirit" through which we can respond "through God's challenging presence" (Hick and Knitter, p. 34).

60. Gilkey, in Hick and Knitter, p. 40. Kaufman explicitly rejects belief in such "rough parity" (personal correspondence with this author, August 23, 1994).

61. Hick, in Hick and Knitter, p. 17; Kaufman's claims about the radical novelty of the nuclear situation (n. 41 above) comprise another commonly accepted element in the portrayal of the present interreligious situation as an unprecedented one.

62. Kaufman, in Hick and Knitter, p. 14. Can they really enable us, then, to encounter other "religions and secular traditions *in their own terms* instead of as defined by our categories" (p. 14)? Tom Driver acknowledges that *The Myth of Christian Uniqueness* "belongs to Western liberal religious thought at the present time. . . . Ours is not a 'universal' point of view but one conditioned by First World liberal Christianity" (p. 206).

63. A significant tension seems to exist between Kaufman's frequent claims that *all* theologies and philosophies are relative, purely human imaginative constructs, and his recommendation that *one* such construct, his bio-historical effort,

Such links between pluralist theology and Western secular norms have received severe criticism. Pluralistic theology has been interpreted as promoting the dominating surge of Western secular ideals around the globe. Though its proponents talk much of respecting particularity, critics claim that a pluralism based on the rejection of each faith's distinctive normative commitments actually levels out and silences significant differences; thereby it shields itself from encounter with genuine others. And though pluralists talk much of fighting oppression, an approach maintaining that "rough parity" among cultures now exists systematically overlooks the gaping and persistent worldwide asymmetries of economic and military power.[64]

Pluralist dialogues — the critique continues — are conducted not in the world marked by real inequalities, but in one of "global media and information networks, international agencies and multinational corporations."[65] They take place among Westernized intellectuals who have rejected the particularities of their traditions and whose basic language is that of Western academia. Such discourse systematically incorporates and dissolves all oppositional spaces — e.g., those occupied by the truly poor, traditional, and uneducated.[66] By employing a homogeneous logic which "irons out the heterogeneous precisely by subsuming it under the categories of comprehensive and totalizing global and world theologies," it "sedately but ruthlessly domesticates the other — *any* other — in the name of world ecumenism and the realization of a 'limitlessly better possibility.'"[67]

Such an imperialism of Western secular processes and norms is allegedly furthered by the two other pluralist norms we have identified. First, normative claims about the religions' relation to an inexpressible, unconceptualizable "Real" reduce all religious differences to cultural ones and strip religions themselves of distinct cognitive and ethical

---

provide norms for evaluating all others. If his pluralistic emphasis is to be taken seriously, it would seem that his own scheme must be just one among many others. If the normativity of his scheme is to be taken seriously, his pluralistic emphasis would need to be significantly moderated.

64. Kenneth Surin, in D'Costa, pp. 196-97.

65. Surin, in D'Costa, p. 201.

66. Surin, in D'Costa, p. 195.

67. Surin, in D'Costa, pp. 210, 200; the quotation in single italics is from Hick's *An Interpretation of Religion* (cf. n. 59 above).

content. This, Jürgen Moltmann notes, can lead to a "repressive tolerance" which allows one to believe whatever one wants so long as those
beliefs do not prompt one to disturb the secular sphere's autonomy.[68]
Such willingness to tolerate a religion relegated to the subjective sphere,
Lesslie Newbigin observes, has strong roots in the Enlightenment.[69]
Both writers warn that religions shorn of distinctive intellectual and
social shape are unlikely to challenge international economic inequalities, but will become, like "brands of toothpaste and laundry soap,"[70]
items in "the consumer society where the choice of the customer is free
and sovereign."[71]

Second, attempts to replace religious norms with social-ethical
ones, and to emphasize interfaith cooperation as shared *praxis*, have
been traced to the imperializing Western mentality. According to John
Milbank, religions differ over political and social practices as much as
anything else. To suppose that common atheological spaces for praxi-
ological concurrence can be found is to assume "that a common secular
realm of human aspiration, relatively free from mythical and
metaphysical elaborations, has always been latent within the religious
traditions, and that the modern distinguishing of the political category
has always been present, albeit obscurely."[72] Interreligious sociopolitical agreement, however, is usually a product of secularization: it "nearly
always betokens the triumph of Western attitudes and a general dilu-
tion of the force of traditional belief."[73] It does not occur apart from
subordination of religion to "the universal sway of the liberal state and
the capitalist market."[74]

68. Moltmann, in D'Costa, pp. 151-52. The phrase "repressive tolerance"
comes from Herbert Marcuse.
69. Newbigin, in D'Costa, p. 136.
70. Moltmann, in D'Costa, p. 152.
71. Newbigin, in D'Costa, p. 138; this sort of analysis illustrates Newbigin's
increasing skepticism about Western trends since the 1960s.
72. John Milbank, in D'Costa, p. 182. Knitter affirms the existence of "a *shared
locus of religious experience* now available to all religions" and apparently concurs
with Aloysius Pieris that "'a revolutionary urge, a psycho-social impulse, to
generate a new humanity . . . constitutes and therefore defines, the essence of *homo
religiosus*'" (p. 188). Suchocki also seeks to replace religious criteria with a social-
ethical criterion, justice (p. 149). Langdon Gilkey wants "the present flood of rela-
tivity" to be "balanced by the stern demands for liberating praxis" (p. 50).
73. Milbank, in D'Costa, p. 184.
74. Milbank, in D'Costa, p. 179.

Based on the foregoing, let us assume, at least for discussion, that (1) commitment to interfaith relations necessarily involves commitment to some ultimate norms, which are not mere opinions but deep convictions without which meaningful participation would be impossible; and (2) pluralistic approaches have not yet satisfactorily dispensed with such norms, and the norms they have proposed are insufficiently disconnected from Western imperialism. If so, can any better norm, or ultimate, be suggested than the one which guided Anabaptists (which they derived from Scripture)? Let me call it the "kenotic lordship" of Jesus Christ. I mean his universal lordship as proclaimed by the early church and indelibly imprinted by his life, teaching, example, suffering, and cross (esp. Phil. 2:5-11).

This lordship is that of one who became a servant, who poured himself out to death for the sake of humankind and creation. It is the lordship of one who identified with the humble and downtrodden, who called for justice and sharing, and therefore implacably opposed the forces of pride, oppression, injustice, and inequality — whose inner logic could only seek his death. This ultimate, therefore, is unalterably opposed to all oppressive cultural, political, and ideological absolutes. If all persons are committed, at some deep though perhaps inarticulable level, to some ultimate(s), Christ's kenotic lordship will most fully free them from their oppressive features. By critiquing the absolutist pretensions of all cultures, systems, and religions, this lordship will make rich, authentic pluralism among them possible (rendering them contrasting, but no longer unalterably opposed, *finite* realities).[75] It will also critique, more thoroughly than anything else, all forms of Christian*ity*.[76]

This kenotic lordship, however, is also personal and living, for the love which grounded the *kenōsis* proved to be that which raises the dead and gives life to all things.[77] Jesus' cross was not simply "an

---

75. See Calvin Shenk, "The Gospel and Pluralism" (unpublished paper, February 1990), discussed in Finger, "What Are Mennonites Saying?" p. 36; cf. Toews, pp. 3, 23.

76. It "drastically relativizes every Christian claim to embody the full truth of God in any intellectual system or to embody the perfect righteousness of God in any political order" (Newbigin, in D'Costa, p. 145).

77. Kenosis, or divine self-emptying, has been suggested as a bridge among religions. For example, Masao Abe, a Buddhist, expresses admiration for the classic

expression" of self-giving love,[78] but its decisive historical actualization. Though something of this love may be expressed through symbols of other religions,[79] its personal, divine reality was fully and uniquely active here. Through his resurrection, this ultimate Lord bestows the grace and companionship essential for walking in his way.

9. *Kenotic lordship functions within a trinitarian dynamic.* The love which raised Jesus was, precisely speaking, not his own, but that of his Father through the Spirit.[80] While Mennonites have not often stressed the Trinity (perhaps because this theme seems somewhat speculative), Jesus' kenotic openness toward humankind, which renders him a "critical absolute," was rooted in reciprocal openness with his Father and

---

kenosis text, Philippians 2:5-11. But he finds in it "a complete abnegation of Christ as the Son of God. . . . the Son of God abandoned his divine substance. . . . Christ's kenosis signifies a transformation in substance . . . a radical and total self-negation of the Son of God" (John Cobb and Christopher Ives, eds., *The Emptying God* [Maryknoll, N.Y.: Orbis, 1990], pp. 9-10). Such a reading, however, dissolves the paradox at the heart of this text, which culminates with the raising to lordship of the one who emptied himself.

78. Hick, in Hick and Knitter, p. 33.

79. Gilkey, in Hick and Knitter, p. 50. In my understanding, historic — and Anabaptist — Christianity regards the divine Self-involvement in this event as so deep and unprecedented that it differs qualitatively from all other manifestations of self-giving love. It cannot be simply one among many "expressions" or "symbols" of this love, even one which brings into sharpest "focus" (Kaufman) many such acts of essentially the same kind. To be sure, the grace overflowing from this event manifests itself in other acts. As Kaufman says, the symbol "Christ" can be applied to communities whose "ethos" is shaped by such acts (cf. material indicated by nn. 49 and 50 above). Yet such communities cannot be literally equated with Jesus Christ in the full, personal sense. As I see it, Mennonite understanding of "the fundamentally historical significance of the Christ-event" (Kaufman) includes such an emphasis on its unique particularity, even though Mennonites have also stressed the church. It is difficult to retain the impact of this particularity in one's theology if it does not function as one of that theology's initial norms. Kaufman surely wishes to emphasize "radical self-giving love" and the Christ-event's fundamental historicity, thereby retaining precious elements of his Mennonite heritage. Yet his theology begins at a point so distant from Jesus (the sweep of bio-history), is so determinatively shaped by current concerns, and comes to "Christ" so late, that Jesus' concrete particularity becomes mixed with and diluted by many other considerations. Jesus' radical self-giving, as I see it, does not sufficiently critique the Western cultural elements in Kaufman's theology, despite its author's intentions.

80. See Finger, *Christian Theology*, vol. 1, pp. 352-54. The original kenosis was also grounded in the trinitarian love.

Spirit. The Christian God's historical activity, then, involves cooperative intertwining of these three agencies. While Jesus the Son provides its basic pattern, the Holy Spirit contributes a dynamism that can operate surprisingly, and beyond the realm where this pattern has been most clearly discerned (the authentic church). This is a basic reason why Jesus is not revelation's sole content, but rather its norm.

The fullness of God's work, then, can never be contained in one institution, historical era, or conceptual pattern. It must continually be discovered. Trinitarian theology, that is, raises a "prohibition against would-be final accounts of divine nature and action."[81] For the relationship between Logos and Spirit, and thus our knowledge of the Logos, remains incomplete and open until history's end. Given this Logos-Spirit interplay, however, we might expect to find God in the "tension between tradition and unforeseen possibilities."[82] This may be occurring in encounters between Christians and other religions. If we want to know how the Spirit is working there, we simply have to become involved and look.[83]

Yet while this continual searching directs attention to history, the Spirit's unpredictability also means, as Mennonites have stressed, that history's overall pattern cannot be discerned from within.[84] The final shape of relationships between religions awaits the eschaton. On the other hand, though the Spirit may work in unexpected ways, these will

81. Rowan Williams, in D'Costa, p. 12. My exposition incorporates some intriguing suggestions in Williams's attempted application of Raimundo Pannikar's approach (pp. 3-15; cf. Hick and Knitter, pp. 89-116; I take no position on the accuracy of Williams's reading of Pannikar).

82. Williams, in D'Costa, p. 13.

83. D'Costa, p. 19. The variety and unpredictability of the Spirit's movement mean that there can be no one goal for interfaith dialogue (Williams [affirming Pannikar], in D'Costa, p. 10). But if the Spirit is active in other religions, this makes them vital to Christians (D'Costa, pp. 22-23). Christianity, then, engages in dialogue to discover itself more truthfully (Williams, in D'Costa, p. 11). At the same time, it can allow other religions to tell their own stories, including "narratives of oppression" relating their negative experiences of Christianity (D'Costa, pp. 23-24). In such discussions, "The normativity of Christ involves the normativity of crucified self-giving love" (D'Costa, p. 20). The trinitarian dynamic prevents Christian witness from "turning into the mirror image of the monolithic empires of 'the world'" (Williams, in D'Costa, p. 13). These are just several of the trinitarian implications for interfaith dialgoue with which Mennonites would likely resonate.

84. Williams, in D'Costa, p. 5.

never be disconnected from the Son. His kenotic lordship provides the norm for assessing claims that God is active, such as in bio-history's general direction, or "wherever there is a costly commitment to the struggle for human justice."[85]

85. Hick, in Hick and Knitter, p. 33. I include this affirmation because many like it appear in ecumenical documents. Whatever serves justice, community, liberation, etc., is frequently declared to be God's activity apart from any careful definition of justice and any application of a christological criterion.

CHAPTER SIX

The Search for a Methodist Theology of Religious Pluralism

NEHEMIAH THOMPSON

Tʜɪs paper tries to answer a specific question: Are there elements in the Methodist tradition that would impel Methodist Christians to engage in dialogue with people of other faiths? The answer is: Yes, there are ample evidences in the Methodist tradition, particularly in the teachings of John Wesley, that would challenge Methodists to engage in interfaith dialogue within a theological methodology which can be established on the basis of the Wesleyan teaching. This paper is an attempt to search for raw materials that would constitute such a theology of religious pluralism in the Methodist tradition. However, I like to warn the readers of a certain dilemma in the Methodist tradition that they should be aware of. The Methodist tradition, like most other Christian traditions, is geared toward nurturing Christians with the faith and proclaiming the gospel to people of other faiths primarily to convert them to Christ or Christianity. But, like most other Christians, Methodists have also realized that the present multifaith society requires a theology of religious pluralism based not only on the theology of evangelism but also on the challenges of this new age in which most world religions have reasserted their validity in terms of providing salvation to the adherents of those faiths.

I must confess my own inadequacy to engage in such a task mainly because I am not a scholar in Methodism. My home is ecumenical Methodism, having originated in the Wesleyan tradition, traveling through the Church of South India into the United Methodist fold. My search for a theology of religious pluralism began during my tenure as an interfaith worker for the United Methodist Church at the General Commission on Christian Unity and Interreligious Concerns and during my participation in the National Council of Churches' Faith and Order study on theological response to religious pluralism. During these years I discovered that there is a clear theological potential in the Methodist tradition to engage in interfaith dialogue. I will continue my search here, and I am absolutely open to the critique of my Methodist colleagues toward perfecting this paper.

A Discussion of Methodist Tradition

Before we get into the major task of identifying some of the theological resources that exist in the Methodist tradition for interfaith relations, it is appropriate to discuss briefly the Methodist tradition itself in order to understand its nature and to assess the extent to which it is an asset to interfaith relations.

Methodism has a unique and identifiable doctrinal emphasis of considerable import both for mission and ecumenism. However, in the words of Albert Outler, the Methodist ecumenical patriarch, Methodist doctrinal emphasis does not add up to a singular system of doctrines, whole and entire, but is rather a delicate balance of emphases and accents.[1] It has a distinct style of integrating the evangelical stress on God's sovereign grace and the Catholic accent on human agency in the history of salvation.[2] Thus according to Outler it is a dynamic mix of prevenience, justification, regeneration, and holiness.[3] A dominant tradition that Methodism nurtures is the teaching of John Wesley on prevenient, sanctifying, and justifying grace. Wesley linked prevenient grace to natural theology in the broad christological context. He opposed the way in which a polarization took place between grace and nature in Reformation theology.

The Wesleyan tradition is often an extracted rather than a literally

---

1. Albert Outler, *The Wesleyan Theological Heritage* (Grand Rapids: Zondervan, 1991), p. 191.
2. Outler, p. 191.
3. Outler, p. 194.

repeated phenomenon.[4] It is the interpretation of persons who experience the Christian teaching as originally expounded by John Wesley, not abstract speculation, that gives flesh to Methodist tradition. As the Methodist scholar Thomas A. Langford indicates, "the Wesleyan tradition is open for interpretation of both its achieved character and its future prospects."[5] The interpretation of Wesleyan tradition has come from a variety of sources, including ecumenical Methodism, the evangelical movement, high-church and low-church circles, the holiness movement, European Methodism, United Methodism, African and Asian evangelical Methodism, and the South American liberation movement. Besides, each generation takes a fresh look at the Wesleyan tradition which, consequently, changes the context of the interpretation from one thrust to another. This nature of Wesleyan tradition has forced Methodists to be sympathetic to the theological pluralism of their religious tradition.

The pluralistic interpretation of Wesleyan tradition may justify some Methodists' choice of title for Wesley as a mentor and not a guru.[6] A mentor is a guide and a guru is one who dictates a direction. Wesley is considered by some as a folk theologian because one of his major concerns was to take religion to the masses — "plain truth for plain people." He combined the Catholic accent of "work" and the Reformation emphasis of "faith alone" into "faith working in love." Thus Wesley transformed Christianity from the personal and philosophical exercise of a few into the practical and public witness of many for Jesus Christ. This prompted Wesley to combine vital religion and social justice as two sides of the same coin, which prompted even secularists to make interesting comments on Methodism: Mahatma Gandhi commended Wesley for taking religion to the poor and the workers of England (Gandhi attended Methodist churches while he lived in England), and E. P. Thompson blamed Wesley for preventing a possible socialist revolution in England. This latter charge implies that Wesley socialized religion, transforming it into the religion of the poor and the working

4. At the risk of inviting certain polemic I equate Methodist tradition to Mr. Wesley's thoughts at least as far as the origin of Methodist tradition is concerned.

5. Thomas Langford, *Wesleyan Theology: A Source Book* (Durham, N.C.: Labyrinth Press, 1984), preface.

6. See Mildred Bangs Wynkoop's article, "John Wesley — a Mentor or Guru?" *Wesleyan Theological Journal* 10 (1975).

class and causing almost a welfare society, which diminished the need for a revolution.

However, Wesley operated on a definite theological base with accurate knowledge of tradition combined with flexibility of implementation. Outler concludes that "it is not Wesley's stature and function as Methodism's cult hero that draws attention but his significant achievements as a theologian in his special historical situation that are significant to Christian development."[7]

Wesley laid some foundational rules for the Methodist orthodoxy upon which various interpretations must be based. The Articles of Religion (of the Church of England), the *Notes on the New Testament*, and four volumes of sermons were given as a distinct Wesleyan guide to the Methodists. But these foundational materials themselves have been interpreted more liberally than Wesley intended by both the left wing and the right wing of the Methodist family.

Scripture is the primary source of Christian faith for John Wesley and the Methodists. While the Church of England gave almost equal status to Scripture, tradition, and reason, Wesley emphasized Scripture as the primary source while relegating reason and tradition to the status of aids for understanding Scripture and the church. One of Wesley's most helpful resources for understanding the Scripture was the literature of the Fathers. He regarded them as "the most authentic commentators on scripture as being both the nearest the fountain and eminently endued with the Spirit by whom all scripture was given."[8] But Wesley added experience to Scripture, tradition, and reason as a source of understanding the Christian faith in order to achieve balance between understanding through tradition and reason and living out the faith through scriptural guidance. Outler described the Wesleyan quadrilateral as follows:

> It was intended as metaphor for a four-element syndrome, including the four-fold guidelines of authority in Wesley's theological method. In such a quaternity Holy Scripture is clearly unique. But this in turn is illuminated by the collective Christian wisdom of other ages and cultures between the Apostolic age and our own. It also allows for

7. Outler, p. 79.

8. David Butler, "The Methodist Perception of Tradition," in *The Quadrilog*, ed. Kenneth Hagen (Collegeville, Pa.: Liturgical Press, 1944), p. 209.

the rescue of the gospel from obscurantism by means of the disciplines of pure reason. But always, biblical revelation must be received in the heart by faith: this is the requirement of "experience."[9]

The quadrilateral is a helpful tool to know and embrace "all" that can be received in order to perceive Christian truth and pursue Christian growth. It also allows prudent theological pluralism in a unique manner. Most of all, through the freedom that it bestows for the existential theological methodology, Methodists can enjoy the inclusivity this system requires. This unique methodology opens the gates of inquiry not only in the area of empirical knowledge but also in the analytical and practical spheres and thus brings relevance to living as individuals and communities. This prompted Wesley to declare that "the world is our parish" because the system that the quadrilateral enhances requires the consideration and reception of the created world with everything that God saw good, and also it provides insight to serve the world without condemning it in the overall goal to save the world not by destroying the systems and ideas that exist in the world but by enabling them to grow into perfection.

Like most other Christian traditions Methodism also has ecclesiastical boundaries. But those boundaries do not limit theological inquiry. Wesley himself did not draw narrow boundaries to his doctrinal standards and did not provide the Methodist people with a confession for subscription. Wesley was convinced that to reduce doctrine to any particular form of words was to misunderstand the very nature of doctrinal statements.[10] It is within this theological openness that the Methodists look at the emerging situations which demand their theological determination. Multifaith society is one such new situation that John Wesley was not aware of and could not address, but modern Methodists are forced to reckon with. However, the barometer that the Wesleyan teaching and the ecumenical Methodist heritage have established can provide major resources for a Methodist theology of religious pluralism. Before we get into such theological speculation we must look at Wesley's own attitude toward other religions.

9. Outler, p. 28.
10. Outler, p. 24.

John Wesley and World Religions

John Wesley lived in the Age of Reason. He allowed the thoughts of the Enlightenment to play a role during the years of his formative as well as developing Christian thought. Wesley's attitude to other religions was not an outright rejection but a nonjudgmental critical reflection. This was rather unique considering the prevailing attitude of British Christians toward other religions. David Pailin has reported that the British Christian attitudes to other religions (pagan and savage tribes) during the seventeenth and eighteenth centuries reflected a strong, confident, aggressive, and often ill-informed type of Christianity.[11] But, as Gavin D'Costa reports, an appreciative attitude toward other religions also existed during that period. Sir William Jones, in his *Philosophy of the Asiaticks* (1794), warned against the "uncandid" asperity toward the wise men of ancient India, pointing out that three centuries before Christ certain Indian texts contained the teaching that evil should be repaid with good. In later days Jones's discordant note and informed respect for other religions became increasingly a dominant theme in the debate concerning attitudes to other religions. This was the time Wesley lived and preached in England.

There are evidences that Wesley knew contemporary Judaism and took the Pauline position as far as the salvation of the Jews was concerned. He refused to condemn the Jews, arguing that Christians must leave them to their God.[12] However, he was more gentle toward Jews than people of other faiths. And yet, as far as Islam was concerned he did forbid a summary damnation of Muslims. He praised the sincerity of their response to the "limited revelation" they have received. He gave credit to their sensibility to God's inward voice.[13] (He had formed his attitude toward other religions because of his theological stand, which we will consider later.) Wesley wrote:

> I have no authority from the Word of God to judge those that are without. Nor do I conceive that any man living has a right to sentence

11. Gavin D'Costa, *Theology and Religious Pluralism* (New York: Basil Blackwell, 1986), p. 1.

12. Wesley, Sermon 106, in *The Works of John Wesley*, ed. Albert Outler (Nashville: Abingdon Press, 1984-), 3:495.

13. Wesley, Sermon 130, in *Works* (Outler), 4:174.

all the heathen and Mohometan world to damnation. It is far better to leave them that made them, and who is the Father of the spirits of all flesh, who is the God of the heathens as well as the Christians, and who hateth nothing that he hath made.[14]

Wesley placed unchanged Christians and heathens on the same level.[15] He adored the search for holiness in Hinduism. Would Wesley have distinguished between the authentic experience of the holy in Hinduism and the authentic experience of the holy in Christianity? The answer may vary. However, Wesley gave equal level of standing between those who experience the holy regardless of their religion. As we know, for Wesley it is perfection (holiness), and not sanctification alone, that forms his soteriological principle. He said:

> I believe the merciful God regards the lives and tempers of men more than their ideas. I believe He respects the goodness of the heart rather than the clearness of the head.[16]

When Wesley used the word "heathen" or "pagan," he did not use it in the religious sense as his contemporaries did. To Wesley anyone who was not morally upright was heathen — including Christians. "There are heathens enough, in practice if not in theory, at home (England). Why, then, should you go to America?"[17] He condemned the way the English rulers in India behaved. He called them "ruffians."[18] He condemned the slavery in Africa.[19] When he compared the Christian morality in Europe with the morality of the "heathen," he commented: "I am afraid truly, that many called Christians are far worse than the heathens that surround them — more profligate, more abandoned to all manner of wickedness, neither fearing God, nor regarding man."[20] Speaking of the Reformation and the reformed Christians of Europe, Wesley said: "How little are any of these reformed Christians better

14. Wesley, Sermon 130, in *Works* (Outler), 4:174.
15. Wesley, Sermon 130, in *Works* (Outler), 4:175.
16. Wesley, Sermon 130, in *Works* (Outler), 4:175.
17. Wesley, "Letter to John Burton," in Frank Baker, ed., *The Works of John Wesley* (Oxford: Clarendon Press, 1975-), 25:441.
18. Wesley, Sermon 69, in *Works* (Outler), 2:579.
19. Wesley, Sermon 69, in *Works* (Outler), 2:579.
20. Wesley, Sermon 69, in *Works* (Outler), 2:581.

than heathen nations? Have they more justice, mercy or truth than the inhabitants of China or India?"[21]

Wesley talked about the "noble savage," the Native American, as possessing a moral and religious clarity, free from the distorting sophistications and ambitions of advanced culture.[22] Commenting on the Native American Christians, he said: "they have no comments to construe away the text (gospel), no vain philosophy to corrupt it, no luxurious, sensual, covetous, ambitious exponders to soften its unpleasing truths, to reconcile earthly-mindedness and faith, the Spirit of Christ and the spirit of the world. They have no party, no interest to serve (alcohol), and are therefore fit to receive the gospel in its simplicity. From these, therefore, I hope to learn the purity of that faith which was once delivered to the saints."[23] But regarding nominal Christians: "myriads of those poor savages know nothing of Christianity but the name."[24] These comments, intentionally made at different times, cause us to come to the following conclusions about John Wesley:

> he did not reject world religions as unacceptable;
> he was willing to learn other faiths and appreciate the religiosity of the people of other faiths;
> he was willing to adopt the best teachings of other faiths;
> he saw Christianity and other faiths as equal as far as the pursuit of holiness was concerned;
> he was open to acknowledge the moral integrity of people of other faiths and place them even on a higher ground than Christians;
> he did not see religions as rivals;
> he would have approved dialogue between religions as far as moral and religious issues were concerned, and especially the issue of holiness would have been a common agenda.

---

21. Wesley, Sermon 61, in *Works* (Outler), 2:465.
22. Wesley, "Letter to John Burton," in *Works* (Baker), 25:439.
23. Wesley, "Letter to John Burton," in *Works* (Baker), 25:439.
24. Wesley, Sermon 122, in *Works* (Outler), 4:122.

Are Religions an Expression of Pre-Christian Light?

Wesley's tolerance of other faiths was not merely prompted by the goodness of his heart, it was intentional and based on his definite theological stand. As Saint Paul declared to the Christians in Rome (Rom. 2:12-16), Wesley also believed that those who have not heard about Jesus or pursue other systems will be judged according to their law, and that God is the God of not only Christians but also people of other faiths. It is not what you believe that will be the basis for judgment; how you pursued your journey toward perfection was the major concern to Wesley, as the following passage suggests:

> Seeing they (people of other faiths) are cut off from faith, for faith cometh by hearing. And how shall they hear without a preacher? I answer (as) St. Paul's words, spoken on another occasion, are applicable to this, "what the law speaketh, it speaketh to them that are under the law." According to that sentence, "he that believeth not shall be damned," is spoken to them to whom gospel is preached. Others it does not concern; and we are not required to determine anything touching their final state. How it will please God, the judge of all, to deal with them, we may leave to God himself. But this we know, that he is not the God of Christians only, but the God of the heathens also; that he is rich in mercy to all that call upon him, according to the light they have and that "in every nation he that feareth God and worketh righteousness is accepted of him."[25]

Wesley here makes reference to Saint Peter's sermon in Joppa in which he emphasized the light that God has left among the Gentiles: "I truly understand that God shows no partiality, but in every nation anyone who fears him and does what is right is acceptable to him" (Acts 10:34-35).

The above passage of Wesley's sermon suggests certain vital teachings of Wesley. It suggests that the exclusive passages in the New Testament were addressed to Christians only and cannot be applied to people of other faiths. It also suggests that God is the final judge of all people. The most important teaching here is the belief Wesley held that all people have received the light and will be judged according to that light and not

25. Wesley, Sermon 91, "On Charity," in *Works* (Outler), 3:295-96.

the light the Christians have received. Invincible ignorance never did nor ever will exclude any man from heaven.[26] However, Christians have a different rule. "I cannot believe he will receive any man into glory (I speak of those under the Christian dispensation) without such an inspiration of the Holy Ghost as fills his heart with peace and joy and love."[27] Wesley preached "unconditional predestination."[28]

These teachings of Wesley should not be taken in isolation from his other teachings and his person as a theologian of the church. He considered himself to be a follower of the best of the Anglican tradition; he preached salvation in Jesus Christ for more than half a century; he was probably the best New Testament scholar of his century; he was a Scholastic and a patristic scholar; he admired Martin Luther; he adopted the best of both Augustine and Aquinas; people in thousands went to hear him preach about God, Christ, and morality. Wesley was the founder of one of the most popular world communions — there are Methodists in almost all countries of the world. However, Wesley accepted the integrity of other religions and firmly believed that people of other faiths will be judged by the light they have received from God and should not be condemned by Christians on the basis of Christian revelation. Wesley was harsher to Anglicans and Calvinists than to Hindus, Muslims, and the native religions of North America because he thought that more will be expected of those who have received more.

Wesley was not a universalist. He believed and preached that Jesus Christ was the savior of the world. But he did not undermine the integrity and the light that exist in other faiths. His position on nature and grace illustrates rather clearly his theological commitment to the above stand.

Wesley on Nature and Grace

Wesleyan scholar Randy Maddox points out that Wesley's dominant concern as far as the discussion of other religions was concerned appeared to focus on the issue of the "reality and implications of a gener-

---

26. Wesley, "Letter to John Smith," in *Works* (Baker), 26:198.
27. Wesley, "Letter to John Smith," in *Works* (Baker), 26:198.
28. Wesley, "Letter to John Smith," in *Works* (Baker), 26:198.

ally-available revelation of God" in religions.[29] Maddox claims Wesley's convictions about revelation appear to be more in line with early Greek perspectives than with late Western theology. Like the Greek theologians, he too came to affirm that there is a basic knowledge of God universally available to those who have not heard of Christ, while insisting that this knowledge is itself an expression of God's gracious activity epitomized in the revelation of Christ.[30] Wesley opposed the dichotomy of nature and grace created by Reformation theology. For him they both belong to the realm of grace. However, Wesley's debates with the Deists reveal that he saw the restoration of grace taking place in Jesus Christ. According to Maddox, the initial universally available knowledge about God, the major source that Wesley consistently identified, was inferred from God's creation.[31]

Wesley lived at a time when it made a great deal of difference how you preached to the "unconverted," whether you assumed or rejected the premise of God's grace as prevenient, preparatory, and morally active in human existence, always and everywhere. Wesley assumed the existence of prevenient grace always and everywhere. Maddox claims that Wesley's attitude toward Native American religions might have something to do with his conception of natural theology. Wesley assumed that they were innocent, humble, willing to learn, and eager to do the will of God. He even claimed that "they would immediately discern if the Christian doctrine was authentic or not" because of the way native religion prepares them to receive the gospel.[32] Albert Outler affirms this perception of Wesley. Outler points out Wesley's assumption that "the power that enables a person to do anything positively is the grace of creation, one of the functions of which was the preparation of the human will that normally precedes the gift and reception of saving grace itself."[33] This was a way of urging that human nature, even at its worst, is never wholly bereft of grace. And thus grace does not destroy nature but perfects it.[34] This is a

---

29. Randy Maddox, "Wesley and the Question of Truth or Salvation through Other Religions," *Wesleyan Theological Journal* (March 1994): 13.

30. Maddox, p. 14.

31. Maddox, p. 14.

32. Maddox, p. 14.

33. Outler, p. 196.

34. Outler, p. 201.

profound Wesleyan contribution to the polemic between Augustinianism which came out of the ruins of the Roman Empire with a denial of human capacity to do good and the Thomistic uncritical synthesis of nature and grace. The result of the Wesleyan synthesis is the notion that while "faith alone" is the general Protestant emphasis, the Methodist accent is "faith working through love" and everything is under grace. Thus the Methodists, generally, have followed the Wesleyan emphasis on grace at work among the "virtuous pagans" and Wesley's implicit appeals for preaching to the "unconverted" in terms of that prevenient, preparatory grace that can be assumed to be active even in the unheeding heart.[35]

The above discussion implies that the realm of grace reaches to all people in all religions. This understanding has come to Christians because of Jesus Christ. Religions, including Christian faith, are preparations to receiving the gospel, and the partial light that exists in all religions is a sign of God's prevenient grace. This understanding must impel Methodist Christians to engage in dialogue with other faiths in order to determine how those lights in other faiths are significant, first, to the salvation of the adherents of those faiths, and secondly, to the full understanding of the gospel that has come to Christians through Jesus Christ.

United Methodist Theology of Religious Pluralism

The United Methodist Church has pioneered among Methodist churches in the area of creating guidelines to interfaith dialogue. The United Methodist statement on interreligious relations made by the 1980 general conference and reaffirmed by the subsequent quadrennial general conferences is a primary resource to United Methodists in their pursuit of relationship with people of other faiths. This statement reflects the Wesleyan heritage of both churches that united in 1968 to become the United Methodist Church: the Methodist Episcopal Church and the Evangelical United Brethren Church.

One of the Wesleyan teachings that is lifted up in the document is the primacy of Scripture. The New Testament image of community is depicted in the statement as a model for interfaith community, a commu-

---

35. Outler, p. 201.

nity which includes the stranger in its midst (Luke 10:29-37), which implies that one's own community does not have to be religiously homogeneous. The basis for communal coexistence is love and compassion — virtues consistently preached by Wesley and adopted by all Methodist traditions. Thus, the community that the statement refers to should be characterized as the coexistence of diverse people in towns and cities. But it affirms and recommends mutual witness, dialogue, and common life.

There are clear Wesleyan syndromes in the statement. The statement proclaims that "the God to whom we point in Jesus Christ is the God who is at work in every society in ways we do not fully understand and who has not left himself without witness in any human community." The statement goes one step further in affirming the prevenient grace that exists in other religions: "Christians witness to God in Jesus Christ in the confidence that here all people find salvation and in the trust that because of what we know of God in Jesus, God deals graciously and lovingly with all people everywhere." It recognize the "rich store of wisdom of the other," and "the truth worth sharing."

The statement calls for dialogue with people of other faiths precisely because God does work in other religions graciously and lovingly and other religions have truths to share with Christians. The statement refers to the new insights that dialogue brings to community. It acknowledges that through dialogue "the depths of another's faith may be so disclosed that its power and attractiveness are experienced." The statement also points out that Christians' self-understanding may be broadened and redefined because of interreligious relations. It says: "interreligious engagement challenges United Methodist Christians to think in new ways about our life in the broader human community, about our mission, evangelism, service and our life together within the Christian church."

This statement reflects a shift in the Christian understanding of other faiths. The earlier missionary theology that existed in the Western churches, including the churches of the Wesleyan heritage, professed superiority to other religions, which in fact turned away the people of other faiths in many parts of the world from considering Jesus Christ as an option for their lives. Even Methodist missionary theologies did not reflect Wesley's attitude toward other religions. The 1980 United Methodist statement on interreligious relations is a significant step toward incorporating the Wesleyan stance on other religions.

Conclusion

There is no uniform conclusion among Methodist Christians about the resources that are available within their tradition for interfaith dialogue. The Methodist tradition allows diversity in the church, and therefore interpretation of the resources that permit interfaith dialogue also may vary. However, this paper has tried to establish John Wesley as the common progenitor of the varied Methodist traditions in order to draw inspiration for interfaith dialogue based on certain of his specific teachings. The following are conclusions inferred from Wesleyan teachings that would serve as raw materials for a theology of religious pluralism that would enable Methodist Christians to engage in interfaith dialogue.

1. Religious pluralism is not an enemy to the gospel. Other religions can be complementary to achieving Christian perfection if the teachings of other religions are perceived positively.
2. Nominal Christians and people of other faiths who do not observe the teachings of their religions are considered the same as far as their religious standing is concerned.
3. God has left God's light in all religions. All people have access to God through their religious practices. They will be judged by the light they have received, not by the Christian revelation through Jesus Christ.
4. Prevenient grace is available to all equally through God's creation. Grace is present in creation. The moral and spiritual life of people of other faiths is an indication as to how they respond to God's grace.
5. Creation is groaning for perfection. All creation, including religions, is called to grow to perfection and should not be destroyed.
6. There is no truth outside God. Other religions also have truth, and God works in other religions.
7. Interfaith dialogue can be the most effective way of knowing the truth that exists in other religions, getting to know those who witness to their truth, and allowing people of other faiths to know the truth that Christians profess. It would also be a channel to recognize the fundamental Christian confession that God was in Christ reconciling the world to God. Because of this knowledge that Christ has brought to us, we have no choice except to dialogue with all people whom God has reconciled in Christ.

CHAPTER SEVEN

Theological Resources for Response to Pluralism from Christian Churches/Churches of Christ

FREDERICK W. NORRIS

BECAUSE Christian Churches/Churches of Christ have no denominational statements or official bodies to make them,[1] the suggestions here are my own.

I. Scriptural Recognition of Truth in Other Religions

In an article requested by one of our missionaries for a book on missions among Christian Churches, I responded to a position of Arthur Glasser, a Fuller missiologist, who had insisted that finding truth in other religions was a step down the slippery slope of dreaded syncretism.[2] In my view the Bible itself declares that important truth resides in other religions. "Yahweh," as God's name, was revealed to Moses, but Eve and certain Philistines also knew God by that name, according to the final redactors. Other scriptural names for God were shared with a number of Canaanite peoples. According to the Epistle to the Hebrews, Melchizedek, the non-Jewish priest of uncircumcision, provided the

---

1. See the appendix at the end of this chapter.
2. "God and the Gods: Expect Footprints," in *Unto the Uttermost: Missions in the Christian Churches and Churches of Christ*, ed. Doug Priest, Jr. (Pasadena, Calif.: William Carey Library, 1984), pp. 55-69.

type for the priesthood of Jesus. A block of verses in Proverbs comes from an Egyptian wisdom book. Luke's rendition of Paul's sermon in Athens has Paul use the statue to an unknown god positively and praise two sayings about God from Hellenistic philosopher/poets.

Although the Bible criticizes false religions, it often indicates that God was already active in other cultures and religions in ways that should be honored; for those concerned with Christian mission, God's work within those cultures and religions provides indigenous truth to be connected with the gospel of Jesus Christ. Indeed, one of the abject failures of Christian mission was the rejection of Matteo Ricci's Chinese translation of Scripture which used deeply rooted Chinese words for God.

II. Missionary Experience of Truth in Other Religions

A number of missionaries from our churches have found that people of other faiths gave them insight into the meaning of the Christian Bible[3] and led them toward greater openness to possible truths which those communities confessed. I first gained this insight by listening to conversations between missionaries and my parents in our home. Recognizing truth in other religions did not move those missionaries to stop preaching Christ as the Lord of the universe, the name above all names. But they also looked for God's activity in the lives of the people to whom they brought the gospel, and were thankful when they found and understood it.

To expand such oral tradition on the basis of adult experience, a Christian Church missionary in Africa told this story. He had completed his language and culture education in central Africa and headed with his family out to an oasis. The people he sought were nomads; he had information that they would make their way to that oasis within the next few months. Only the director in Africa knew exactly when this

---

3. In an unexpected way I find Wesley Ariarajah's description of certain veteran missionaries at the Edinburgh Conference in 1910 in his *Hindus and Christians: A Century of Protestant Ecumenical Thought* (Grand Rapids: Wm. B. Eerdmans Publishing Co., 1991), particularly pp. 17-31, to be similar to my childhood memories. Yet Ariarajah interprets the views of those missionaries as the strong beginnings of the type of religious pluralism which he embraces.

missionary and his family had left for that remote region and where they intended to locate. When the family arrived they set up their tent and were looking around. Across the desert came an African, dressed in white, walking toward the water. When he arrived and they had shared their food with him, he told them that he had been sent there to learn more about God. The shaman had been told in a dream to go to the oasis for that purpose.

This story may strike you from different directions, but it taught a conservative Christian Church missionary that his God operates in ways the missionary had not imagined. When you are in Africa to preach Christ, and a shaman's God told him to come and learn from you, it is a bit difficult to start your lessons by rebuking his God. Notice, however, that this type of experience does not necessarily lead one to the acceptance of foundational religious pluralism. It can be accepted as yet fuller evidence that God, the Father, Son, and Holy Spirit, does more in more places than many in our churches have dreamed.

Such oral tradition which shows that people of other faiths have brought insight into Christian Scripture and were led by their God to search for the Father, Son, and Holy Spirit is one of the least-developed resources within our heritage. To date I know of no collection of these anecdotes, although they often continue to form the center of table talk. The lack of such a collection may well be because these experiences are still difficult to process.

III. *Consensus Fidelium*

William Robinson, perhaps our most important theologian, insisted that *consensus fidelium* is what we seek to restore for the unity of the church in the pursuit of its mission. Other leaders also have felt the force of this understanding; some have discussed it under the rubric of catholicity.[4]

4. See Robinson's contribution in *The Ministry and the Sacraments: Report of the Theological Commission Appointed by the Continuation Committee of the Faith and Order Movement*, chairman A. C. Headlam (London: SCM Press, 1937), esp. pp. 254-58. Also see Robert O. Fife, *Celebration of Heritage* (Joplin, Mo.: College Press, 1992); Dean E. Walker, *Adventuring for Christian Unity and Other Essays* (Johnson City, Tenn.: Emmanuel School of Religion, 1992); and my "Apostolic, Catholic, and Sensible:

The acceptance of *consensus fidelium* has meant that we could develop growing relations with Anglicans, holiness groups, Orthodox, Pentecostals, Protestants, Roman Catholics, and others,[5] both in order to learn from these folk about such a *consensus* and to encourage those points where we have seen them expressing it.

Within that historical and theological understanding, my work as a patristic scholar for over a quarter century primarily has involved more than the guild.[6] It has been part of my tradition's search for *consensus fidelium*. As a free church catholic I need not leave my heritage to explore the guidance that comes from church history. Although not all believers who called themselves Christians would feel at home in such a *consensus*,[7] I find a rather well-worked-out confession in early Christian documents which claims that Christianity does not have a corner on all truth but that ultimate truth and salvation are in Jesus Christ.

Kwame Bediako, an African theologian of the Presbyterian Church of Ghana, has found the second-century theologians Justin Martyr and Tertullian to be helpful for responding to and affirming important parts of African cultures and religions.[8] He preaches Christ and finds truth in indigenous Africa. His model is a good one for a tradition interested in *consensus fidelium*.

The patristic figure I know best from the so-called golden age,

---

The Consensus Fidelium," in *Essays on New Testament Christianity in Honor of Dean E. Walker,* ed. C. Robert Wetzel (Cincinnati: Standard Publishing, 1978), pp. 15-29.

5. Through the good graces of Joseph Kelly, chairman of the Department of Religious Studies at John Carroll University in Cleveland, I was the Tuohy Visiting Professor there for a semester. The evening public lectures resulted in *The Apostolic Faith: Protestants and Roman Catholics* (Collegeville, Pa.: Liturgical Press, 1992).

6. In May 1994 I gave the presidential address at the international meeting of the North American Patristic Society held in Chicago at Loyola University. It appeared in the winter 1994 issue of the *Journal of Early Christian Studies.*

7. The earliest Gnostics called themselves Christians. Mani saw himself as a Christian and yet was the founder of a world religion that lasted a thousand years. Hans-Joachim Klimkeit, *Gnosis on the Silk Road: Gnostic Parables, Hymns, and Prayers from Central Asia* (San Francisco: Harper, 1993), provides evidence of Christians who met Persian dualists and Zoroastrians and found ways to merge their doctrine and practice with their own.

8. Kwame Bediako, *Theology and Identity: The Impact of Culture upon Christian Thought in the Second Century and Modern Africa,* Regnum Studies in Mission (Oxford: Regnum Books, 1992).

Gregory the Theologian, mounted a vitriolic attack on the emperor Julian's attempt to renew Greco-Roman religion. His Orations 4 and 5 are unusually strong invective from a man who loved philosophy and rhetoric, but who loved Christ more. Yet he did not castigate all aspects of the other religions he knew. His poetry reveals examples of piety and contemplation among some who worship pagan gods, models that he thinks Christians themselves might emulate.[9] Quite unexpectedly, after denouncing the errors of the Hypsistarii, a Jewish Hellenistic sect to which his father's family belonged, he says of his father during that time:

> Even before he was of our fold, he was ours. His character made him one of us. For, as many of our own are not with us, whose life alienates them from the common body, so, many of those without are on our side, whose character anticipates their faith, and need only the name of that which indeed they possess. My father was one of these, an alien shoot, but inclined by his life toward us.[10]

Christian Churches' search for *consensus fidelium* not only encourages but also underwrites careful study of early Christianity's relationships with other religions as preparation for contemporary relationships. It is probably true that the size of present-day great world religions is not a feature of the religions which early Christianity knew. Yet few if any around the Mediterranean in the early part of our common era understood the size of our globe. Their experience of other religions well into the eighth century may have been more overwhelming for them than our present experience of other world religions is for us.

What Christians face today is not totally different from what was the case then. It would be difficult to predict by looking at first century C.E. documents about Christianity and other religions that Christianity would become the dominant power. Students of antiquity often tend to see the weaknesses of ancient non-Christian religions because they know what occurred later. Yet I am not certain that anyone would have guessed that the pantheons of Greece or Rome and the local gods of

9. *Carm.* 1.2.25, 253-303, *PG* 37, 831-34. See my "Gregory the Theologian and Other Religions," *Greek Orthodox Theological Review* 39 (1994): 131-40.

10. Gregory Nazianzen, *Or.* 18.5-6, *PG* 35, 989D-992D, trans. C. G. Browne and J. E. Swallow, *NPNF* 7 (1894), 256.

specific regions and towns would collapse as they did. Pliny, the second-century governor of Bithynia, said Christianity was represented within wide strata of the society in which he lived, but he told Trajan it could be handled and was not dangerous.[11]

During the fourth century, when imperial government was turning the screws, Emperor Julian wanted a revival of the ancient order in terms of a monotheistic religion. He certainly faced a pluralistic religious situation; near the end of the third century Maximus of Tyre had estimated there were more than thirty thousand gods when those with recognizable names, the stars, the "sons and friends of God," and the daimons were also counted.[12] Julian hated the people of Syrian Antioch because they had forgotten their rich and varied religious heritage that was praised lavishly by Libanius.[13] Yet Roman, Egyptian, Cypriot, Persian, and Chinese influences were present there, as well as strong Syrian and local traditions. It was precisely within that bustling metropolis, the third-largest city of the ancient world, that Christianity thrived. Christianity was urban; if you will allow the pun, paganism lost and became rural. Although much less information is available than we would like for detailing the plurality of religion in Antioch before Constantine, it is a much more pluralistic picture than many moderns carry of the area and the period. Because its local traditions were healthy, absorbing and/or enriching the Greco-Roman pantheon, it reminds one more of New Delhi than of New York.[14]

Doctrinally within early Christianity, even the use of the term *kurios* as a title for Jesus fits plurality. It may have come from Hellenistic Jewish circles like those that produced Greek translations of the Old Testament. In any event it served mission well since it was also a title for at least Zeus and Serapis. The point I make here is that early Christianity faced plurality and usually stood against what we call "pluralism," although not always in the sense we give the words "exclusivist" or "inclusivist."

11. Pliny, *Ep.* 10.96
12. Maximus of Tyre, *Or.* 11.12.
13. See Julian's *Misopogon* and Libanius's *Or.* 11, "In Praise of Antioch."
14. See my "Antioch-on-the-Orontes as a Religious Center, I. Paganism before Constantine," in *Aufstieg und Niedergang der römischen Welt* 18.4 (Berlin: Walter de Gruyter, 1990), pp. 2322-79. The destruction of evidence has been monumental. Theodor Mommsen noted that Antioch's inscriptions could be matched by a number of small North African villages.

If we turn to a consideration of how ancient Christianity reacted to some of the great world religions, again the responses do not always settle into exclusivist, inclusivist, or pluralist categories. The Dunhuang documents from seventh-century China represent efforts to explain Christianity within the terms of Chinese culture and the religions then "native" to it. *The Treatise on Jesus the Messiah* — perhaps the work of A-lo-pen, an East Syrian (Nestorian) Christian who reached Xi'an, then the capital of China, by 635 — tells the story of Jesus in a manner that is recognizable to any who know the New Testament Gospels. It is clumsy Chinese, probably an early translation unaided by a skilled Chinese-speaker who understood Christian faith well. But it begins the story in forms common to a Buddhist sutra and works within concepts used by Confucianists and Taoists. It teaches "The Way" through the life of Jesus, but it affirms significant aspects of Chinese culture and religion. Truth in other religions and cultures, but the ultimate way in Jesus Christ. The emperor Tai Tsung (627-49) lent his support to these Christians by requesting translations of their books for his library and by allowing his portrait to be put on the walls of Christian monasteries as a sign of that support. An eighth-century stele which tells part of the tale of A-lo-pen also speaks of a contemporary named Chin-Chin, "Adam," who was a skilled Chinese scholar as well as a witnessing Christian.[15]

The East Syrian (Nestorian) patriarch of Baghdad, Timothy I, an eighth-century figure, was called into Caliph Mahdi's palace. The caliph wanted to know why an upstanding man such as he was not a worshiper of Allah. The attempt by Timothy to reproduce the dialogue is still extant in Syriac. Since the treatise is written from the Christian perspective, we should expect that from a Muslim point of view the caliph's case was more persuasive than it appears in Timothy's recounting. But for my purposes here, the important milieu is intact. Muslim culture and religion are in part affirmed while Trinity and Christology are respectfully proclaimed. Timothy sees no reason to become a Muslim even in the presence of the caliph. But when asked what he

15. For an English translation and notes on the text see Y. Saeki, *The Nestorian Documents and Relics in China,* 2nd ed. (Tokyo: Academy of Oriental Culture, Tokyo Institute, 1951), pp. 125-61. The best short treatment of this expansion is David Bundy, "Missiological Reflections on Nestorian Christianity in China during the Tang Dynasty," in *Religion in the Pacific Era,* ed. Frank K. Flinn and Tyler Hendricks (New York: Paragon House, 1985), pp. 14-30.

thinks of Muhammad, he offers one of the most remarkable affirmations that I have ever read from a Christian, one in direct contradiction to some Christian statements that prophecy stopped with John the Baptist, thus eliminating the prophecy of Muhammad.

> Muhammed is worthy of all praise, by all reasonable people, O my Sovereign. He walked in the path of the prophets and trod in the track of the lovers of God. All the prophets taught the doctrine of one God, and since Muhammed taught the doctrine of the unity of God, he walked, therefore, in the path of the prophets. Further, all the prophets drove men away from bad works, and brought them nearer to good works, and since Muhammed drove his people away from bad works and brought them nearer to good ones, he walked, therefore, in the path of the prophets. Again, all the prophets separated men from idolatry and polytheism, and attached them to God and to his cult, and since Muhammed separated his people from idolatry and polytheism, and attached them to the cult and the knowledge of one God, beside whom there is no other God, it is obvious that he walked in the path of the prophets. Finally Muhammed taught about God, His Word, and His Spirit, and since all the prophets had prophesied about God, His Word and His Spirit, Muhammed walked, therefore, in the path of the prophets.[16]

These examples deny that once Christians find themselves living as a minority among a world religion they must either revert to a sectarian fundamentalism which is exclusivist or move to positions which are inclusivist or pluralist.

IV. Rejections of Foundational Religious Pluralism

One can read the position taken thus far as exclusivist at its core. Ultimate salvation in Jesus Christ is central. But I and others in my heritage do not claim the label "exclusivist" as long as some wear it

---

16. Timothy I, *The Apology of Timothy the Patriarch before the Caliph Mahdi*, Syriac text and Eng. trans. by A. Mingana, Woodbrooke Studies II (Cambridge: Heffer, 1928), pp. 1-163. The analogies he uses to explain his Christology are well contextualized.

with pride and refuse to recognize any truth whatsoever in non-Christian religions.

Nineteenth-century Christian Churches depended in large part epistemologically on the Scottish "common sense" philosophers' responses to the skepticism of David Hume. Various projects outside our churches have looked again at Thomas Reid and Dugald Stewart. Some Christian Church scholars are drawn to philosophical theology within evangelical circles because the questions of transcendental truth are asked in ways that speak to them. The president of my seminary, C. Robert Wetzel, an American who was for eleven years principal of Springdale College in the Selly Oak Colleges at Birmingham, England,[17] was an original member of the team that formed the project The Gospel and Our Culture, which Lesslie Newbigin leads. Both Newbigin and Wetzel find relativism to be one of the more destructive aspects of contemporary culture and thus respond to pluralism from within that critique. Richard A. Knopp, who teaches at Lincoln Christian College (a Christian Church school), has developed an interesting attempt to look for "intercontextual argument and evidence" in the construction of apologetics which goes beyond "uncriticizable commitment." In this effort he argues for a rationality that can be defended over against other worldviews and religions.[18] Paul Marvin, a Ph.D. student in philosophy at the University of Nebraska, has compared that "common sense" tradition within our heritage to the work of Alvin Plantinga.[19] He is presently pursuing questions about the nature of knowledge as it impinges on epistemic justification, particularly externalist reliablism.

Others take a somewhat different tack.[20] The dean of our missiolo-

---

17. Wetzel and a group of Emmanuel faculty have begun to explore the possibility of creating a special mission institute in cooperation with Milligan College.

18. See his "On the Value of the Philosophy of Science: Some Implications for Theology and Apologetics" (paper given at the Wheaton Theology Conference, February 1993).

19. Paul Marvin, "Whatever Shall We Do with Alexander Campbell? An Examination of the Epistemology of Alexander Campbell in Light of the Reformed Epistemology of Alvin Plantinga" (MAR thesis, Emmanuel School of Religion, 1993).

20. My own views are succinctly stated in my review of *The Bible and People of Other Faiths* (Geneva: World Council of Churches, 1985) and *Hindus and Christians: A Century of Protestant Ecumenical Thought* (Grand Rapids: Wm. B. Eerdmans Pub-

gists, Charles Taber, for years has been a champion of contextualization. Former president of both professional associations of missiologists in the United States, he is presently involved in the study headed by Wilbert Shenk: Towards a Missiology of Western Culture. Taber's work as a linguist, sociologist, and anthropologist leads him away from a return to positivism in any of its forms. His own critiques of so-called First World culture and its churches are devastating. He emphasizes community and practice while rejecting any sense of ultimate religious pluralism as it is commonly described. For him such pluralism appears to be the most culturally conditioned position, the one most caught up in a European Enlightenment sense of universalism that is foreign to Christianity's sense of itself. For Taber Christianity has adapted to many different cultures and accepted important parts of those cultures and their religions as it has developed within them. Inclusivism lacks clarity. Plurality is clear, but pluralism is an ideology. It posits a reality called "religion" under which every belief in some power beyond humanity is organized, and thus it too seldom takes notice of difference and particularity.[21]

Two young scholars within our heritage are making interesting contributions to the critique of foundationalism and the Enlightenment structures that support Western sociopolitical pluralism. Philip Kenneson teaches at Milligan College, Emmanuel's sister undergraduate institution. He has developed an ecclesiology that roots discussions with members of other communities within the communities themselves, avoiding the creation of theoretical overviews and expecting such discussions to be intensely ad hoc. Among the many interesting influences on Kenneson's work are the liberation theology of Clodovis Boff and the literary deconstruction of Stanley Fish.[22] Robert Parsley, a Ph.D.

---

lishing Co., 1991) by S. Wesley Ariarajah in *Ecumenical Trends* 22 (April 1993): 58-61. To date I find the two most helpful modern volumes to be John Milbank, *Theology and Social Theory: Beyond Secular Reason* (Oxford: Blackwell, 1990) and Joseph DiNoia, *The Diversity of Religions: A Christian Perspective* (Washington, D.C.: Catholic University of America Press, 1992).

21. See in particular his *The World Is Too Much with Us: "Culture" in Modern Protestant Missions* (Macon, Ga.: Mercer University Press, 1991), his "God vs Idols: A Model of Conversion," *Journal of the Academy for Evangelism in Theological Education* 3 (1987-88): 20-32, and the article mentioned in note 6.

22. Philip Kenneson, "The Reappearance of the Visible Church: An Analysis of the Production and Reproduction of Christian Identity" (Ph.D. diss., Duke University, 1993).

student at the University of Virginia, has developed a critique of the Western liberal political project not only through the writings of ethicists such as Alasdair MacIntyre and Stanley Hauerwas, but primarily through a study of John Cassian's interpretation of Scripture from within a community of faith and spirituality.[23]

In sum, my tradition in Christian Churches/Churches of Christ employs an understanding of Scripture, insights from contemporary missionaries, a reading of *consensus fidelium*, and critiques of specific Western Enlightenment theories in responding to religious pluralism. I have tried to show that a position which attempts to affirm at least in part both other cultures and the religions within them while preaching the good news of Jesus Christ as ultimate for every human person need be neither exclusivist nor inclusivist, and cannot be pluralist. It is more proscriptive and eschatological, acting on what the community believes and trusting in what we hope. For us that is a sensible approach for the twenty-first century.

Appendix

Christian Churches, Churches of Christ, and Disciples of Christ, the Restoration Movement or the Stone-Campbell Movement — all are names for a nineteenth-century reform movement within Christianity. Born in the minds of father Thomas and son Alexander Campbell, one in the United States and one in Scotland, and joined in this country by Barton Stone, it spread throughout Great Britain, Australia, and New Zealand and flourished in the United States. This heritage originally centered on the restoration of the ancient New Testament order for the unity of the church so that the world might believe in Jesus Christ as Lord and Savior.[24] It looked to the Bible in a manner which makes it

23. Robert Parsley, "Understanding Means Living: Interpretation of Scripture according to John Cassian" (M.Div. thesis, Emmanuel School of Religion, 1994).

24. Thomas Campbell, *Declaration and Address*, published in 1809. Frederick D. Kershner, *The Christian Union Overture: An Interpretation of the Declaration and Address of Thomas Campbell* (St. Louis: Bethany Press, 1923), is a useful edition and commentary. For a continuation of those themes within Christian Churches see Dean E. Walker, "Restoration? . . . Unity? . . . Mission!" and "An Approach to Reconciliation," in *Adventuring for Christian Unity and Other Essays* (Johnson City, Tenn.: Em-

clearly appear to be a Protestant tradition. Many of these congregations still practice immersion baptism of believers as the New Testament model,[25] related to the Anabaptist heritage, but also as the one form of baptism recognized by the whole church. All congregations of this shared tradition celebrate the Lord's Supper each Sunday and leave it open to any who call themselves Christian.

Tragically these churches have fractured into three groups in this century. Congregations called Christian Churches and Churches of Christ, sometimes referred to as Independent Christian Churches, have been distinguished from Churches of Christ who refuse the use of instrumental music and from Christian Churches (Disciples of Christ). In round numbers these Christian Churches worldwide involve 6,500 congregations, 1,100,000 members, and 1,000 missionaries.[26] They have not belonged to the National Council of Churches.

Being people who honor congregational autonomy but who also enjoy fellowship at our North American Christian Convention each summer, we are difficult to describe. Our convention is a preaching/teaching gathering organized by a one-hundred-person committee, exclusively men. (There has in recent years been a shadow cabinet of women whose advice is sought.) The convention presidency changes each year, as do certain seats on the steering committee, but that committee and the director of the convention serve over long periods. There are no delegates and nothing to vote on. The convention has no detailed business agenda and makes no pronouncements. During the fundamentalist troubles of the Missouri Synod Lutherans and the Southern Baptists, our lack of centralized organization open to capture by skilled Protestant canon lawyers has proved to be a gracious gift. Yet because of these features there are no official statements to quote because intentionally none exist.

---

manuel School of Religion, 1992), pp. 583-603, and Robert O. Fife, "The Stone-Campbell Movement: Toward a Responsible Future," in *Celebration of Heritage* (Joplin, Mo.: College Press, 1992), pp. 443-62.

25. Christian Churches (Disciples of Christ) accept a series of forms of Christian baptism. Some Christian Churches and Churches of Christ do not accept the validity of sprinkling or pouring and reject infant baptism. Others practice only the immersion of adults but leave the salvation of the pious unimmersed to God's grace.

26. *Directory of the Ministry: A Yearbook of Christian Churches and Churches of Christ* (Springfield, Ill.: Directory of the Ministry, 1994).

The word "independent" is a misnomer which arises from a twentieth-century debate. Christian Churches were "independent" because their missionaries were sent out by local congregations, not agencies. Christian Churches (Disciples of Christ) were "cooperative" because their missionaries were sent out under a denominational agency. Christian Churches do not have an episcopal, presbyterial, or delegate convention structure, but we do work together for various projects.[27] Christian Missionary Fellowship is the largest of a number of mission agencies that now support missionaries. Educational enterprises, benevolent associations, church-planting groups as well as mission endeavors often have national or regional organizations that assist local churches in efforts too large for a single congregation. Yet each of those organizations must make its appeal for funds directly to individual persons and congregations. The national convention and the few state conventions which exist seldom if ever underwrite any such project. On occasion men's or women's regional or district associations may support some particular effort.

After an interesting nineteenth-century history in which the church brought about some unions and worked rather hard at restoration and unity for Christian mission, our twentieth-century history has been somewhat shortsighted, marked by internal polemic. In this century many Christian Churches/Churches of Christ and many Churches of Christ noninstrumental have emphasized the restoration theme and left the unity theme to the Disciples of Christ.[28] While a number of my Disciples friends tell me that one of their difficulties is that people join their congregations as a place where they need not believe any specific

---

27. From a sociologist's perspective we do have leaders who fill the functions of bishops or archbishops. When congregations search for leadership they often call the offices of college or seminary presidents. In any region one may find an older minister who serves younger ministers through counseling and advice. But no such offices are occupied for life with final authority. Such "bishops" must operate by persuasion and example.

28. My hometown newspaper, the *Johnson City Press*, reported on July 6, 1994, a meeting of 10,000 members of the Churches of Christ (noninstrumental) in Nashville. Some who attended expressed their worries about the organizers' attempt to call for open relationships within "ecumenical circles." Some in the Christian Churches' North American Christian Convention held in Orlando during the same week applauded conversations with the Churches of God (Anderson, Indiana) that are now going on, but others found that a dangerous precedent.

119

doctrine, a number of Christian Churches have found a home in sectarian fundamentalist camps. There is a line that can be drawn from aspects of Alexander Campbell's writings on through J. W. McGarvey in the 1880s directly into the fundamentalist side of the debates with "modernists" of the 1920s and beyond.

To use the popular terminological triad of our era in asking about Christianity's relationships with other religions,[29] the world mission of Christian Churches appears exclusivist, neither pluralist nor inclusivist. From our perspective a great evangelical, catholic, and orthodox consensus runs from the earliest centuries into the present. We do not view this line as needing great revision; when we attend to it, many among us find it to be both biblical and traditional. Some in our congregations primarily think of "tradition" in terms of the biblical phrase "the traditions of men," and thus as something to be avoided. But the center of our faith has in many ways been carried forward by the consensus: Jesus Christ is the Savior of the world. The liturgical structure of our worship services continually emphasizes that commitment, particularly our weekly celebration of the Lord's Supper and our hymnody. From this perspective, someone who thinks that being a Christian does not involve taking Jesus Christ as ultimate Lord of all and working within the mission of the church so that "every knee may bow and every tongue confess" appears decidedly odd to us. Our sense of the mission of the church within and for the world is inviolate.

Although this heritage began as a church-uniting movement, it has found foundational religious pluralism, inclusivism, and exclusivism to be church-dividing issues. The accommodation of the gospel so that people of other great world religions may be seen as without need of Christ has been fiercely rejected. One reason for the division between Christian Churches and Disciples of Christ was whether or not missions were true to this confession. Even in a land as overwhelming as early-twentieth-century China, conservative Disciples refused to work in comity agreements with Protestant missionaries for two reasons: partly because of a sense that Jesus Christ as Lord and

29. I use the term "religion" here in a very broad sense with a critique of its employment in much Enlightenment and modern literature. See my colleagues Charles and Betty Taber, "A Christian Understanding of 'Religion' and the 'Religions'," *Missiology* 20 (1992): 69-78.

Savior was being compromised and partly because denominational traditions were viewed as defeating the unity of the church as it grew in China and thus as deeply wounding the mission of the church. When the Disciples national convention would not heed their warnings, many of these conservatives felt frozen out and eventually formed their own convention.

My immediate tradition is a community within this heritage. Our best recent theologian, perhaps described in some ways as a conservative Disciple of Christ or better yet as a free church catholic, was William Robinson. An English theologian, he was for some years principal of Overdale College in the Selly Oak Colleges near the University of Birmingham. (You may know that the Federation of Selly Oak Colleges has hosted several mission colleges representing a number of Christian traditions in Great Britain.) Robinson believed in restoration and unity as the two poles of the ellipse necessary for the mission of the church. He was a part of early meetings of the World Council of Churches. Thus my involvement with this consultation fits into that model; I follow his lead and that of his pupil, Fred P. Thompson, Jr. About three decades ago the National Council held a Faith and Order Colloquium with evangelicals whose churches did not belong to the council. Thompson, the president of Emmanuel School of Religion when I joined the faculty in 1977, had participated for two years in those discussions.

CHAPTER EIGHT

All Things New:
An Orthodox Theological
Reflection on Interfaith Dialogue

MICHAEL OLEKSA

"Behold, I make all things new."

Revelation 21:5

I<small>T</small> may seem strange to start at the end and move toward the beginning, but, in a sense, that is what Christianity always challenges us
to do. With our lives totally oriented toward God, focused on the Holy
Trinity, on Christ and his eternal reign, we are commanded to live and
act in this world faithful to this vision, this "impossible dream" of a
"new heaven and earth" (Rev. 21:1). For this reason, I offer these few
pages of reflection as an Orthodox Christian, active for many years on
the Dialogue Subunit Working Group for the World Council, beginning
with the ultimate goals, the "last things" toward which we strive as
human beings created in the image and likeness of God, summoned to
become "new" (2 Cor. 5:17).

The newness to which all creation is summoned is described
elsewhere in the New Testament. Saint Paul, writing to the Colossians,
speaks of Christ in cosmic terms, proclaiming him "the image of the
invisible God, the firstborn of all creation. For by Him all things were
created that are in heaven and on earth visible and invisible. . . . He is

before all things and in Him all things consist . . . for it pleased the Father that in Him all fullness should dwell" (Col. 1:15-19). The new heaven and new earth are already present to the Christian believer. Christ is identified with life and all life-sustaining, life-affirming, and nurturing elements — "all things." The reign of God includes the whole created universe, *ta panta*. Too often in the last five centuries Christians have forgotten the cosmic, and therefore the ecological dimension of their faith, fearing, perhaps, a confusion with pantheism or paganism. But in these and other texts, looking at the message from the perspective of its *telos*, its ultimate goal, the whole creation is the focus, the concern, the object of Christian witness and action. Nothing and no one can be excluded. In the eschaton, Christ will be "all in all" (Eph. 1:23), and for Christians, he already is.

"For God so loved the world that He gave His only begotten Son that whoever believes in Him . . . should have everlasting life." How familiar this verse is, of all those memorized in the Gospel of John. And yet it loses a critical dimension in English translation; the word "world" in the original text is not, as might be assumed, *oikoumenoi,* the inhabited world, the people of the world, but *kosmos,* the whole created universe. Too long abandoned as a legitimate concern of Christian action, the creation is to be blessed, sanctified, restored, saved along with humanity. The "new heaven and new earth" are this world, this earth, this galaxy, this forest, beach and ocean, blessed, transfigured, renewed. This is the world God loves. He did not undertake the entire saving plan, the divine *oikonomia,* just to destroy it all and start again after all. God loves this cosmos of his, and it is to the shame of Christians that they have apparently forgotten this truth.

"The heavens are telling the glory of God and the firmament declares his handiwork," wrote the psalmist (19:1). Is not God revealed in his works? Does not our concept of majesty derive from mountains, our ideal of beauty from the natural beauty around us? Does not the grandeur and power of canyonlands and seascapes inspire us with awe, with spiritual yearning, do they not offer a religious experience known to sensitive Homo sapiens for millennia? If so, we have much to discuss with traditional tribal peoples whose entire spirituality centers on these experiences of majesty, beauty, grandeur, and power and their attempt to live in harmony within this sacred context.

While western Europe was in its own Dark Ages, the Christian East actually debated such questions as the spiritual value of the created universe. In the mid–seventh century, Saint Maximus the Confessor articulated a view of the world that the church accepted as her own vision at the Sixth Ecumenical Council. Saint Maximus spoke of the Logos, the Word of God "embodied," several times, for the Word of God establishes the universe, not just in a chronological sense, "in the beginning," but at every moment from that point onward. God sustains the cosmos "by his Word" in each second, so that creation is not so much a chronological process but an instant miracle. The energies of the Word in God, the dynamic Presence of the Logos in each of what Saint Maximus called the particular "logoi," create the world, so to speak, from moment to moment. And these energies are what theologians call "grace." It is more appropriate to speak of *tota gratia* rather than *sola gratia*.

> We believe that the logos of the angels preceded their creation; that the logos of each essence and of power which constitute the world above, the logos of all human beings, the logos of all that to which God gave existence — and it is impossible to enumerate all things — is unspeakable and incomprehensible in its infinite transcendence by being greater than any creature . . . but this same logos is manifested and multiplied in a way suitable to the good in all the beings who came from Him . . . and He recapitulates all things in Himself. . . . For all things participate in God by analogy, insofar as they came from God.[1]

Traditional tribal peoples know and love their homelands, treating them as "holy lands," as the tribes of Israel regarded theirs. For centuries they have been the target of tremendous Christian missionary efforts — some remarkably successful, others catastrophically disastrous. Where tribal peoples embraced Christianity, they underscored and reaffirmed the cosmic dimension of the gospel which the Western Christian missionaries seldom recognized. Where they rejected the gospel message as it had been presented to them, it might be argued, they did so because they saw no cosmic dimension in it or, in fact, came to believe that Christianity was hostile to what was, for them, the essence of religious experience. This is again true today in modern

1. Quoted from John Meyendorff, *Christ in Eastern Christian Thought* (Crestwood, N.Y.: SVS Press, 1969), p. 102.

Western society, where people are searching for a spiritual home which includes their reawakened consciousness of the sacredness of the natural world. Not finding any such approbation in Christianity as they understand it, they go elsewhere, to East Asian or Amerindian traditions, seeking a wholeness they do not believe exists within the Judeo-Christian tradition.

For Christianity to be complete, full, according to the whole *kathoulou*, it must take its own cosmic dimension seriously. There are those, not only traditional tribal peoples but also Hindus and Buddhists, Chinese philosophers, Taoist and Shinto, whose spiritual lives are grounded firmly and deeply in their experience of the sacred in the natural world. Christians may insist that there is more to religious experience than what nature can provide, but they must not exclude nature from their own spirituality. Making *ta panta* new requires taking *ta panta* into account. The Word is first embodied in the whole creation, then in the Scriptures. We know God from revelations outside the Bible. We Orthodox embrace Scripture, but not *SOLA scriptura*.

The sacramental and liturgical life of the Eastern Orthodox Church certainly affirms the cosmic dimension of the Christian message. Architecturally in the very structure of a traditional Orthodox temple, this all-embracing vision is expressed in the overall plan and in the iconography.

> The architecture of the interior of an ancient Russian church expresses the ideal of the all-embracing church, where God Himself resides, and beyond which there is nothing. Naturally the dome represents the highest extreme limit of the universe, the crowning celestial sphere where the Lord of Hosts reigns. The outside is a different story: there, above the church, is the real sky, a reminder that the earthly church has not yet reached the highest sphere. To reach it, a new surge, a new fervor is needed. That is why the same dome assumes on the outside the mobile form of an upward-pointing flame.
>
> Need I say that the interior and the exterior are in perfect harmony? It is through the flame that heaven descends to earth, enters the church, and becomes the ultimate completion of the church, the consummation in which the hand of God covers everything earthly, in a benediction from the dark blue dome. God's hand, vanquishing the world's discord, leading to universal community, holds the destinies of humanity. . . .

Thus the church affirms the inner communal unity destined to overcome the chaotic divisions and enmity in the world and in humanity. A "Sobor" (cathedral/council/assembly) of all creatures as the coming universal peace encompassing angels and people and every living creature on the earth — that is the basic idea of the church that dominated both ancient Russian architecture and icon painting. St. Sergius of Radonezh himself expressed it quite consciously and in a remarkably profound way. He erected a church to the Trinity, as a mirror for those he had gathered into a monastic community, so that the sight of the Holy Trinity "might vanquish the fear of the world divided by hate." St. Sergius was inspired by the prayer of Christ for his disciples, "that they may be one as we are one" (John 17:22). His ideal was the transfiguration of the world in the image of the Holy Trinity, that is, the inner union of all things in God. All of ancient Russian religiosity, including icon painting, lived by this ideal. Overcoming hateful discord, transforming the world into a church uniting all creation as the Three Persons of the Holy Trinity are united in one Godhead — to this basic theme everything in old Russian religious painting was subordinated.[2]

Orthodox church architecture and iconography are an attempt to make theology, the reality of the eschaton, manifest. Orthodox Liturgy is an attempt to make it tangible, active, dynamically present. This is not escapist. It is a deliberate, conscious effort to place the ultimate goal constantly before the Christian community — an all-embracing unity in peace, harmony, freedom, beauty, truth, and love. The destination must logically be known before one embarks on a journey. For Christians the journey is to the eschaton, the new heaven and the new earth, this world in its transfigured condition. The saints are the historical evidence that "new creaturehood" is already to some extent attainable, if believers take their Christian vocation to grow to "the measure of the stature of the fullness of Christ" seriously. But this is a struggle, spiritual warfare (Eph. 6:10ff.). Climbing the mountain is very different from owning a map of it. The saints have accepted and journeyed according to the map and attained the summit, but they will not be complete without us (Heb. 11:40). For the Christian vision to be realized requires

2. Eugene Trubetskoy, *Icons: Theology in Color* (Crestwood, N.Y.: SVS Press, 1973), pp. 18-19.

each person to follow their lead, for the goal is panhuman *agape*, unity-in-love, in the image and likeness of God.

This all-embracing unity is revealed in the mystery of the Holy Trinity, for it is essentially a unity of free persons. The first eight centuries of conciliar debate and eventual consensus centered on the person of Christ and the Christian vision of God. The issues were critical since human persons are created in God's image and likeness. We can only know our own nature and destiny by knowing God. And this was impossible before God revealed himself to us. The third "embodiment" of the Word is the incarnation: "And the Word became Flesh and dwelt among us" (John 1).

> The great teachers of humanity, the authors of the Upanishads, Lao-tzu, Confucius, Buddha, Mohammed, Socrates, Plato and others perceive the truth like the summit of a high mountain which they climbed with the greatest difficulty. This was justified because truth does not lightly yield itself up. It is really like a high mountain that has to be climbed, breathing heavily and feeling that a steep slope still lies ahead. . . . Yogis, philosophers' way. But Jesus came from a simple village, where he lived the life of an ordinary person. In him everything was ready made. He did not ascend to any place. On the contrary, he came down to the people.
>
> Every sage has been conscious of his ignorance. Socrates said, "I know that I do not know anything." The great saints of every age felt themselves to be sinners much more acutely than you and I do because they were closer to the light and every stain on their life was beheld more consciously than for us in our gray lives.
>
> In Jesus Christ there was no consciousness of sin, nor any consciousness that he had attained something or other. He came to people bringing to them something that was in him from the beginning, by nature.[3]

Here is a distinguishing characteristic of the Christian faith: Its Founder is unlike all others. He proclaims himself eternal, united with the Father in a unique way, as a Person who has preexisted and voluntarily entered this world, who willingly suffers and dies and takes up

3. Alexander Men', "Christianity," in *Sourozh* (Oxford, UK), August 1994, pp. 7-9.

his life again and returns to his original, true place with God and in God. Such a person is not a great religious philosopher, teacher, mystic, or genius. He is either what he claims to be or completely insane. He either fulfills the Law and prophets, as he said he would, or he doesn't. He is either God-with-us, Emmanuel, or a lunatic.

Those who knew him personally and directly accepted his claims were deeply disappointed, totally shaken at his arrest, crucifixion, and death. They lost confidence and ran for their lives. It is the resurrection that is the source of Christian faith, Christian hope, Christian love, for if there had been no resurrection, Christ's birth, the birth of a Galilean charlatan, certainly would never have been celebrated. It is the paschal event that constitutes the essence of the gospel, the good news. If Christ is not risen, as the apostle Paul commented long ago, "our preaching is empty and your faith is also empty" (1 Cor 15:14).

Christ's resurrected body is, in fact, the very image and evidence of the "new earth," for it displays all the properties of this new reality. He is certainly in some sense a physical reality, for Thomas doubts that his fellow disciples have seen anything more than Jesus' ghost (which was also their first reaction). But when he touches the nail print in Jesus' hand, he confesses, "My Lord and my God!" The doors are locked and suddenly Jesus is there. They walk with him on the road to Emmaus and fail to recognize him. When they do, he vanishes. This resurrected Lord is the same and yet different — the image of the new reality which first manifested itself in him but will ultimately extend to the whole created universe in its renewed, transfigured, sanctified condition. Every traditional icon attempts to portray this "new" reality, for the image is "the same and yet different."

The self-revelation, therefore, of God in Jesus Christ is personal, tri-personal. The ancient councils did not so much attempt to explain God, which is impossible, as to set certain parameters, exclude certain possibilities, which, given what Jesus taught and exemplified, were no longer "in the ballpark." Jesus had to be fully God, not a uniquely constituted liaison between God and humanity, for the whole point to God's plan was to unite himself to us. Only God himself can unite us to himself, not a semidivine being. But only if he was completely like us could we identify with him, be united to him. In uniting ourselves to Christ we unite ourselves to the Unifying Principle of the Universe, the Divine Logos. And he is united totally and completely to the Father, as he testified so often. In and through the Holy Spirit, we are united to Christ and thus enter the community of life and love which is God, Father, Son, and Holy Spirit.

The mystery of the Holy Trinity is not a theological abstraction concocted by philosophically minded professors of doctrine. It is the central affirmation of the Christian faith. God is a community of Persons, and human persons have been invited to join them, to unite themselves freely in faith, in truth, hope, and love, to God, Father, Son, and Holy Spirit. Indeed, this is the reason for which each person was created, called from nonexistence into being, each according to God's eternal *oikonomia*, his saving plan. Each divine Person is unique, sharing with the other two all the characteristics of divinity — omniscience, omnipotence, eternal existence, etc. Each human person is unique, sharing with all other human beings a common humanity. But whereas Father, Son, and Holy Spirit are totally and forever united because of the infinite love each has for the other, there is never any division among them. The Son and the Spirit eternally, in love and humility, fulfill the will of the Father. There is humility "built into" God as well. This is how human beings are to be united to God and to each other, then, with persons freely accepting to fulfill the will of the Father in their own existence, as they discern it in the circumstances of their lives. For God, this unity is, one can say, "natural," but it was meant to be our natural condition as well. Some ancient Christian writers believed that, from this perspective, the incarnation was part of the divine plan from the very beginning, but that the fall of Adam only delayed and complicated the process. Sin, as refusal to fulfill the will of the Father, as separation from God and therefore from life, is unnatural and suicidal. The human machine was meant to be fueled by God, but since the beginning human beings have sought inappropriate and self-destructive substitutes — power, money, physical pleasures, sexual satisfaction, delusions, escapist remedies, and drugs — rather than "the Real Thing." All the substitute "fuels" offer some sort of pleasure, while the fullness of human potential can be achieved only in communion with God, by participating in his energies, his love, his *agape*. The opposite of pleasure is not pain, but *blessedness*.

To "climb the mountain" means to live in a particular way, as Saint Gregory Nazianzus wrote in the fourth century. He noted that human persons were given four divine attributes — existence, eternal existence, goodness, and wisdom, the first pair constituting the image of God in humanity, the latter two the likeness. The image is indelible and "given," so to speak, but likeness had to be developed by effort and commitment. All people are God's image in that they are alive and have eternal souls, but only those who seek and live by goodness and wisdom develop their potential for likeness to God. Saint Maximus, commenting on this, wrote:

> Do you want to be righteous? Give to each part which constitutes you what it deserves — I mean your soul and your body — to the reasonable part of your soul give readings and contemplations and prayer; to the irascible part, spiritual love and the adversary of hatred; to the concupiscible part, chastity and temperance; to the flesh, food and clothing, which alone are indispensable.[4]

The Son and the Spirit not only fulfill the will of the Father but are totally united to each other in infinite and eternal love, so that while each Person remains distinct, they share one will and one action. They are "one in essence and undivided." This is the image in which human persons are created as well. We are meant to fulfill freely the will of God the Father in our lives and so totally love one another that there is never any division among us, that all the human race, taken as a whole, would also be "one in essence," sharing the same humanity, and also "undivided," acting according to one will, united in love. Attaining this condition is the Christian vision of life: "That they may be one as we are" (John 17). Such interpersonal unity is hardly attainable even in the most intimate of relationships in this world, within the community of marriage. But the vision of "the new heaven and the new earth" challenges Christians to strive toward that type of unity-in-love, fulfilling the will of the Father, with all other persons, living and departed, together with those not yet born. By human effort and willpower, of course, this vision is unattainable. That is why Christ, the center, the "hub" of all things, provides the key. In and through him we are united to the Personal Unifying Factor of the Universe. By being united to him, like spokes on a wheel we are placed in a condition of unity with the

4. Meyendorff, p. 104; also see L. Thunberg, *Man and the Cosmos* (Crestwood, N.Y.: SVS Press, 1985), and J. Zizioulas, *Being as Communion* (Crestwood, N.Y.: SVS Press, 1985).

Father and with all others who are united to him. And this includes the whole cosmos, all realities visible and invisible in heaven and on earth. Christ is central, absolutely central in this vision of the world. But it is more accurate to speak of *totus* Christus rather than *solus* Christus.

The search for the appropriate center and source for life, for the meaning and purpose of existence, has inspired the philosophers and ascetics of all cultures and generations. The thirst for this truth is universal. When we encounter the adherents of other major world religions, we are meeting other human beings who have followed other paths in their search for the truth about life, about humanity, about God. They have begun the ascent up the mountain path. We Christians claim to have a map of that terrain, not because we have ourselves already climbed, but because Christ has come down, has descended and led the way for us to ascend, too.

Here we must clearly distinguish between the map and the climb. We must also consider the destination. In interfaith dialogue we need to consider all three. The map is what theologians have debated and discussed for centuries. Doctrines are the broad contours that chart the spiritual journey for the adherents to a given faith tradition. Whether the world is eternal or not; whether it is created or not; whether there is one God or many; whether the power of evil is equal to or even superior to the power of goodness; whether people are capable of free choice or are totally depraved and predestined to act in a certain way in their lives; whether there is heaven, hell, purgatory, transmigration of souls, and reincarnation — all are doctrinal positions that affect each person's spiritual pilgrimage. And doctrinal positions are seldom assumed on the basis of purely analytical, philosophical reflection. Prior to embracing a particular religious or doctrinal system one needs to decide whom one trusts and why. There are thousands of conflicting authorities, hundreds of sects, dozens of distinct religions. A Christian believes the apostolic witness. A Christian confesses that Jesus is the Lord. A Christian affirms the death, burial, and resurrection of Christ. But a Christian cannot prove any of these. To accept the Christian message is to accept the Christian map, buy the Christian atlas. This is an act of faith. But it is not yet the mountaintop, nor even the journey. Faith is absolutely necessary, but it is not in itself sufficient: *fide*, yes, but not *SOLA fide*.

A Moslem, on the other hand, posits the divine inspiration of

Muhammad, and through him the Koran. A Hindu may venerate the Vedas and Upanishads, a Baha'i the writings of Bahaullah, a Mormon the *Book of Mormon.* Why one accepts a certain corpus of writings as sacred and rejects all others is, in most cases, a matter of culture, of the social norms and expectations with which one is raised. Increasingly, especially in the West in the late twentieth century, people are growing up in a religious vacuum, with no particular spiritual orientation or grounding at all. This is becoming the norm rather than the exception, so that the formerly "Christian" West is confronted not only with religious indifference and secularization but also with an increasing interest in a plurality of religious traditions across an extraordinarily wide spectrum.

In such a situation it is easy, perhaps expectable, that misunderstandings and controversies should arise. Those who have not journeyed very far on their own pilgrimage are most likely to get drawn into controversies about whose map is the most accurate. Doctrinal controversies are legion, but few ever get down to basics deep enough to realize that maps and journeys are different realities. It seems to me to be much more interesting and fruitful to discuss destinations, but it is hardly ever done. A "new heaven and a new earth" is not such a boring or unproductive starting point for interfaith discussion. Total unity-in-love among all people is not such a worthless goal. It may be the only ultimate goal worth pursuing. But it requires all those in dialogue to be genuine pilgrims, not cartographers or atlas owners. The "holy fathers" were not judged holy by virtue of being on the winning side in various theological disputes. They were holy because their guidance and teachings came from the summit, the mountaintop they had attained. Their writings came not only from logical analysis of scriptural data but from their own spiritual quest and experience. Only prayerful, spiritual warriors, communicants, and celebrants in the liturgical and sacramental life of the church, ascetic heroes in "the good fight," can speak with authority, from experience. Having followed the spiritual map, they have, by their lives, explored and verified its accuracy. These are the kind of Christians we need in interfaith dialogue. It was such Christians who were able to reintegrate Arians, Nestorians, and iconoclasts in the faith community. The church has always been "in dialogue," and those who oppose ecumenical discussions (and misquote the holy fathers and the canons to justify this isolationist position) fail to understand the mind of the fathers, their vocation, their vision. We must be in dialogue with everyone everywhere: our vision of "all things new" demands it. If the ultimate goal is total interpersonal unity-in-love, no one can be excluded on any basis whatsoever. We can never say "I have nothing to say to you, nothing to do with you." To the extent we do, we ourselves are not saved.

The "new person" each human being is challenged to become has certain divine characteristics, as Saint Isaac of Nineveh described:

> The perfect person has a kindling of the heart for all creation — for humanity, the birds, the animals, the demons, the whole universe. And whenever he thinks of them, or contemplates them, tears pour from his eyes because of the strong sympathy which possesses his heart. And his heart feels itself touched and possessed and he cannot endure to see or to hear of any creature suffering any harm or even the slightest pain.[5]

If we keep the goal to attain such spiritual perfection (Matt. 5:48) in mind, certain attitudes and tactics, certain beliefs and behaviors, are precluded. There is no place, if we keep our focus on the ultimate goal, for bigotry, intolerance, coercion, or persecution. The goal becomes unattainable under these conditions, and so resorting to force, injustice, or violence is antithetical to the goal. They violate the God-given freedom of the person, violate the will of the Father, violate love. Certainly one of the main justifications for interfaith dialogue is this simple: believers of all traditions must as a minimum cease slandering each other. Bearing false witness is viewed as a sin in nearly everyone's catechism. Before members of one tradition make pronouncement about what another tradition believes or teaches, they should be sure they are speaking with honesty and integrity, as members of that tradition themselves might want their faith to be described. It is a matter of applying the Golden Rule to interfaith discussions.

Besides conversations about the map and/or the destination, interfaith dialogue needs to focus more fruitfully on the journey. All else is idle chatter. If we have a clear vision of our goal and the most accurate possible doctrinal map for reaching it and then never leave the comforts

5. Saint Isaac, Homily 48, quoted in N. Arseniev, *Mysticism and the Eastern Church* (Crestwood, N.Y.: SVS Press, 1979), p. 52.

of home, our spiritual status quo, neither the vision nor the map profits us anything. Bragging about what a fine atlas we own does not make us world travelers. Arguing over the maps and insisting on reexploring everything, rechecking all the cartographer's work, also makes little sense (although many "believers" love to engage in such controversies, no doubt to avoid setting a departure date). It is precisely in discussions focusing on the spiritual climb — the work the individual must do to become the open, loving, trusting, and faithful Christlike being the Christian is sincerely and earnestly trying to become — with adherents from other faiths that one suddenly realizes that at this level there are tremendous similarities on the human side of the struggle. This is perfectly consistent with Christian doctrine, which posits the fundamental unity of humanity and the human condition. Regardless of the map or vision of the ultimate destination, all travelers will encounter similar terrain, parallel obstacles, even identical pitfalls and temptations. Especially at the initial stages of the ascent, climbers will have quite similar experiences. Most of the differences on this level appear only toward the end, toward the top. According to some maps, some visions, there is oblivion, according to others passionlessness and peace, to others physical pleasures and rewards, and others continued but effortless, joyful ascent, "further up and further in," as C. S. Lewis described it.

In the end, Christ will have us all in his eternal, loving embrace — Christians, Hindus, Buddhists, Jews, Moslems, traditionalists, atheists, agnostics. God has not constructed a celestial pleasure palace for those who have obeyed his will or in faith purchased the most correct doctrinal "map" on one hand, and a subterranean torture chamber for those who have not on the other. The Gospel stories that discuss heaven and hell in these terms are all parables: "the Kingdom of God is like . . ." (Matthew 25).

Our God is a "consuming fire" (Heb. 12:18), but the fire is the brightness, warmth, and light of *agape*, divine love which unites Father, Son, and Holy Spirit, a community of interpersonal love humanity has been invited to enter "by faith, by grace, by Christ." Once again Saint Isaac offers some wonderful insight into the nature of salvation and eternity:

> Those who find themselves in hell will be chastised by the scourge of love. . . . For those who understand that they have sinned against

love undergo no greater suffering than those produced by the most fearful tortures. The sorrow which takes hold of the heart which has sinned against love is more piercing than any other pain. It is not right to say that sinners in hell are deprived of the love of God. . . . But love acts in two ways, as suffering for the reproved and as joy for the blessed.[6]

Even within this context, the process of growth in unity, growth in love, does not end. There is nothing static about the "new heaven and earth," for loving relationships will continue to develop "further up and further in" but, in the reign of God, without the struggles, imperfections, frustrations, suspicions, and misperceptions that plague all interpersonal relationships in this fallen world. Each person will grow in love with all other persons, both those one has known and loved in this life and those billions of strangers one has never known or perhaps toward whom one was merely indifferent. The process of increasing each person's capacity to love continues in this world only with effort, commitment, and struggle — the cross. In the new reality, this effort, begun so haltingly and inadequately here, will be the very content of eternal joy. From this perspective salvation is never fully attained until each person has freely committed himself/herself in love to God and to all other persons, to the entire created universe, and has entered into a fully loving relationship with everyone and everything. Salvation is an eternal process and everyone is part of it. Each person must accept the challenge to grow, to change, to undergo a metamorphosis. (We have been collectively summoned to become butterflies, but the choice to remain caterpillars is still an option.) We must respond personally, but salvation is never individual. It is a communal and cosmic task we undertake together with all Christians, in and through the church.

Christians engaged in interfaith dialogue are approaching the encounter from a Christian perspective, with the Christian vision, map, and certain expectations about their spiritual journey. These will all inevitably differ from other faith traditions in greater or lesser degrees. It is not true that "there is only one God," in the minds and visions of religious people. The descriptions and articulations vary. The paths do

6. Quoted in Thomas Hopko, *Spirituality* (Syosset, N.Y.: DRE, 1976), p. 134.

not necessarily converge. Not all atlas owners are on their own journeys, and not all atlases are equally accurate. But the Christian vision of total unity-in-love — complete interpersonal harmony and *agape* in the image and likeness of God — demands that Christians pursue, work, and strive toward this goal as the very purpose for their life, the very meaning of their faith. We have no choice but to dialogue. It is but the initial phase of unity — getting acquainted. And we are commanded to go much, much further, to fellowship, mutual respect and appreciation, kindness, humility, generosity, forgiveness, patience, tolerance — to exhibit in our relations with each other and all others, to the best of our abilities and energies — all the gifts of the spirit, culminating in love. Nothing else, as 1 Corinthians 13 reminds us, really matters. In the end, there may finally be one *sola*, but it will be *agape*.

CHAPTER NINE

An Anglican Perspective on Our Interreligious Situation

PETER SLATER

IN this paper I propose to give a sense of how Episcopalians have addressed questions concerning interfaith relations and how our traditional reliance on a Logos Christology may be reconceived to affirm the surprise element in the guidance of the Holy Spirit. I shall look at one way of construing the authority of Scripture and tradition for theology and reflect on appeals to baptism as a basis for ecumenical relations among denominations. Then I shall consider the call to be Christlike as the basis for relations among religions and, finally, the Anglican ideal of a sacramental "communion of communions" as the basis for affirming plurality without succumbing to relativism.

I

Episcopalians are members of the worldwide Anglican Communion. Most Anglicans like to be seen as incorporating the best of the Protestant and Catholic traditions in churchmanship and as historically akin to the Orthodox in theology. The English heritage of church rather than sect, where parishes are geographical areas more than specifiable worshiping communities, means that one usually can find the whole spectrum of theological opinion among Anglicans. The creeds are integral to baptismal and eucharistic liturgies, but narrow doctrinal conformity is not required for membership. Consequently, while it is possible for a theologian to offer *an* Anglican perspective on a given topic, it is not possible for him or her to give *the* Anglican position, without some sort of conciliar confirmation.

We sometimes forget that there are more Anglicans in Kenya than in Canada, more in sub-Saharan Africa than in all of England or the USA. Historically, the Anglican ethos has been shaped by Thomas Cranmer's rendering of the Book of Common Prayer. What exercises many Anglicans today is not theology but prayer book revision. In the Anglican cycle of prayer churches on one side of the world regularly pray for churches on the other and are reminded of the very different conditions under which all Christians live and work. The common British heritage fosters a global vision of what it is to be a Christian. Being an Anglican requires a sense of both "vertical" and "horizontal" relationships crossing many ethnic and social barriers.

Anglicans exist in North America and elsewhere because in modern times missionary societies sent preachers to the colonies, often despite opposition from traders who were nervous of interference. First the evangelicals joined the waves of European Protestants moving across the oceans, then the Oxford movement inspired high-church emissaries to follow suit. What they typically did on arrival was to establish hospitals and schools. For instance, the Cambridge lecturer in theology who nurtured Mahatma Gandhi's interest in the Sermon on the Mount was one such — C. F. Andrews of Saint Stephen's College, Delhi.[1] The men and women who responded to the missionary call were certainly culture-bound in their conceptions of Christianity and "civilization." But they were not all minor talents supporting the mercenary interests of their secular compatriots.

Two results of the churches' missions overseas have been slow in coming but are important. First, many missionary educators engaged in dialogue with local religious leaders long before this became fashionable. When they returned home they disseminated specialist knowledge of world religions through the churches and universities. For example, George Appleton, compiler of the Oxford Book of Prayer, wrote on Buddhism, Kenneth Cragg on Islam, and John V. Taylor on

---

1. See *Gandhi and Charlie: The Story of a Friendship,* ed. David McL. Gracie (Cambridge, Mass.: Cowley, 1989).

African traditional religion.[2] All three became respected bishops. Second, and in the long run more important, indigenous leaders among the churches overseas have begun to find their own voices, addressing the question of other religions afresh.[3]

The emphasis on communal liturgy means that for many Anglicans the question of interfaith relations is more often a question of common worship than of conflicting beliefs. Can my daughter marry her Muslim fiancé in our parish church? Can the rector attend a function involving worship when the Dalai Lama is on the platform? These are the kinds of questions bishops refer to their interfaith consultants these days. When those consultants attend joint meetings with representatives of other traditions, talk is more likely to turn to how to combat discrimination than to points of doctrinal disagreement. *The truth sought is the truth of living relationships.*

Like many others, the Episcopal Church in the USA situates its interfaith concerns among the terms of reference for its Standing Commission on Ecumenical Relations of General Convention. What in 1979 was predominantly preoccupation with Jewish-Christian relations, in 1994 culminated in adoption of intelligently nuanced guidelines on dialogue, from a committee including experts on Buddhism and Islam. These reflect earlier initiatives by the British Council of Churches.[4] Also

---

2. Appleton wrote *On the Eightfold Path.* Cragg's books include *The Call of the Minaret, The Dome and the Rock,* and *Sandals at the Mosque.* John V. Taylor wrote *The Primal Vision.*

3. See the overview by Wesley Ariarajah, *Hindus and Christians: A Century of Protestant Ecumenical Thought* (Grand Rapids: Wm. B. Eerdmans Publishing Co., 1991). For an Anglican note see, e.g., Michael Nazir Ali, *Frontiers in Muslim-Christian Encounter* (Oxford: Regnum, 1987). For an African note see, e.g., Joseph Omosade Awolalu, "Traditional African Religion and Christianity," in *African Traditional Religions in Contemporary Society,* ed. Jacob K. Olupana (New York: Paragon House, 1991).

4. Official documents are available from the Archives of the Episcopal Church, 606 Rathervue Place, P.O. Box 2247, Austin, TX 78768. The most important is the Supplemental Report of the Presiding Bishop's Advisory Committee on Interfaith Relations, Blue Book for the 1994 General Convention, pp. 186-91. This alludes to Kenneth Cracknell's British Council of Churches guidelines and a 1986 Anglican Church of Canada report, on which see Peter Slater and others, "An Anglican Basis for Inter-Faith Encounters," *Toronto Journal of Theology* 2, no. 2 (1986): 204-14. U.S. Episcopalians working on these issues include Malcolm David Eckel of Boston University and Robert D. Hughes III of the University of the South.

a sign of the times, however, is the loss of the services of the ecumenical officer staffing this committee, due to budget cuts.

In theology, Anglican faculties and colleges used to emphasize the common mind of the churches up through the first four ecumenical councils, before the great schism between "East" and "West." The result was generally a Logos Christology and Neoplatonic orientation open to finding glimpses of eternity in the faith of others. Anglican divines were confident that we may know, or are known by, absolute truth, without confusing this with provisional statements intended to warn us against untruth, such as the Chalcedonian definitions. Anglicans have never given much heed to the thirty-nine "Articles of Religion" printed in the Prayer Book. They do emphasize the Chicago-Lambeth Quadrilateral as the basis for future ecumenical dialogues.[5]

In philosophy, the British empiricist tradition tempered the Platonic bent of Anglican divines by teaching them to value facts over theories. If it seems to be the case that the Holy Spirit is heeded as much among Catholics as among Protestants, or vice versa, and is apparently to be met on the slopes of the Himalayas as well as in urban ghettos, then most Anglicans are ready to assume that this is according to God's will. Any doctrine limiting God's presence to one creed or code or episcopal jurisdiction must be false, no matter how rational the argument to the contrary or how eminent the rationalizer. At the same time, English-speaking people tend to assume that theirs is the superior language and culture. Accordingly, in ordinary circumstances, there is no impulse among Anglicans to want to become anything else. Many agreed in the nineteenth century with the hymn writer who found Jerusalem more discernible in England's green and pleasant land than in modern Palestine.

My graduate professor, Paul Tillich, showed his Lutheran pre-

5. Note Oliver O'Donovan, *On the Thirty-Nine Articles: A Conversation with Tudor Christianity* (Exeter: Paternoster, 1986), and Paul J. Griffiths, "The Uniqueness of Christian Doctrine Defended," in *Christian Uniqueness Reconsidered: The Myth of a Pluralistic Theology of Religions,* ed. Gavin D'Costa (Maryknoll, N.Y.: Orbis, 1990). Also in the latter volume is Kenneth Surin, "A 'Politics of Speech': Religious Pluralism in the Age of McDonald's Hamburger," and Rowan Williams, "Trinity and Pluralism," cited below. On the 1886 Chicago-Lambeth Quadrilateral (Scriptures, Creeds, Sacraments, Historic Episcopate), see *Quadrilateral at One Hundred,* ed. J. Robert Wright (Cincinnati: Forward Movement Publications; London: Mowbray's, 1988).

dilections by declaring that the trouble with English theology is that it is written on tea. Had he known Oxford and Cambridge better, he would have said sherry. I doubt that he could have named a British philosopher after Locke and Hume (unless we count Toynbee or White-head), or any British theologian ever. Given that official Anglican/Epis-copalian doctrinal statements are the work of church commissions, not named individuals, this is not surprising. Interestingly, considering our topic, his only Anglican colleagues at the Harvard Divinity School were the professors of the history of religions and of "world" religions.[6] We can produce Anglican theologians with sensible things to say — I shall name some in what follows — but *my first point is that the more typical Anglican positions are found in the ethos of the worshiping communities worldwide, not in theological statements.*

The relevance of referring to our specific history comes from the current emphasis on contextualization and/or inculturation in theol-ogy.[7] Tillich and his contemporaries still assumed that their philosophi-cal categories were universal. Today, under the impact of liberation theology, we are taught to start where we are and work outwards, moving from the concrete to the universal, not vice versa.[8] Kenneth Surin, for example, berates Wilfred Cantwell Smith and John Hick for advocating "global" philosophies and theologies which seem to float above the turmoil of Third World struggles.[9] In the name of decon-structionist "post-pluralist" thinking, he dismisses indigenous spokes-persons as cultural clones of their First World mentors. This is certainly

6. Arthur Darby Nock, author of *Conversion: The Old and the New in Religion from Alexander the Great to Augustine of Hippo* (Oxford: Clarendon, 1933), and Robert Lawson Slater, founder of the Center for the Study of World Religions and author of *Can Christians Learn from Other Religions?* (New York: Seabury, 1963) and *World Religions and World Community* (New York: Columbia University Press, 1963).

7. See Aylward Shorter, *Towards a Theology of Inculturation* (Maryknoll, N.Y.: Orbis, 1988), and Peter Schineller, S.J., *A Handboook on Inculturation* (Mahwah, N.J.: Paulist, 1990). I owe my introduction to this topic to Carl Starkloff, S.J., of Regis College, Toronto.

8. For a critique of Tillich and exposition of Wittgenstein and Panikkar, see David J. Krieger, *The New Universalism: Foundations for a Global Theology* (Maryknoll, N.Y.: Orbis, 1991).

9. For Surin see the D'Costa volume cited in note 5. D'Costa was in response to John Hick and Paul F. Knitter, eds., *The Myth of Christian Uniqueness: Toward a Pluralistic Theology of Religions* (Maryknoll, N.Y.: Orbis, 1988).

unfair to Smith and hardly describes Chung Hyun Kyung. But it is symptomatic of a hermeneutics of suspicion which focuses more on the powers of the presently privileged than on the abiding power of ideas.

The assumption seems to be that "global" theology is only for jet-set Christians, not for the long-suffering people in the pews. In fact, in most urban clusters, as remarked earlier, the parent in the pew as likely as not has a wholly secular son or daughter and a daughter or son-in-law from a quite different religious tradition. What Surin neglects is Whitehead's point, that today's philosophy (and theology) is tomorrow's common sense. He is right to challenge Hick's Kantianism as a basis for assessing Hindu and Buddhist epistemologies and is justly skeptical of any move to minimize essential differences among us. But he confuses "virtuoso" with "popular" religion when he chivvies Hick, in effect, for not entering into dialogue with Calcutta street people as well as with his intellectual peers.[10]

For Anglicans the emphasis on local theologies means that we can no longer assume a Logos Christology as common ground or that the English speak for anyone but themselves. A politically correct God may only remain Greek for the Greeks.[11] Both the Greek fathers and British institutions remain part of our tradition. But it is traditionalism, not tradition, to affirm only past perspectives. Tradition itself comes from the healing interplay between a usable past and a salvific vision of our mission.

A contemporary example of the present interplay between past tradition and eschatological vision is Rowan Williams's essay on Raimundo Panikkar's trinitarian doctrine. Panikkar's aphorism is: "Jesus is Christ: but Christ is not only Jesus."[12] This neatly encapsulates the classical Logos Christology which allowed most church fathers to

10. For the concept of "virtuoso" religion see Melford Spiro, *Buddhism and Society: A Great Tradition and Its Burmese Vicissitudes* (Berkeley: University of California Press, 1970), and Steven Collins, *Selfless Persons: Imagery and Thought in Theravada Buddhism* (Cambridge: Cambridge University Press, 1982).

11. The allusion is to Robert Hood, *Must God Remain Greek? Afro Cultures and God-Talk* (Minneapolis: Augsburg Fortress, 1990).

12. Williams, "Trinity and Pluralism." Panikkar's best-known work is *The Unknown Christ of Hinduism*, 2nd ed. (Maryknoll, N.Y.: Orbis, 1981). See also *The Trinity and the Religious Experience of Man* (Maryknoll, N.Y.: Orbis, 1973), and his essay in Hick and Knitter (n. 9).

incorporate Plato along with Moses as a forerunner of Jesus, on the grounds that both were inspired by the one eternal Word. But then Panikkar juxtaposes Logos with Mythos in an un-Platonic way. The Word is now linked with the wisdom of the Spirit moving through history to account for the presence of others and the vision of their ideal harmony. For Panikkar the significant other is Hindu. Time is no longer, as for Plato, "the moving image" of eternity. It is where the truth of creation and redemption is disclosed in the inspired actions of successive generations of women and men, using their own cultural idioms.

What Williams draws from Panikkar is readiness to find novelty in how the Spirit enlivens the Word in our words, often in surprising and untraditional ways. Echoing Orthodox objections to the *filioque* clause, Panikkar and Williams give the Spirit priority in defining divinity. The Spirit is not a late arrival, supplementing the work of the Logos, but the creative ground of the latter's harmonizing presence. An impetus to freedom is there from the beginning, of and for the other in relation to the self. We are to image this Trinity in our plurality.

My own gloss on Panikkar is to underline the contrast between archetypes and prototypes when invoking the authority of Scripture and tradition. An archetype is an eternal form to which every temporal instance must forever conform in all essential respects. Thus an archetypal reading of doctrine assumes that the Word is so invariable that every deviation from canonical definitions is heresy. A prototype, by contrast, is the first in an ongoing historical series which defines the genre while allowing constant development as contexts and conceptions change. For instance, reading the Chalcedonian definitions as prototypical allows us to honor the intentions affirming the two-natures Christology, without restricting us to that vocabulary in order to describe the conjunction of God's time and ours in what modern theologians have called the Christ-event. On this view, *our task as theologians is to assist in the disclosure of timely truth, not act as if we are the custodians of timeless truth.*[13]

Supposedly timeless talk is myth, not history. Myth is unavoidable in religion. But human histories cannot be transposed into divine sagas

---

13. Note similarly Gadamer's discussion of the classical. Hans-Georg Gadamer, *Truth and Method,* trans. Joel Weinsheimer and Donald G. Marshall, 2nd rev. ed. (New York: Crossroad, 1991), pp. 285-90.

of salvation without much more attention than used to be given to the question: for whom is this good news? It is this more substantive question that Surin raises against Hick, but then confuses with his psychologizing and third-generation Marxist emphasis on class conflict. What is important about proponents of pluralism is not their motives but their challenge to the "myth" of incarnation. They question claims to Christian uniqueness supposedly stemming from the neo-Chalce-donian Christologies invoked by those mistrustful of interreligious dia-logue. The error of many on both sides of the debate is to assume that Chalcedon must be read as timeless truth, either to be accepted as such or replaced as such. For them history is the unpacking of invariant truth, not creatively living truly in new ways and old.

What Williams following Panikkar proposes is a revision of what has been called the "inclusivist" position, but based on the freedom of the Spirit rather than the formality of the Word. This freedom allows Christians to accept as grace the plurality of creation and project this into the new creation. If both Logos and Mythos are construed as prototypical, not archetypal, then theologians are released from the mythic demand to speak timelessly. They are also released from the assumption of the monomyth to the effect that everyone ("in Adam") must have undergone exactly the same "fall" and therefore must follow exactly the same pattern of redemption in order to be saved.[14] As we shall see with reference to baptism, at one level this is true: everyone must die with Christ to be raised with Christ. What Williams and Panikkar are addressing is the spirit of this transformation when it occurs outside the context of salvation history, traditionally understood.

The *emphasis on prototypes makes us take history more seriously* than our predecessors without collapsing into historical relativism. *This is my second main point.* In Augustine's time, with the Vandals on the doorstep and corruption eating at the Roman Empire from within, a supernatural heaven plausibly conveyed good news in a way that a secular vision could not. But in this century, even with Hitler on his doorstep and Marxists making more sense than Christians about conditions in the slums, Archbishop William Temple could declare that *we* are the "early" Christians, whose actions will serve as prototypes for

14. Note on the fall, Jon D. Levinson, *Creation and the Persistence of Evil: The Jewish Drama of Divine Omnipotence* (San Francisco: Harper & Row, 1988).

Christians in industrial centers for centuries to come.[15] The advent of the nuclear age since World War II may make him sound unduly optimistic. But the point is that Augustine and Temple responded to the crises of their day differently, yet with fidelity to the cumulative tradition, creatively appropriating Platonic (and, in Temple's case, process) philosophy. This enabled them to speak for their generations and to ours. As such, they serve as secondary prototypes of what it means to follow Jesus in a very different world from that of first century C.E. Israel. The conception of primary and secondary prototypes allows for continuity in tradition while affirming the importance of local contexts for each new generation in the faith.

II

Since World War II we have been moving slowly from conceptions of the church triumphant or the church militant — the church versus sect debate — to that of the church penitent. We are no less sure of God in Christ, but we are no longer so sure that our collective witness to the God relationship has been true in all respects.[16] Williams accepts Panikkar's division of our history in terms of Christianity, Christendom, and Christianness.[17] Instead of "Christianness" I would emphasize the call to be Christlike. We understand what this means from the prototypes set forth in the New Testament.

Where we differ biblically even from the time of Tillich and Temple is in being trained to give priority to the Synoptic Gospels over the Fourth Gospel. Not the Logos but the inbreaking of the kingdom has become the central focus of the baptized community. The Gospels are, so to speak, the early church's campaign statements in the politics of the Spirit. With respect to joint action and group loyalties, an analogy

15. On Temple see Joseph Fletcher, *William Temple: Twentieth Century Christian* (New York: Seabury, 1963), and Owen C. Thomas, *William Temple's Philosophy of Religion* (New York: Seabury, 1961). Note also Owen Thomas, ed., *Attitudes towards Other Religions* (New York: Harper & Row, 1969).

16. In this connection see John C. Meagher's *The Truing of Christianity* (New York: Doubleday, 1990).

17. So Panikkar in Hick and Knitter, chap. 6 on "The Jordan, the Tiber, and the Ganges: Three Kairological Moments of Christic Self-Consciousness."

may be drawn from our experience in secular politics. To become involved typically means joining a political party. Today the priority is to be democratic, to which end Americans may join the Democratic Party. But to say "my party, right or wrong" can lead to decidedly undemocratic practices. And not all democrats are Democrats.

With reference to the church-sect dichotomy, the third option is not to blur the lines in mysticism, as Troeltsch supposed, but to follow H. Richard Niebuhr in identifying ourselves as denominations.[18] Denomination means naming, and naming entails naming what empowers, that is, grace, and what corrupts, that is, sin. To be a denomination is to name the truth that is in us and to inquire after the truth in others. Whether our leaders admit it or not, the result of the schisms in our history is that none of us alone embodies the church universal. We are denominations — Catholic, Protestant, and Orthodox — collectively constituting the church penitent.

To be the church penitent is to acknowledge our respective and collective need for continuous transformation, as we use our traditions to approach the call to be Christlike. This is *my third point: We do not assume when we engage in dialogue that we are perfect, with nothing to learn, or that we are nothing and that the others are perfect, with nothing to learn from us.* Nor do we as "insiders" assume that we know ourselves in all respects better than "outsiders" can.[19] A polite way of noting this in Catholic theology is to distinguish between the promulgation of doctrine and its reception. Validity requires reception. What the surprise in talk of the Spirit adds is the warning that, often, what we have to learn from others is not what we expect to learn.

The concept of dialogue is of talking things through with others ("dia" not "duo"), in ways that allow the truth to be heard. Consider the experience of those engaged in Buddhist-Christian dialogue.[20] The typi-

18. See H. Richard Niebuhr, *The Kingdom of God in America* (New York: Harper Torchbooks, 1937), and *The Social Sources of Denominationalism* (Cleveland and New York: Meridian, 1957; first published 1929).

19. On insider-outsider perspectives see Robert J. Schreiter, *Constructing Local Theologies* (Maryknoll, N.Y.: Orbis, 1985).

20. Note, e.g., Paul O. Ingram and Frederick J. Streng, eds., *Buddhist-Christian Dialogue: Mutual Renewal and Transformation* (Honolulu: University of Hawaii Press, 1986); David Lochhead, *The Dialogical Imperative: A Christian Reflection on Interfaith Encounter* (Maryknoll, N.Y.: Orbis, 1988); and Susan Walker, ed., *Speaking of Silence: Christians and Buddhists on the Contemplative Way* (Mahwah, N.J.: Paulist, 1987).

cal reactions of participants is to come away even more convinced than before of their previous commitments. It often shocks Christians to learn that our traditional portraits of God in Christ seem to Buddhists to be *sub*-Christian. By comparison with the bodhisattva's vow, our concept of God seems lacking in compassion.[21] The same Augustine who made so much of the love of God could, at least hypothetically, consign the majority of God's creatures to hell.[22] His Buddhist contemporaries, on the other hand, were teaching that, even though a bodhisattva merits life in heaven, he or she vows not to enter into bliss as long as there is one creature left in hell. Even to consider enjoying heaven while others are in torment, however well deserved, seems to such observers a defective understanding of ultimate wisdom and love. Should we allow our triumphal theories to override such dissonant facts?

Our traditional conceptions of heaven and hell have owed too much to tribal conceptions of retributive justice and too little to what Tillich called creative justice.[23] Augustine's sense of order in times of chaos meant that for him it was good news that, at least in the afterlife, evil does not go unpunished. The shift of emphasis from Augustine to Temple involves a shift of focus from heavenly order to earthly ministry. Temple remarked that Christianity is the most materialistic of religions. He made the sacramental principle his key and social justice his passion.[24] Taking this shift further, we now value freedom over order, to the point where we cherish the right to be different more than conformity to a party line. This freedom is accorded to other religions and secular philosophies, not just to Christians.

If God makes every individual and every group of individuals different, then theology should teach us to celebrate such differences. On the personal level, we celebrate this fact at baptism when we name our children. Typically, we affirm our ancestors by recycling their names. But in order to live together we do have to give our children their own

21. See, e.g., Donald S. Lopez, Jr., and Steven C. Rockefeller, eds., *The Christ and the Bodhisattva* (Stony Brook: State University Press of New York, 1987).

22. On Augustine see John Burnaby, *Amor Dei* (London: Hodder & Stoughton, 1947) (a reply to Anders Nygren).

23. See Paul Tillich, *Love, Power, and Justice* (New York: Oxford University Press, 1954).

24. See William Temple, "The Sacramental Universe," lecture 19 in *Nature, Man, and God* (London: MacMillan, 1953), p. 478.

distinctive names. In this connection, what is important about other religions is that they are *not* Christian and therefore may have something new to teach us about the good news and about life before and after death.

However, whereas modern Christians have found in our common baptism a basis for interdenominational dialogue, we have yet to find a comparable basis for interfaith relations. Karl Rahner built on a Catholic conception of "the baptism of desire" to describe others as "anonymous" Christians. But such "verbal baptism" moves the relevant network of intentions so far below the level of conscious Christian self-identification that most commentators are unwilling to follow him.[25] To the extent that much that shapes us *is* below the level of consciousness, he was right. The insider-outsider and other forms of dialectical interplay are part of history, whether or not we choose to engage in dialogue. But it may not foster meaningful dialogue to give the category of "Christian" such universal application.

Reflections on the missionary and evangelical movements of the past two centuries are bringing at least some to conclude that God does not want all Hindus or Buddhists to become Christians (or vice versa).[26] Further, historians and sociologists are finding that hard-sell mass evangelism only works with a minority in any population and that the day of imperial takeovers and dollar evangelism appears to be waning.[27] Circumstances have inspired some ecclesial cousins to merge. But as long as we can afford them, denominations seem here to stay, and so do other religions. So the questions are: how do we discern God's will in this situation and witness to the truth that is in us?

With hindsight we can identify Augustine and Temple among our acknowledged ancestors. But how do we discern authenticity in the middle of change? Against too much tradition, Luther cried *"sola scriptura."* But four centuries of reflection on this maxim have forced all but the most fideistic to acknowledge the plurality in the witness of Scripture.

25. For an Anglican on Rahner see Maurice Wiles, *Christian Theology and Inter-religious Dialogue* (London: SCM, 1992), chaps. 3-4.

26. So, e.g., Wilfred Cantwell Smith in *Towards a World Theology* (Philadelphia: Westminster, 1981). For a survey of the history see David J. Bosch, *Transforming Mission: Paradigm Shifts in Theology of Mission* (Maryknoll, N.Y.: Orbis, 1992).

27. An Episcopalian statement on evangelism is given in Howard Hanchey, *Church Growth and the Power of Evangelism* (Cambridge, Mass.: Cowley, 1990). On the relevant history see the works of George Marsden and William G. McLoughlin.

We have to discern what Sandra Schneiders calls the world "before" the text (the one we bring to it), as well as the worlds behind and of the text.[28] As David Kelsey has demonstrated, Scripture alone is not enough for Lutherans, Barthians, or anyone else. He also shows that each denominational community tacitly or explicitly works from within its own developing paradigm, drawn simultaneously from traditional, philosophical, and experiential sources.[29] Actual theological argument is not a matter of quoting canonical axioms and *then* drawing deductively on reason and experience. It requires spiraling out of the hermeneutic circle compounded from all sources to allow disclosure of what the Spirit is saying concretely to us through the transforming movements of the day. To this end, dialogue is an inescapable part of the process.

Once we admit that our present sense of what religion is about and that a tacit or explicit philosophy is an element in any theological thinking, then the door is open to admitting that these elements of our thought and experience may in principle be Hindu or Buddhist in origin, not just Hebrew or Greek. Whether we consider them orthodox or not, there are in our time Christian Buddhists and Hindu Christians, just as there have been Christian Platonists and Christian existentialists in the past.[30] An orthodox response is not achieved by denouncing alien imports but by baptizing all the elements in our operative paradigm. With respect to Platonism, Augustine did this better than most, as Aquinas did with Aristotelianism, which is why they serve as *the* prototypes for Western theology. I would say the same of Barth, Tillich, and Rahner with respect to existentialism.

As Maurice Wiles points out, the Neoplatonism imbibed by the church fathers was not religiously neutral.[31] Creative appropriators such as Augustine were converted in part by their change in philosophy. They in turn changed that philosophy into a Christian exercise. Examining our secondary prototypes with this in mind, we recognize today

28. See Sandra M. Schneiders, *The Revelatory Text: Interpreting the New Testament as Sacred Scripture* (San Francisco: Harper, 1991).

29. See David H. Kelsey, *The Uses of Scripture in Recent Theology* (Philadelphia: Fortress, 1975).

30. On being a Buddhist Christian or Christian Buddhist, see Roger Corless and Paul F. Knitter, eds., *Buddhist Emptiness and Christian Trinity* (Mahwah, N.J.: Paulist, 1990).

31. Wiles, p. 16, and Nock, chap. 14.

that the churches have almost always lived in pluralistic situations and that, in those situations, their best thinkers have been syncretistic. Such syncretism is decried by essentialists looking for only one correct and invariable form of a doctrine. If instead we adopt the conception of prototypes rather than archetypes and the Wittgensteinian metaphor of family resemblances, we shall not look for rote repetition of past formulae but for continuity in the Spirit.

Taking the root sense of syncretism as growing together, we can say not only that the churches have always been syncretistic but that they ought to be so. *One test of authenticity is the inclusiveness or univer-sality of our vision of God's kingdom.* The question is not whether but how we appropriate alien customs and ideas, affirming our identity as Chris-tians in the process. Notice here that the metaphor of baptism comes into play now, not with respect to individuals belonging to institutions but with respect to myths and rituals. In this connection, we must note that there is no such thing as cultureless Christianity. The question concerning Christianity and Christendom is whether all the elements in them were fully "baptized." Thus, for example, Anglicans affirm the broad sacramental principle undergirding the adoption of Christmas trees and wedding rings, while guarding against the commercialization of the festivities.

III

There is nevertheless an unresolved tension in all talk of Christ, culture, and other religions, due to *the second test of authenticity: the affirmation of the uniqueness of each individual,* group, and movement in the eyes of God. Those who stress "inculturation" as the key to finding the uni-versality of Christ stress a Catholic sense of "the" church as the exten-sion of the incarnation. Protestants talk more of "contextualization" and individual commitment, focusing on the distinctive patterns of life, death, and resurrection in the Gospels.[32] Certainly the image of baptism presupposes the latter, while the vision of eschatological Eucharist

32. Note the issues reported in Max L. Stackhouse, *Apologia: Contextualization, Globalization, and Mission in Theological Education* (Grand Rapids: Wm. B. Eerdmans Publishing Co., 1988).

builds on the former.[33] By tradition, baptism is the prerequisite to receiving the Sacrament. But in the tradition, we also have the story of Peter and Cornelius (Acts 10), suggesting once again that the Spirit moves in extraordinary ways in directions that apostolic successors have not anticipated. What is the vision of mission in relation to other religions that this surprise element entails?

The point in Catholicism is not just to have a pope in Rome but thereby to foster a worldwide communion of saints. The point in Protestantism is to recognize institutional, not just individual, sin. The point about localizing theology is to recognize our uniqueness in our specific situations while acknowledging that these are all in need of healing transformation. Part of the Anglican experience emerging out of the shadow of the British hegemony is that we can celebrate relations with others in their otherness, without denying our history or minimizing our differences. The gospel is not a call to self-forgetful globalism. But neither is it the sanctification of tribalism. This reminder applies as much to prayer book tribalism as to papal or southern white Protestant tribalism. We are all called to affirm our identities as people of color. (The Japanese described the first European missionaries as pink people.) We are to continue to speak our own languages — not just Hebrew, Latin, Sanskrit, or Arabic.[34] But what comes out of our mouths is to be good news for all. Our difference from others does not make us superior to them.

As Anglicans shedding the vestiges of our colonial past and celebrating diversity within the commonwealth of nations, our ideal of the church is of a communion of communions. This fellowship is predicated on the healing presence of the triune God wherever two or three are gathered "in his name." Ideologically and practically we prefer the historic episcopate to the idea that every person is his or her own pope. The theological basis for this suggested by Williams and Panikkar is in a revised sense of the creative and redemptive work of the Spirit, the definitive revelation of which for us is still the renewing Israel movement inaugurated by Jesus. But we are more aware than ever that there are other sheep in other folds.

---

33. For an Anglican overview see William R. Crockett, *Eucharist: Symbol of Transformation* (New York: Pueblo, 1989).

34. On this subject see Lamin Sanneh, *Translating the Message: The Missionary Impact on Culture* (Maryknoll, N.Y.: Orbis, 1989).

From our perspective, continuing the Jesus movement is the ordinary way "home." But *this does not preclude others having saving knowledge engendering ways which to us seem extraordinary. A "christomorphic" — as contrasted with a "christocentric" — sense of mission invites us to celebrate deeds done in a Christlike spirit, wherever and whenever we encounter them.*[35] We do not use our traditions to build a fence around but to provide guidelines for discerning the disclosure of enlivening truth.

The contrast between ordinary and extraordinary ways of salvation seems a more fruitful model for Christian relationships with other religions than that between consciously professing and unconsciously reflecting followers of what is asserted to be at bottom the same faith with the same ends in view.[36] The same Spirit and the same Logos need not translate into the same letters or "logoi" of faith.[37] But taking history seriously means looking into how others embody living truth.

In the Hebraic tradition, we do not deal in disembodied spirits. We know what "spirit" is by contrasting a living body with a corpse. So we ask: what defines the life of living bodies and living institutions, such as the denominations? To answer, Temple for one drew on theories of evolution and talked of levels of being: To those with personalities needing healing, good news can only come by making a breakthrough in spirituality. As feminists remind us, being embodied means being vulnerable and being connected. In traditional language, our connection to God's only begotten Son is by adoption. Among other things, what this means is that our identity is no longer *just* that of our ancestors.

Tension comes when too much talk of the universality of Christ cuts all ties with the historical Jesus.[38] The sticking point is not uniqueness — in a trivial sense, everyone is unique — but once-for-allness. If we use

35. See Christopher Morse, *Not Every Spirit: A Dogmatics of Christian Disbelief* (Valley Forge, Pa.: Trinity Press International, 1994), p. 105, on whether Christian faith is theocentric or christocentric: "Such faith may more aptly be described as christomorphic."

36. On this see Heinz Robert Schlette, *Towards a Theology of Religions* (Freiburg: Herder, 1966), and Monika Hellwig in D'Costa. On the differences see Joseph A. Dinoia, O.P., *The Diversity of Religions: A Christian Perspective* (Washington, D.C.: Catholic University Press of America, 1992).

37. See Stanley J. Samartha, "The Holy Spirit and People of Other Faiths," *Ecumenical Review* 42, nos. 3-4 (July-October 1990): 250-63.

38. For a brief survey see Lucien Richard, O.M.I., *What Are They Saying about Christ and World Religions?* (Mahwah, N.J.: Paulist, 1981).

event language, the question is whether or not something decisive in history occurred that is inextricably linked to the Jesus movement. As one of my students used to ask: why Jesus and not George Washington? Theologically, the question is one of election and mission. The answer is the "scandal of particularity": it just happens that, in the Mediterranean world, the war against evil magic was most enduringly waged by the Israelites and what universalized that mission most enduringly was the Jesus movement. If someone thinks otherwise, we should invite him or her to offer us a more salvific vision and then compare notes.

Now the question becomes: must the process of salvation be tied to history? For most Christians, the answer was worked out in the dialogue and dialectic called Gnosticism. Buddhists, by contrast, chose an answer emphasizing psychology — the psychology of meditation. Unlike the Trikaya doctrine in Buddhism, which discerns ultimate reality not in the historical figure of Gautama but through the Dharma or Teaching of Enlightenment, the doctrine of the Trinity in Christianity holds us to the paradox of knowing everlasting love in the transformed flesh of historical individuals bound together in spirit.

While we cannot escape from employing some philosophy in our theology, the freedom of the Spirit means that we are not tied to any one philosophical school. In analyzing the movement for which Jesus and the women and men around him are the prototypes, we are no more tied to event language than to two-natures language. But we do still have to find some particular language in our specific cultures to name how the Spirit draws us into healing relationships. And we do have to show how our language is congruent with that of our predecessors in the faith.

In the present context, it is noteworthy that the new Anglican prayer books shift the focus of the eucharistic prayer from echoes of debates over transubstantiation to invocation of the Spirit on those gathered around the table and commissioned to bear witness in the world, once again linking mass to mission. In this lies our key to what it means to be Christlike.

At the heart of the sacramental principle is the accent on life in spite of death in the sacrificial cultus.[39] On this view, what is central to the story is not the judicial murder of Jesus but the quality of life offered

39. For the emphasis on spirit/life see F. C. N. Hicks, *The Fullness of Sacrifice* (London: Macmillan, 1930).

to the community after his death.[40] This is seen to be continuous with the spirit in which he conducted his mission, despite the threat and experience of martyrdom. It is Jesus' sacrifice in the sense of life-offering, then that of his disciples after the resurrection, received and blessed by God and then returned to the ongoing community, which is the basis of full communion, celebrated both in baptism and the Eucharist. In this connection, what Peter learned from the Cornelius episode was not to call unclean any life offered in this Spirit, however alien the offering seems at first sight.

It follows that our question of people from other religious traditions is not "Are they crypto-Christians?" but, when they are at their best, "Are they Christlike?" The honest answer is, "Sometimes, and sometimes more than professing Christians." Then the question is not about other religionists but about other religions as ways of life, that is, whether more or less independently they enable their adherents to celebrate what we call the saving presence of God in Christ. We should no more want to love Hindus in spite of their Hindu background than we want them to love us in spite of our Christian background.

Whether non-Christians find these ways of putting things congenial is beside the point. (The question and its explication could be a fruitful topic for dialogue.) For Christians what identifies saving power and presence is what is known from the paradigmatic narrative of Jesus and his disciples. When describing this in any detail, we have initially no other vocabulary or experience on which to draw.[41] The paradigm for us *is* one of dying and rising in Christ. But the key is not the literal dying: it is the quality of life offered in one historic existence and shared with others.[42] This is the measure by which we assess the churches' claims to be the body of the risen Christ. On the road to Emmaus we do not ask first whether the stranger who fires our imagination is wearing the "Jesus" label. But after he has broken bread with us, we do look back and see the connections.

40. Note Edward Schillebeeckx, *Christ: The Experience of Jesus as Lord,* trans. John Bowden, vol. 2 (New York: Seabury, 1980), chap. 1, "God Does Not Want Mankind to Suffer."

41. On this topic note George Lindbeck, *The Nature of Doctrine: Religion and Theology in a Post-Liberal Age* (Philadelphia: Westminster, 1984), chap. 2.

42. For some amplification see Peter Slater, "The Kerygma and the Cuckoo's Nest," *Scottish Journal of Theology* 31 (1979): 301-18.

The challenge for Christians today is to say what being Christlike means for the world without sounding self-serving or afraid of the truth. Most of us have come to where we are from knowing people who were Christlike to us. Others may not know their names. But having known them by name we are able to pass on something of their vision for us and our neighbors. For example, in my family the paradigm of true piety was my mother, a medical missionary in Burma before World War II. For her it was her uncle, an Anglo-Catholic priest in a slum parish at the turn of the century, and so on through the centuries to the real lives of Jesus and Mary. The difference between philosophy and religion is that the former deals in types while the latter deals in cases. Concrete faith grows out of a network of historic relationships in which the names of most of the links have been lost. What is not lost is the name that brings us all together.

When we talk of quality of life we include individual flourishing and enrichment in community. Bearing witness to this is what Temple meant in calling us materialists. Our history only becomes demonic when we absolutize particulars. The sacramental principle is not about how we use but about how God uses particulars to draw all into an absolutely universal vision affirming the value of each. The difference between the divine and the demonic is that the former maintains the finite-infinite relationship of true communion, where the latter mistakes the finite for the infinite and so loses contact with the Spirit that unites us.

For most Anglicans, the context in which faith is acted out paradigmatically is the celebration of Holy Communion. Kelsey's contention is that theology depends upon such Communion to maintain its vitality.[43] The ecumenical movement arose out of awareness that we seldom live up to the ideal that this suggests. The Anglican Communion is testimony to the fact that we can still retain a sense of family and family resemblances, even though we are all adoptees who only imperfectly recollect our prototype. By now in such an extended family the similarities are sometimes hard to see. One benefit from learning about other religions is that this helps us to discern through the contrasts what it means to be Christian and become Christlike.

43. See David H. Kelsey, *To Understand God Truly: What's Theological about a Theological School* (Louisville: Westminster/John Knox, 1992), chap. 7.

Today, on every continent, we have to face the fact that, if people are formally religious at all, they are plurally so. Our mission is to those without any religion on our own doorsteps, not to denigrate those from other cultures whose religious traditions are different. If they have knowledge of the One we call God, this too must be saving knowledge — God offers nothing less. For that we should rejoice and learn from them how their religion transforms their culture, not act like the disgruntled older brother spoiling the party. For us being Christlike means both knowing how to name the saving experience and knowing that we do not have the last word on what salvation means for each and all. The last word, like the first, is with the Spirit.

CHAPTER TEN

Discovering Christian Resources for a Theology of Interfaith Relations from the African Methodist Episcopal Zion Church

MOZELLA G. MITCHELL

T HE AME Zion Church is a black church. It belongs to the black church tradition in America, and it cannot be separated entirely from that tradition, not even in discussion of its present realities. Before dealing with live resources in the AMEZ Church that provide orientation in the area of interfaith relations and dialogue, it is necessary to look at the self-understanding and existence of this communion as a church within the African American, American, and world traditions of Christianity. It seems common knowledge in American religious circles that the black church is unique in its origin and development and role not only in the general African American community but also in American society. It is a complex and multifaceted phenomenon that has been successfully analyzed, criticized, and interpreted by expert sociologist E. Franklin Frazier,[1] anthropologist Melville Herskovitz,[2] sociologist of religion C. Eric Lincoln;[3] historians such as Carter G. Woodson[4] and

---

1. E. Franklin Frazier, *The Negro Church in America* (New York: Schocken Books, 1964).

2. Melville Herskovitz, *The Myth of the Negro Past* (Boston: Beacon, 1969).

3. C. Eric Lincoln, with Lawrence H. Mamiya, *The Black Church in the African American Experience* (Durham, N.C.: Duke University Press, 1990).

4. Carter G. Woodson, *The History of the Negro Church* (Washington, D.C.: Association for the Study of Negro Life and History, 1919).

Hart M. Nelsen and Anne K. Nelsen;[5] and theologians such as James Cone,[6] Benjamin Mays,[7] and James H. Evans, Jr.[8] Both the uniqueness and complexity of the African American church stem from its successful blending of seemingly contradictory or incompatible elements and/or components, such as the spiritual with the social, political, cultural, and economic; the individualistic and the communal; the sacred and the secular; the African and the Euro-American; the liberal and the conservative.

In a short article, "Christian Unity from a Black Perspective," published in 1988, Lawrence N. Jones, then dean of the School of Divinity at Howard University, summed up significant aspects of the uniqueness of the African American church vis-à-vis the rest of organized Christianity. Jones opens his article with the following statement:

> Even a cursory review of the efforts made to give institutional structure to Christian unity in America reveals the conspicuous absence of Black involvement. To be sure individual blacks have played a major role in movements towards Christian unity from the earliest time, but the organized Black churches have not. Black denominations have not *refused* to join ecumenical bodies, they have tended, rather, to ignore invitations to membership or have endorsed participation but never accepted fully the obligations and responsibilities of membership.[9]

As Jones proceeds to account for what he sees as the "apparent indifference of Blacks toward movements for Christian unity," he not only gives us a snapshot view of the character and nature of the black church, but he also presents us with some challenging, living realities we will have to grapple with in considering the possibilities and potentialities of a

---

5. Hart M. Nelsen and Anne K. Nelsen, *Black Church in the Sixties* (Lexington: University of Kentucky Press, 1975).

6. James Cone, *Speaking the Truth: Ecumenism, Liberation, and Black Theology* (Grand Rapids: William B. Eerdmans Publishing Co., 1986).

7. Benjamin Mays, with Joseph Nicholson, *The Negro's Church* (New York: Russel and Russell, 1969, reissue).

8. James H. Evans, Jr., *We Have Been Believers: An African-American Systematic Theology* (Minneapolis: Fortress Press, 1992).

9. Lawrence N. Jones, "Christian Unity from a Black Perspective," *AME Zion Quarterly Review* 97, no. 4 (January 1988): 18.

black church such as the AME Zion Church for conversations or dialogue with Christians of other communions in the vast multicultural complex of the Christian faith.

One of the reasons Jones gives for the apparent indifference is that of the primary focus of the African American churches in general contrasted with what has been the primary focus of movements toward Christian unity. Freedom and justice have always been the vital and central concern of African American Christianity, Jones states, while Christian unity movements have been focused mainly on doctrinal, creedal, organizational, and theological precision. "Employment, education, political participation, civil and legal rights and other factors" affecting the quality of life of communities and contributing to the "abundant life of all persons in this world" — these Jones rightfully discerns as being primary in African American religion. On the other hand, movements toward Christian unity, such as the National Council of Churches of Christ (NCCC) and the World Council of Churches (WCC), have "traditionally focused upon creedal and doctrinal issues (Faith), structure and authority (Order), witness and mission (Life and Work)." This latter area, life and work, has been relevant to the vital concerns of the black church, while the first two (faith and order) have been the chief concentration of the majority Christian community.[10]

Jones's second reason for black Christian indifference toward movements for Christian unity is the "lukewarmness" of these movements "towards the oppression and deprivation of Black people." Blacks perceive these movements as mirroring invariably the discriminatory practices of the larger society, and therefore, as being a part of the problem black people face rather than part of its solution. The evidence of this is seen, of course, in the continuing segregation of the religious community along racial lines — "in the existence of racially exclusive congregations and denominations, in the existence of racially distinctive councils and conventions, in the existence of [ethnically] defined theologies, in the special departments of 'minority affairs,' in majority group denominations and in the existence of 'black caucuses' in a number of historically white denominations." All such structures, Jones says, "point to the festering racism that has resisted eradication among Christians of diverse ethnic origin." And he denies the claim

10. Jones, p. 18.

that cultural differences account for the separations by asserting the fact that the early builders of the church, such as Paul, addressed the matters of cultural differences more seriously than today's leaders.[11]

Jones closes his short article by lifting up contemporary efforts to come to grips with the problems of cultural diversity on the part of black theology and the various Third World theologies (African, Asian, Latin American). These theologies have seriously challenged the church's historical assumption that "the theologies generated in the Euro-American Caucasian communities are the only authentic theologies," he says. Jones draws the conclusion that "The unity of the Christian community will not be achieved unless and until a serious dialogue is entered into with a view towards arriving at a theology that adequately takes into account the theological understandings of all its constituents irrespective of race or ethnic origin." And finally, in regard to the black community and church, he says, "There is no disposition to settle for the appearance of community which is not supported by the active involvement of the whole church in combatting racism, and in the effort to secure equality of access for all to the rights which are available to members of the majority community."[12]

Lawrence Jones has framed the context within which we must view the AME Zion Church and its possibilities and potentialities for carrying on conversations with other Christian communions. For he speaks from the standpoint of historical fact regarding the nature and attitudes of the African American church community. And his position is corroborated again and again by historians, theologians, and other scholars of the church. For instance, C. Eric Lincoln sums up the views of many in assessing the current situation in his recent publication *The Black Church in the African American Experience.* "The hopes among some black and white Christians that the Black church will eventually merge itself into mainline white Christianity seem increasingly unrealistic as these racial communions seem more and more resigned to the realities of religious separation in a society where secular separation remains the ideological norm."[13]

11. Jones, pp. 18-19.
12. Jones, p. 19.
13. Lincoln, p. 394. See also part 2, "Black Churches, Ecumenism, and the Liberation Struggle," in Cone, pp. 81-110; "Humanity, Sin, and Forgiveness," in Deotis Roberts, *Liberation and Reconciliation: A Black Theology,* rev. ed. (Maryknoll,

A brief look at the origin and development of the African Methodist Episcopal Zion Church reflects its grounding in this black church tradition. It is fairly common knowledge that all of the predominantly black Methodist churches came into being through separation of African American members from the Methodist Episcopal Church because of racial prejudices and discrimination within the mother church. The African Methodist Episcopal Church (AME), the African Methodist Episcopal Zion Church (AMEZ), and the Christian Methodist Episcopal Church (CME), the three major black Methodist churches,[14] were organized in the nineteenth century for similar reasons.[15] All came into being as a protest against dehumanizing and

---

N.Y.: Orbis Books, 1994), pp. 51-67; and "On Being Black" and "The Community of Faith and the Spirit of Freedom," in Evans, pp. 99-140.

14. There are four smaller black Methodist bodies: the Union American Methodist Episcopal Church (UAME) with approximately 28,000 members; the Reformed Methodist Union Episcopal Church with about 16,000; the Reformed Zion Union Apostolic Church, claiming 16,000; and the Independent Methodist Episcopal Church, with about 8,000 members; Lincoln, pp. 48-49. The largest black Methodist church is the AME Church, numbering about 2.2 million members; next in size is the AMEZ Church with about 1.2 million; the CME church has about 900,000; Lincoln, pp. 54, 58, and 63.

15. "The initial impetus for black spiritual and ecclesiastical independence was not grounded in religious doctrine or polity, but in the offensiveness of racial segregation in the churches and the alarming inconsistencies between the teachings and the expressions of the faith. It was readily apparent that the white church had become a principal instrument of political and social policies undergirding slavery and the attendant degradation of the human spirit. Against this the black Christians quietly rebelled, and the Black church emerged as the symbol and the substance of their rebellion" (Lincoln, p. 47).

Specifically, the three major black Methodist bodies came about as a bold step for freedom in the face of religious and racial oppression. The AME Church resulted from a movement of black members of Saint George's Methodist Episcopal Church in Philadelphia (Richard Allen, Absalom Jones, and others), who were pulled from their knees during worship in a gallery they did not know was closed to black Christians. This was in 1787. At this time they along with other black members withdrew from the church and began the process which led to the establishment of the AME Church in 1816. The AME Zion Church was the result of a similar withdrawal of black members from the John Street Methodist Episcopal Church in New York City in 1794. Peter Williams, William Miller, Francis Jacobs, and others led a group out of the church because of discriminatory practices against the 40 percent black membership. And by 1821 the AME Zion Church was founded. The AME Church resulted after the Civil War when black members of the Methodist Episcopal Church, South, became less and less tolerant of their segregated and subservient

161

demeaning practices against African Americans in either the predominantly white Methodist Episcopal Church or the Methodist Episcopal Church, South.

Although black people were involved in the establishment of the Methodist Episcopal Church in America from the beginning,[16] they were not accorded the dignity and respect as equal participants in the Christian fellowship. Bishop John J. Moore (1804-93), of the AME Zion Church, described the conditions and treatment against which black communicants rebelled in withdrawing from the John Street ME Church in New York City in 1896 and began steps in the formation of the AME Zion Church.

> As the church grew popular and influential, the prejudice of caste began to engender Negro proscription, and as the number of colored members increased, the race friction and proscription increased which finally overcame the tolerance of the colored members of the M.E. Society. Again the M.E. Church in New York, licensed a number of colored men to preach, but prohibited them from preaching even to their own brethren, except occasionally, and never among the Whites. The colored preachers, being thus deprived of the opportunity of improving their gifts and graces, as they stood connected with the white M.E. Society, and prohibited from joining the annual M.E. Conference, as itinerant preachers, with their white brethren; thus restricted in their church relations, they were prompted to seek the privilege of holding meetings among themselves.[17]

---

status in the church. At the urging of both black and white members who recognized the need for separation, the ME Church, South's General Conference in 1866 made separation possible. And in 1870 in Jackson, Tennessee, the Colored Methodist Episcopal Church was established. (The name was changed to Christian Methodist Episcopal in 1954.) Lincoln, pp. 50-62.

16. "In 1766, when Irish Philip Enbury, who had been licensed by John Wesley, held the first Methodist meeting on American soil in his home in Augustus Street (then Barrack Street), exhorting to an audience of five, one black person was present. She was Betty, the slave of Barbara Heck, who had requested the meeting of her fellow countrymen out of necessity to save their people from 'hell'. . . . As they grew, their slaves and other blacks were privileged to join the movement"; William J. Walls, *The African Methodist Episcopal Zion Church: Reality of the Black Church* (Charlotte, N.C.: AME Zion Publishing House, 1974), p. 39.

17. John J. Moore, *History of the AME Zion Church in America* (York, Pa.: Teachers Journal Office, 1884), pp. 15-16, quoted in Walls, pp. 43-44.

Such stories have been repeated in innumerable cases and detail the non-Christian treatment of black people in Euro-American Christian settings that occasioned their separation and the formation of their own institutions in freedom and self-sufficiency. James H. Cone laments, "It is unfortunate that the black separatists did not write creeds or doctrines to define theologically the difference between black faith and the white churches from which they separated." Thus, he believes that their "failure to reflect intellectually on the meaning of their faith has led many black Christians to assume that there was no theological difference between white and black views of the gospel, as if what one does has nothing to do with the definition of faith itself."[18]

It is true that there has been, regrettably, in so many ways, little effort to put forth systematically an ecclesiology of the black church. Much has been written about the sociology and history of the black church, as we see in E. Franklin Frazier and C. Eric Lincoln, Benjamin Mays, and Carter G. Woodson. Numerous works have been done on black preaching and its distinctiveness, on the music of the black church, on the uniqueness of black worship, but in the AME Zion Church and other black Methodist, and Baptist, traditions, not much has been written on black church ecclesiology. James H. Evans, Jr., in his recent attempt at putting together an African American systematic theology, notes certain factors that impede such an ecclesiological task, such as heterogeneity or diversity in the various Baptist and Methodist, Pentecostal, and other black congregations, including those which are a part of predominantly white denominations. He sees that the "unique context and the array of traditions, customs, and styles within African-American Christianity make the formulation of a black ecclesiology difficult."[19]

Another impediment to the formation of an ecclesiology, he says, is that the "notion of community is so basic to African-American religious experience that the normal doctrinal explanations for church formation are not sufficient." The fact that the black church was not born of doctrinal disputes and heresy, as is typical in the history of church development in the Western world, but emerged out of "deep-seated cultural tendencies toward solidarity and association among

18. Cone, p. 91.
19. Evans, pp. 119-20.

African-American Christians" causes it another difficulty in formulating an ecclesiological statement.[20]

Nevertheless, Evans does arrive at some theological frameworks for understanding the nature of the black church which I believe are quite applicable to the AME Zion Church's self-understanding, as well as that of other black churches. He asserts:

> Although the creative and expressive traditions of African-American Christianity have provided numerous ways of speaking of the church, there appear to be three primary modalities around which most of the early ecclesiological discourse was centered. These are "the company of the elect," "the family of God," and "the nation of God."[21]

We can see the application of each of these characterizations to the AME Zion Church (as well as to other black churches or denominations) in its development and present construction.

Though very much aware of its origin and heritage, the AME Zion people saw themselves as a part of God's elect and chosen people who were called to a special mission in this country and in the world. This mission was to create a truly free and godly people. The second modality, "family of God," Evans says, has an emphasis on "internal survival, psychological affinity between the members, and the nurturing of the community."[22] This, too, is certainly descriptive of the AME Zion Church. The history of any local AME Zion Church would no doubt reveal a group of families coming together to form an organization, secure property and build a place of worship, etc. From that point onward the life and vitality of the church consist in the group's regard for themselves as one extended family under the parenthood of God. Andrew L. Foster, Jr., makes the point regarding slave and free blacks in the nineteenth century: "The Black church served as a family to the slave and as an extended family to the free black. Blacks were no longer stranded individuals in the midst of a prejudiced society. They were a part of a family, a community, a society within the society, that was found wherever Black people lived."[23]

---

20. Evans, pp. 119-20.
21. Evans, p. 128.
22. Evans, p. 130.
23. Andrew L. Foster, Jr., *The Saying and the Doing: Zion Methodism at the Lord's Table* (Columbus, Ga.: Brentwood Christian Press, 1990), p. 132.

Certainly, the third modality, "nation of God," is found to be characteristic of the AME Zion Church experience. Evans says this nationalism "refers to the bond that is created among a people based on a common history, common values, and common political aims."[24] Among African Americans it consisted, he says, in our attempts as enslaved Africans to survive and overcome bondage. The AME Zion Church has always recognized their link with other African peoples and their mission to seek and fight for the freedom of all African Americans, as well as other African peoples. In choosing their name, it was explained, the "Methodist Episcopal" was to exhibit the retention of the doctrine and form of government under which the denomination originated. "African was prefixed to the rest of the title of this church because it was to be controlled, by descendants of Africa, in the interest of humanity, regardless of race, color, sex or condition."[25] In light of this conception of itself, the AME Zion Church became known as the "Freedom Church"[26] because of its central role in the nineteenth-century abolition movement known as the Underground Railroad and maintains this characterization even to this day.

> Long known as "The Freedom Church," A.M.E. Zion claims such abolitionist luminaries as Sojourner Truth, Harriet Tubman, Rev. Jermain Loguen, Catherine Harris, Rev. Thomas James, and Frederick Douglass who was licensed as a local A.M.E. Zion preacher. Like the A.M.E.'s many members, pastors and church officials were abolitionists and were intensely involved with the Underground Railroad. That commitment to social justice has persisted to the present time. The A.M.E. Zion Church was the first among all the Methodist denominations, including the Methodist Episcopal Church, to extend the vote and clerical ordination to women.[27]

At this point we should take a closer look at the AME Zion Church and assess its potential and possibilities for dialogue or conversations with the rest of Christianity. First of all, let me say that from my estimation the AME Zion Church has excellent potential for dialogue and

---

24. Evans, p. 131.
25. C. R. Harris, *Zion's Historical Catechism*, p. 8, quoted in Walls, p. 50.
26. Walls, p. 45; Cone, p. 92; Foster, p. 27.
27. Lincoln, p. 58.

conversations with other denominations. It has a strong foundation, history, and heritage of development of two hundred years (it observed its bicentennial in 1996). It is well established in the Methodist Episcopal tradition. Like other black Methodist churches, when the separation from the ME Church took place and the founding of the new institution was effected, the shapers of the AME Zion Church maintained the government and doctrines of the mother church. The organization and structure, polity, articles of religion, sacraments, etc., closely paralleled those of the church from which the members had withdrawn. The *Book of Discipline*, which outlines the procedures, structures, and operational bases of the denomination, is very sound and cogent. Being well situated and operationally sound, the church can operate from a position of strength as it enters into conversations with other denominations. And while the doctrines and polity as written in the *Discipline* are not highly divergent from Methodists and some other denominations, there is much freedom and diversity among the AME Zion churches in their interpretation and actual practices of the different aspects of their church, especially in liturgies, rituals, programs, and worship procedures. For instance, some large AMEZ churches in cosmopolitan settings like Detroit, Chicago, New York City, and Saint Louis are highly liturgical and ritualistic; while in more rural and small town southern and northern settings such as East St. Louis, Illinois, Tampa, Kissimmee, and Melbourne, Florida, small churches, especially, approach worship much more informally, with a style close to that even of Pentecostal or charismatic churches.

It must be noted that even though the AME Zion Church has kept intact in their *Discipline* the doctrines and practices of the mother white church, as a black church they do not operate primarily out of close observance of those teachings as they are stated. There is almost unlimited freedom of interpretation and actualization of the teachings. For instance, how they see God and Jesus Christ and the Holy Spirit and how they interact with them may vary from person to person and group to group, and comes out of their experiences as Africans in a strange land, deprived of all the visible signs of their former religions and cultures and struggling for humanhood and dignity and freedom and justice in a new world. This is primary with black people in the Zion Church, as it is for those in all black churches. What is important is how our faith, beliefs, and religious practices jibe with our lives in this world and help us find authentic meaning in our own communities and in our relations with other peoples in our pluralistic society. The church has meant and means everything to us. Jesus, God, and the Holy Spirit have been everything to us as we have encountered them first in the church and in our individual and corporate lives, but not in exactly the same sense in which these have had meaning among white Christians. Our religious music attests to this.

Yes, we have our uniqueness and our distinctiveness of which we are duly appreciative; but we realize that we are Christians in the same sense that others of different denominations are Christians. We experience repentance and forgiveness, we worship God and Jesus Christ and are imbued with the Holy Spirit, and we have a mission to fulfill in the world as ambassadors for Christ. We realize, too, that we must unite in some way with other Christians unlike ourselves and work for common goals as commanded by our Lord. At the same time we cannot lose perspective on ourselves; we cannot give up our humanity which our faith has won for us. We can and do participate in the Christian unity movements. We AME Zions were there in 1948 when the World Council of Churches (WCC) was founded, we were there in 1956 when the National Council of Churches of Christ (NCCC) was founded, we were there when the Consultation on Church Union (COCU) hammered through its processes, and we are still a part of the unity efforts. But ecumenism cannot be our primary concern until, as Lawrence Jones says, "the church recognizes [the general Christian community, that is] that it is a pluralistic community and that pluralism must be honored in its theologies, its structures, its mission foci, in its fellowship, and in its proclamation of the Gospel."[28]

The AME Zion Church has much to offer in conversations with other Christians. Long known as the "Freedom Church," it has at the core of its self-understanding and its ecclesiology what James H. Evans, Jr., describes as liberation. He states:

> Liberation is not what the church *does*; it is what the church *is*. . . . This liberation involves the liberation of the self and the liberation of the community. . . . The African-American church is based on the African notion of "self-in-community." The self has no being apart

28. Jones, p. 19.

from the community, and the community is an abstraction apart from the collection of selves. The liberation of one implies the liberation of the other.

The kerygma of the African-American church is the preaching that proclaims the past, present, and future liberation that takes place in Christ.

The church is always involved in ushering in the reign of God. It is always seeking to establish peace and justice where they do not yet exist. This impulse points to the meaning of the claim that the church is holy. There holiness has very little to do with asceticism, other worldliness, or superhuman perfection. Rather, holiness refers to the persistent discomfort of the church with the unchallenged existence of oppression and exploitation in the world.[29]

In these statements Evans has captured the essential meaning of the African American church in its general development and present existence. The meaning of the gospel, the meaning of the church, is liberation. God has liberated us. We have participated in and do participate in God's ongoing liberation of people. The Zion Church has this to offer in conversations with other Christians: its history as an ongoing participant in God's liberation process and its present actions and interests in the liberation process. As a major force in the Underground Railroad of the nineteenth century, as the first major Methodist denomination to ordain a woman clergy (Mary J. Small, 1850-1945) in 1898, and, according to Sandy D. Martin, as the "only mainline Christian body" that officially recognized women's ordination throughout the denomination as early as 1900,[30] the AME Zion Church has not abandoned its leading role in the liberation process.

Though in our local church settings we often tend to lose sight of the marvelous moment of which we are an integral part — Christ's church militant, which, under the headship of Christ and the constant empowerment of the Holy Spirit, is embarked and embattled on the work given to us as a legacy to carry on for our Savior — the AME Zion

29. Evans, pp. 135-36.
30. Sandy D. Martin, "The African Methodist Episcopal Zion Church and the Women's Ordination Controversy, 1898-1900: A Case Study on the Value of Racial Inclusivity in Religious Studies," *Journal of the ITC* 21, nos. 1 and 2 (fall 1993/spring 1994): 107.

Church generally retains the ecumenical vision of working together with other Christians to help build the kingdom of God both in our midst and beyond the confines of church walls and grounds. We are well aware that Jesus declared us, his followers, the branches connected to himself as the vine of God, the vine grower, and urged us to bear fruit (John 15:1-4). We know that he prayed that we should have unity and oneness in love, that God would protect and keep us; and that he sent us into the world, the world that hated him and hates us, in order that we might complete his work of reconciling the world unto himself (John 17:14-24; 2 Cor. 5:17-20). We take to heart Ephesians 4, which reminds us of this unity and of our duty to grow as the body of Christ and to build up that body until all of us come to the unity of the faith and of the knowledge of the Son of God, to maturity, to the measure of the full stature of Christ (Eph. 4:12-14).

The Zion Church takes this obligation to heart, and taking the cue from Jesus as he preached and demonstrated on many occasions (such as in his Sermon on the Mount in Matthew 5–7; the parable of the last judgment in Matthew 25:31-46; Luke 4:18-19; and many healings, feedings, exorcisms of demons, raisings of the dead, restorations of sight, etc.), the church on various levels — local, state, national, and international — continues to engage in numerous types of ministries, programs, services, missions, and activities in order to realize its divine mission and goals. We regret the divisions in Christianity by denominations great and small, the frictions and schisms, confrontations and resistance, economic hard times of ecumenical efforts, but over the years we have maintained the energy, courage, devotion, and commitment to persevere and push forward against all odds in doing our part to keep hope alive and achieve whatever goals we can in the great mission of Christ for the church.

Though we in Zion maintain our denominational structures and commitments, we see evidence around us that denominationalism is on the decline in the present age, especially on local levels. In the present-day crises that shake our faith, people are more acutely concerned about personal faith and values that will sustain them and their families. Realizing this and the overwhelming spiritual, social, economic, cultural, ethnic, and environmental problems facing our society, the churches and denominations are becoming more and more involved in ecumenical or joint efforts of Christian ministry, service, and development. The AME Zion Church is very much a part of these efforts and remains on the cutting edge of vital movements for social betterment, social justice, and equality.

We see much evidence of these efforts in highly visible activities that have gone on in the past year (1993-94). The AME Zion Church holds membership on the Central Committee of the World Council of Churches (WCC), which met in Johannesburg, South Africa, January 20-28, 1994. Notable among the accomplishments of the meeting was the choosing of Harare, Zimbabwe, as the site of its Eighth Assembly in 1998. The meeting of more than four hundred persons took place three months before the national elections and was the first in South Africa, after more than thirty years of the WCC's concerted campaign against apartheid which had made it a target of bitter opposition from South Africa and some churches.[31] It is notable that the Zion Church has a large annual conference in South Africa presided over by Bishop Enoch B. Rochester, and AME Zionite Dr. Naima Quarles, from New Rochelle, New York, was among the observers of the recent election in the Ecumenical Monitoring Programme (EMPSA).[32]

On the national level, the AME Zion Church takes an active part in the National Council of Churches of Christ, USA (NCCCUSA), which through its many programs, branches, and activities has been making strides. The NCCC Executive Coordinating Committee (ECC) is appreciated for reiterating its concern about violence in U.S. society and its plans, divulged at a recent meeting in Baltimore, for the NCCC's efforts against urban violence, violence in the media, and violence against women.[33]

Aside from involvement with the NCCCUSA and the WCC, the Zion Church is intricately engaged in numerous ecumenical or combined ministries and programs of service with the other three main Methodist bodies (United Methodist Church, the African Methodist Episcopal Church, and the Christian Methodist Episcopal Church. These churches organized the Commission of Pan Methodist Cooperation in 1985. Meeting in Birmingham, Alabama, March 10-12, 1994, this commission took more practical steps toward realization of its goals.

31. *Ecumenical Courier,* U.S. Office, vol. 54, no. 1 (1994): 1.
32. *Star of Zion,* April 14, 1994, pp. 1 and 7.
33. *Star of Zion,* January 27, 1994, p. 8.

One of the main proposals was to implement cooperative local ventures, to urge annual conferences to create commissions on pan-Methodist cooperation, a proposal to be presented to the respective general conferences of each Methodist body. There were also proposals urging local churches to get involved in health-care issues such as AIDS, drug and alcohol abuse, sexually transmitted diseases, and violence. United Methodist bishop Felton E. May is the chair of the commission, and AME Zion bishop Clarence E. Carr is the vice chairman.[34] The four Methodist denominations have also taken a first step toward union. In an earlier meeting in Birmingham (March 9-10, 1994), an official study commission, chaired by AME Zion bishop Richard K. Thompson and cochaired by CME bishop Richard O. Bass, heard many expressions given by bishops and laypersons concerning the possibilities of cooperation and union. They acknowledged that union may not take place in their lifetimes, but they were not averse to cooperative efforts now beginning.[35]

These efforts on the part of the three black and one white Methodist bodies are indeed laudable and do get at the social justice, economic, and social problem issues that are primary in the African American church tradition. It is hoped that they will lead to more local action and cooperation among these churches at the grassroots level. However, the three black Methodist bodies and other black churches in the Congress of National Black Churches (CNBC) — Church of God in Christ; National Baptist Convention, USA; National Missionary Baptist Convention of America; and Progressive National Baptist Convention — may be the ones most likely, through ecumenical efforts, to attack problems that are more vital to the interests and central concerns of black churches. Organized in 1978 for the purpose of collective church action, this organization has a history of getting at conditions plaguing the black community. Representing 65,000 churches and over 19 million members, the association met in New Orleans, December 7-9, 1993, and their concern was with the plight of black American families and violence in our communities. Approximately five hundred clergy and laypersons attended. Some success stories were shared, such as congregations turning crack houses into recreational centers for chil-

34. *Star of Zion*, April 7, 1994, pp. 1-2.
35. *Star of Zion*, March 31, 1994, pp. 1-3.

dren, programs established to strengthen families, and health programs promoted within the community.[36]

As its involvement with the Consultation on Church Union (COCU) has demonstrated, the AME Zion Church along with other black churches can serve as a challenge to white churches and other ethnic churches in dialogue.[37] This is one of the main functions we have always served in interaction with the Euro-American churches. James Cone points this out:

> The impact of black religious thought on American religion has been significant. During the slavery era, it challenged the white interpretation of Christianity by creating the "invisible institution"[38] and separatist churches which emphasized God's justice and love as being identical with the liberation of slaves from bondage. . . .
>
> From the time of its origin in slavery to its contemporary embodiment in the civil rights and black nationalist movements, black religious thought has challenged segregation and discrimination in the society and the churches. It has contended that God's justice and love cannot be reconciled with racism [and one might add, in more recent times, sexism, classism, handicapism, etc.].[39]

James Cone expresses what I believe the Zion Church and most churches know to be true but have not the visible resources with which to remedy the situation: "the separation of black and white churches in worship and other aspects of their life is a scandal, because each claims that Jesus Christ is Lord." He also has a sound notion of what it would take to overcome the impasse:

36. *Star of Zion*, January 13, 1994, pp. 1-2.
37. COCU came fairly close to union or communion with the nine churches involved in conversations over a twenty-five-to-thirty-year period, as its latest document, *Churches in Covenant Communion: The Church of Christ Uniting* (Research Park, N.J.: COCU, 1989), indicates. The AME Zion Church is involved with this along with eight other churches: African Methodist Episcopal Church, Christian Church (Disciples of Christ), Christian Methodist Episcopal Church, Episcopal Church, International Council of Community Churches, Presbyterian Church (USA), United Church of Christ, and United Methodist Church.
38. The "invisible institution" is a term referring to the secret gatherings of slaves in the South in bush arbors, etc., in order to worship in their own way, as they were denied the right to do so by Southern plantation laws and practices.
39. Cone, pp. 109-10.

This separation cannot be reduced to social realities unrelated to their theological identity. To worship together as a community, persons must live together in community, and to live together as one people of God, white and black Christians must believe and act as if God has given them an identity that transcends the human barriers designed to separate them.[40]

Cone has a highly valid point here, and how such a lofty ideal can be accomplished can be the fruitful topic of dialogue of the AME Zion Church and other Christian communions.

There remains to be said a word about the AME Zion Church and resources for dialogue in a religiously plural society. The question is, are there living resources here for interaction with other world religions?

In critically examining liberation theology's approach of focusing on local theology, or ideological focus, Patrick Bascio speaks of the difficulty this approach poses for Christian unity. The need for particular peoples to find their own identity before they can join in unity with others poses a problem for Christian unity initially. But it is a necessary step when these peoples have spent so many years trying to conform to the dominant culture, not realizing the richness of their own. But Bascio rightly points out that while seeking self-identity and dealing with particular problems, the need for unity with the larger Christian community is never far from the minds of those who are doing theology in particular racial or cultural groups or communities.[41]

This is the case with the AME Zion Church as a part of the black church in America. But it is also true of this church, as with other African American churches, that we have a basic propensity for openness to peoples of other ethnic groups, races, and world religions. We have some specific well-known examples historically of such persons as Howard Thurman (and certain of his followers such as Luther E. Smith, George Thomas, and numerous others), Martin Luther King, Jr., and his followers (the World House concept King strongly promoted), and even Malcolm X. Nikki Giovanni expresses this propensity for African Americans' involvement in dialogue with and even identity with other

40. Cone, pp. 81-82.
41. Patrick Bascio, *The Failure of White Theology* (New York: Peter Lang, 1994), p. 35.

nationalities and religions. In a rather radical way, in dialogue with the Russian poet Zhenya and in other contexts, Giovanni declares that because of the particular way in which generally we were brought (rather than came) to this country, along with our experience here, we are not Americans as such (but rather a nation within a nation). Because of this, in contrast to the "twoness" expressed by W. E. B. Du Bois, we have no attachment to the land (America) as such, and therefore we can go anywhere in the world and feel at home, once we learn the language (she uses such famous persons as Baldwin, Du Bois, Chester Himes, and Richard Wright, who became sort of expatriots).[42]

While I may not agree with it entirely, Giovanni has touched upon a partial truth that has significance for religious pluralism. For instance, while black people may be in the various Baptist, Methodist, Lutheran, Presbyterian connections, we are not bound theologically, doctrinally, and creedally by any of these Western-based manifestations of Christianity. Instead, our churches are African-based in religious thinking and practices, which is already pluralistic. Howard Thurman, for instance, as a black boy growing up in Daytona, Florida, in a *Baptist church* which was segregated in an apartheid-like situation, entirely unrelated to mainline Baptist churches, found his identity and integrity as a person with the natural surroundings: the *oak tree, storms,* the *sea,* the *stars,* the *fauna* and *flora* — he often saw himself *as one* with all of these of God's creation. All of this, which is African in origin, served to inform his later spirituality, which embraces all religions and led to his cofounding what is thought to be the first interracial, interreligious church in America, the Church for the Fellowship of All Peoples in San Francisco, in 1944 (which still exists). But Thurman, like other black religious thinkers, was well anchored in his own black American religious tradition so that he could enter into dialogue with all these different religious traditions and yet return to his own. We are not bound by the Western conception of the Trinity. There is diversity with the Spirit in African American Christianity. There is diversity in Jesus images and functions among African American Christians that have an African origin and orientation. But all are *one* in God, who in African American religion is the father/mother of all peoples everywhere.

42. Virginia C. Fowler, ed., *Conversations with Nikki Giovanni* (Jackson: University Press of Mississippi, 1992), pp. 142-43.

CHAPTER ELEVEN

Lutheranism and Interfaith Dialogue

DANIEL F. MARTENSEN

L UTHER's essay of 1543 entitled "On the Jews and Their Lies," when placed next to his equally vitriolic comments about the Turks (read Muslims), indicates that Lutheranism was off to an early and bad start in interfaith relations.[1] The authoritative Lutheran Confessions have virtually nothing directly to say about the matter. Too, it must be stated at the outset that even with the significant authorship of people like Wolfhart Pannenberg, Paul Tillich, Paul Althaus, and Nathan Söderblom, Lutherans have played a rather unimportant role in the lively theological discussion on interfaith issues which has taken place in the last few decades.

Written in the hope that this situation will change for the better in the coming years, this paper will attempt to do the following. First, some theological-doctrinal resources central to Lutheranism will be catalogued. Second, brief comments will be made on the role played by the cultural diversity, race, and gender issues in Lutheran interfaith relations and dialogue efforts. Lastly, two modest proposals for ways into the future will be explored from a Lutheran perspective.

---

1. The Church Council of the Evangelical Lutheran Church in America (ELCA) released a "Declaration to the Jewish Community" on April 18, 1994. In it the church officially repudiates the anti-Judaic writings of Martin Luther, particularly the 1543 essay.

DANIEL F. MARTENSEN

I. Theological and Doctrinal Resources

Lutherans often react to the prospect of interfaith dialogue with quiet reservation if not fear and anxiety. Playing into this reaction is fear of loss of Lutheran identity, expectation of a compromise of doctrine, worry about syncretism, and suspicion that there will be a loss of the missionary imperative and/or ecumenical theological focus. One way to explore the dynamics of all this is to compare two Lutheran theological postures, each of which draws upon classical Lutheran theological and doctrinal resources in addressing the interfaith question. The first position is represented by Carl Braaten, the second by Theodore Ludwig.[2]

Braaten asserts that Lutherans should recognize the importance of other living faiths in history and in the created world, but he accents the absolute necessity of making a christological critique of other faiths.[3] As is to be expected, in light of his other writings, Braaten begins to develop an eschatological perspective on the interfaith dialogue process. His arguments go somewhat as follows.

Exploring the three-way relationship among the gospel, Christianity, and other world religions requires that we ask what kind of theology of religions can be developed on the basis of a distinctively Lutheran witness to the gospel.

A basic element in a set of Lutheran theological resources, according to Braaten, is the first article of the creed — the doctrine of creation. He argues that Lutherans affirm in the religious experience of humankind an original and continuing revelation which may even be called a kind of natural theology. Typical of the thought of Martin Luther and of Lutheran theology through the centuries has been the

2. For a more extensive representation of these positions see Carl Braaten's "The Identity and Meaning of Jesus Christ," in *Lutheranism and the Challenge of Religious Pluralism,* ed. Frank Klos, Lynn Nakamura, and Daniel F. Martensen (Minneapolis: Augsburg Press, 1990), pp. 103-39. See also Carl Braaten's *Principles of Lutheran Theology* (Philadelphia: Fortress Press, 1993). See also the essays by Braaten and Ludwig in *Religious Pluralism and Lutheran Theology,* ed. J. Paul Rajashakar, LWF Report 23/24 (Geneva: LWF, 1988). Essays in this last volume cited are drawn upon very directly in the development of this first section of the paper.

3. See "Lutheran Theology and Religious Pluralism" in the LWF Report 23/24 cited above.

positing of a twofold revelation of God, one through creation and one through covenant and gospel. It may be, Braaten says, that for Lutherans in this day the new shape of natural theology will be that of a theology of history of religions.

The soteriological core of Lutheran theology, according to Braaten, forces us to ask about the necessity of Christ. Here is where the basic principles of Lutheran confessional theology apply to the theology of religions. Included among these principles are the law/gospel distinction, the doctrine of justification by grace through faith, and the three *solas* — by grace alone, by faith alone, by Christ alone.

Because of the necessity of Christ, seen both ontologically and epistemologically, Braaten says Lutherans see the gospel of Christ as the final medium of revelation and the critical norm in the development of any theology of religions.

The eschatological aspect of Braaten's argumentation is limited to a few introductory comments. He observes that just as religions are relativized from the perspective of the gospel, Christianity itself is relativized when placed in context of the absolute future of the kingdom which Christianity is to serve. Inevitably, Christianity will continue in a process of formation in dialogue and mutual exchange with other religions.

Theodore Ludwig enters the discussion reminding Lutherans that the law/gospel principle is not in itself the proclamation of the faith of Christians, but rather it provides a paradigm for the proclamation according to a specific vision of Lutherans.[4] He argues that the Lutheran principles which were formed in heated debate about issues of great moment in Catholicism of the medieval period, and later as over against Reformed and left-wing Reformation positions, have been valuable for Lutherans through the centuries. However, he notes, the two-kingdoms principle when applied to twentieth-century church and society circumstances functions in a dramatically different fashion than it did in the sixteenth century. The fact that people of other living faiths are not too impressed when presented with a set of theological rules forged in the midst of medieval European intra-Christian conflict should not come to us as much of a surprise. Ludwig argues that Lutheranism should

---

4. See "Some Lutheran Theological Reflections" in the LWF Report 23/24 cited above.

look upon its doctrinal prescriptions as grammatical paradigms of a Lutheran Christian life story which give guidance in understanding the gospel. So doing should enable Lutherans to bring these paradigms to bear upon new situations of interfaith relations with freedom and flexibility. Other faith communities have their own grammars of understanding related to their own histories, he notes.

With Braaten, Ludwig affirms the importance of the doctrine of creation in exploring resources for interfaith dialogue. He sees it to be a helpful thing that some Lutheran theologians are attempting to develop a positive God-given role for other religions within the doctrine of creation. The problem Ludwig sees with this is that space is found in God's plan for other religions, but this is done without challenging basic Lutheran doctrinal rules. If other religions are not seen as ways of salvation, there is no conflict with the rule of "by Christ alone." If other religions represent only a human striving for self-salvation, "by faith alone" is not threatened. One does not have to be in dialogue with others in order to engage in such theological reconstruction. For this reason Ludwig says the "creation" avenue of approach is at a very early stage of development. In all of this he sees little evidence that Lutherans are willing to give deep respect to neighbors of other faiths and, hence, should not expect them to be interested in dialogue. There is a definite need for Lutherans to recover doctrinal principles, reformulate them, and find new ways of applying them.

It is shocking to note, Ludwig says, that Lutherans do not have an explicit doctrine of salvation. The Lutheran Confessions have no description of salvation and no suggestion as to what it might mean now. He sees this fact to be an important clue about the character of Lutheran Christian doctrinal principles. If Lutherans cannot describe salvation in terms of present life or verify it in the daily life of Christians, how can they say anything definite about its being present or absent in the experience of people of other living faiths?

> The main point is that we err in taking a particular doctrine from within our system and using it to evaluate a doctrine in another system without understanding the total contexts of which both are a part.[5]

5. "Some Lutheran Theological Reflections," p. 145.

In a very preliminary fashion Ludwig makes some suggestions about which theological principles interfaith dialogue experience has helped Lutherans recover in a fresh way. One which he believes is key to all the rest is the mystery of God. Luther talked a lot about the hidden God, so this is nothing new for Lutherans. The problem has often been that a doctrinal statement over time takes on a life of its own and can lead to a sterile kind of orthodoxy in which answers about God reside in the statements themselves. Silence, Ludwig notes, is one reminder coming from people of other living faiths about the mystery of God; Jews, Muslims, and Buddhists all accent its importance. Herein certainly lies one potentially important Lutheran theological resource.

A second resource Ludwig sees to be of potential significance in the task of engaging in interfaith dialogue is the concept of *simul*. This word is used to describe the sense of double-sided divine activity as well as the double-sided human relationship to the saving work of God. Lutherans speak of the modes of God's activity in terms of law and gospel, the left-hand kingdom and the right-hand kingdom; they speak of being simultaneously saint and sinner, free and slave. In these expressions and in Lutheran sacramental theology, Ludwig sees fertile ground for probing the question of God's gracious operation in the religions of the world.

The Lutheran sensitivity to a theology of the cross is lifted up by Ludwig as a third resource worthy of exploration and further development. Living in light of a theology of the cross permits us to respond to and to share in the lives of people of other faiths in their immediate situations of life — that is, three-fourths of the people of the world who live by other sacred stories.

II. Cultural Diversity, Race, and Gender

Of approximately 80 million Lutherans in the world, about 55 million are related to each other through the Lutheran World Federation (LWF). More will said about this later; suffice it now to indicate that the 114 member churches of the Federation see themselves as part of a "communion of churches," which, since 1990, has been the official definition and self-understanding of the LWF. In addition to or instead of the two North American theologians drawn upon earlier to assist in laying out some basic Lutheran theological resources operative in interfaith dialogue, theologians, women and men, from Asia, Africa, Latin America, North America, Europe, and Scandinavia, could also have been cited. For example, Notte Thelle from Japan uses a method of cross-reference in alluding to concepts and language in Eastern cultures in order to illuminate Lutheran Christian reflection on God. Simon S. Maimela from South Africa wrestles with some of the issues raised by Carl Braaten and Theodore Ludwig but relates them to the often neglected phenomena of traditional religions. Wi Jo Kang of Korean origin moves into the discussion with an exploration of the sense of community in Asian religions as it relates to the Christian community.

The Evangelical Lutheran Church in America (ELCA), 5.3 million members in size, slowly is becoming more aware of the challenges of cultural diversity. An official document affirmed by the ELCA at its 1993 churchwide assembly entitled "Freed in Christ: Race, Ethnicity, and Culture" is suggestive of the effort of the church to address the new pluralistic environment.

One of the things Lutherans have been learning, particularly through the work of the LWF programs on interfaith dialogue and on the relationship of women and men in church and society, is that they rarely live up to their own vision of life as known through the Scriptures, creeds, and confessions. Ethical challenges abound in interfaith dialogue and relations. One example can be cited.

The subjugation of women as it is justified in the many sayings in the Islamic Hadith, in Christian biblical language, and in Buddhist texts is being discussed increasingly by Lutherans.

Kristen Kvam is presently coediting a book of readings on the gender question drawn from Islamic, Jewish, and Christian holy books.[6] In her recent doctoral dissertation entitled "Luther, Eve, and Theological Anthropology: Reassessing the Reformer's Response to the Frauenfrage," she investigates Luther's "Great Lectures on Genesis." In this study the tense relationship between perpetual hierarchy and original equality in Luther's work is examined. One of her conclusions is that by presenting Eve as one who sees that God's promise for the future

6. Kristen E. Kvam teaches theology at Saint Paul's School of Theology in Kansas City. The title of the book referred to here is *Genesis and Gender: An Anthology of Jewish Christian and Islamic Reading*.

relates not only to the past, but shapes life now, Luther argues in one sense against himself; he offers an endorsement for construing equality as God's original intention for gender relations. The work of Kristen Kvam is one example of how Lutheran resources and memory are being reworked and linked to interfaith dialogue challenges.

Slowly Lutherans are integrating classical theological concerns and formulations with what one can hope is a sensitive response to the powerful contemporary facts of cultural diversity inseparably tied to race and gender inequities.

III. Ways into the Future

Lutherans generally are both disinclined and ill prepared to face the challenges of interfaith dialogue. The tasks they will have to take up in order to change this situation are gradually being more clearly defined. Some of the tasks are unique to the Lutheran communion; some are shared with other Christian communions. Two stand out as the most urgent — the epistemological and the ecclesiological.

As Western Christians, Lutherans carry with them epistemological roots which are an impediment to dialogue with people of other faiths. As daughters and sons of the Enlightenment, Lutherans assume the self-sufficiency of the thinking person. Too, in Kantian fashion, Lutherans tend to think in transcendent categories unimpeded by a consideration of identity and location.[7]

At a Bangkok consultation on Islam in Asia held in 1991, Charles Amjad-Ali said that we post-Enlightenment Christians tend to see dialogue as something we do after our theology has been articulated, or worse yet, we have attempted to construct through dialogue a transcendent, rational "theology of religions." Doing so minimizes the identity of people and their communal religious life. We have replaced *dia* (going through) by *di* (two) in the word "dialogue." *Logos* itself in the word "dialogue," he notes, has been changed from its original meaning

---

7. For a more complete discussion of this see Charles Amjad-Ali, "Theological and Historical Rationality behind Christian-Muslim Relations," in *Islam in Asia*, ed. J. Paul Rajashakar and H. S. Wilson (Geneva: Lutheran World Federation and the World Alliance of Reformed Churches, 1991).

of "principles and significant coherent realities" to mean simply "words exchanged." In our common language the opposite of dialogue has become monologue, an unfortunate development. One result of all this, Amjad-Ali notes, is that even when we refer to two religious communities we treat them as two individuals. Hence, we reduce two communities to two isolated entities having a conversation.

In rethinking epistemological assumptions, Lutheranism has some relatively untapped resources upon which to draw. One is the Lundensian theological tradition, particularly the work on motif research initiated by Anders Nygren of Lund University in Sweden. Nygren argues that the real epistemological issue involved in theological work is not what answers we get to the questions we pose, but rather what it is that shapes both the questions and the answers which we consider to be adequate. In thinking this way, one is drawn to the context, the matrix in which patterns of *pre*suppositions are shaped — inevitably, this involves a communal dimension.[8] This points to a second task relating to ecclesiology.

Up to now there has been a remarkable lack of concentration on the church as community in Lutheran reflection on interfaith relations and dialogue. Happily, this situation is now beginning to change, primarily through Lutheran involvement in the Lutheran World Federation (LWF) and ecumenical conciliar bodies such as the World Council of Churches and regional and national councils. Membership in interfaith councils and local interfaith conversations also serve to nudge Lutherans to do more serious work in the area. Our focus here is on distinctively Lutheran initiatives, accenting the programmatic efforts of the LWF.

After the 1984 Budapest Assembly of the LWF, *communio* became a predominant ecclesiological concept for the Federation. As a result of that the LWF revised its constitution at the 1990 Assembly in Curitiba, Brazil, defining itself as a "communion of churches which confess the triune God and are united in pulpit and altar fellowship." The Federation is just now beginning to make a serious effort to explore the implications of the 1991 decision. The church and its relationship to people of other faiths is one component of the exploration.

8. Nygren's last publication in the field of philosophical theology is *Meaning and Method* (Philadelphia: Fortress Press, 1972).

Islam, Hinduism, Confucianism, Buddhism, and African traditional religion are all being studied by regional working groups, each relating to one of the other faith communities in a specific context somewhere in the world. A more general LWF study process deals with the challenge of religious pluralism as it relates to theological education and training in a multifaith context. These programs of study have just begun; results should be available by the time of the next LWF Assembly planned for 1997 in Hong Kong.

Closely related to the interfaith emphasis are LWF study initiatives dealing with ecclesiology and ethics, *communio* and church structure and common decisions in the history of Lutheranism. Some of the questions posed in these initiatives are: What does communion among Lutherans mean in multifaith and multicultural settings? What are the ecumenical relations implications of the LWF's *communio* self-understanding?

Bilateral dialogue work being done at the international, regional, and national levels also poses fundamental ecclesiological questions for Lutherans. The LWF/Roman Catholic dialogue is now considering the church in light of the doctrine of justification. The LWF/Orthodox dialogue is addressing authority *in* and *of* the church. The USA Lutheran/Orthodox dialogue is looking at the ecclesiological ramifications of the doctrine of the Trinity.

The most dramatic challenge to Lutheran ecclesial self-understanding right now comes from the results of regional and national bilateral dialogue. Here one can cite "The Church as Community Called and Sent Forth by Jesus Christ," discussed at the 1994 Leuenberg Assembly held in Vienna, and the Meissen and Porvoo agreements involving the Lutheran and Anglican churches in Europe. With these must be mentioned the proposal for full communion between the Evangelical Lutheran Church in America and the Episcopal Church in the USA, and a comparable one proposing full communion with the Presbyterian Church (USA), the Reformed Church in America, and the United Church of Christ. Action on all of these proposals is expected no later than 1997. Whatever changes in ecclesial self-understanding emerge from these processes will have a direct effect upon Lutheranism's relationship to other faith communities.

World-level conciliar relations also represent an ongoing challenge to Lutheranism and its identity which is increasingly defined in *com-*

munio terms. Creative tension at best, conflict at worst, has characterized the relationship between the LWF and the World Council of
Churches since the 1940s. Now that *koinonia* (or *communio*) in faith, life,
and witness has become a central theological focus in the work of the
Faith and Order Commission of the World Council, new opportunities
present themselves for cooperation between the two organizations. This
conciliar connection for Lutherans is inseparable from its links with
other organized Christian world communions such as the World Alliance of Reformed Churches, the Anglican Consultative Council, the
Baptist World Alliance, the World Methodist Council, the Roman Catholic Church, and pan-Orthodoxy. All of these relationships presuppose
sensitivity to the importance in our common life of new ecclesial expressions such as the independent churches, women-church, house
churches, base communities, peace and justice coalitions which claim
ecclesial foundations, Pentecostalism, and neo-evangelicalism.

Time alone will tell whether or not, given the scope and complexity of current reflection on ecclesiology, Lutheranism will move to a
more responsible posture in relating to the sisters and brothers of other
faith communities. One thing is certain: Lutherans will not be able to
do it in isolation from other Christian communions, and without tap-
ping neglected resources in the history of Lutheranism.

Assuming that the tasks of developing an epistemology, i.e., finding common ground for speaking about "human knowing," and relating that to the communal, ecclesiological dimension of life are important ones for Lutherans in the coming years, one set of theological
resources can be suggested. In a sense it is one strand in the fabric of
Lutheran self-understanding which originates with Irenaeus and runs
through N. F. S. Grundtvig to twentieth-century theologians such as
the Lundensians and the late Joseph Sittler of the University of Chicago.
Least visible and known in this strand is certainly Nikolaj Frederik
Severin Grundtvig.[9]

The life of Grundtvig spanned the late eighteenth century and
most of the nineteenth century. Integral to his thinking was the convic-

9. The most recent book on N. F. S. Grundtvig in English is *Heritage and
Prophecy: Grundtvig and the English Speaking World,* ed. A. L. Alchin et al. (Norwich:
Canterbury Press, 1994). See also Hal Koch's *Grundtvig* (Yellow Springs: Antioch
Press, 1952) and also Johannes Knudsen's *Danish Rebel* (Philadelphia: Muhlenberg
Press, 1955).

tion that the world was spirit bearing. He affirmed that God is working through the whole of history and made an attempt to write a universal history. "Interaction" was the key to his theological methodology. He was a personalist rather than an individualist in his anthropology. He believed that human freedom rested upon "reciprocity," agreeing with F. Dostoyevsky that all are responsible for all. Grundtvig was fascinated by the distinctive roles of "man" and "woman," basically affirming a complementary relationship between the two. People live in community, he said, and "towards the future."

Grundtvig's basic contribution as a resource in reflecting upon the challenge of interfaith dialogue rests in his view of the created world. Redemption for Grundtvig presupposes a vital "folk-life" in the culture of the hearers of the Word. We humans echo God's Word in our words, he said. We encounter God's Word in what Grundtvig called the folk-spirit.

Kai Thaning, one of Denmark's leading Grundtvig scholars, has said that what Grundtvig is driving at here is a concept of preunderstanding. Needless to say, there is a connection between Grundtvig's epistemological assertion of the importance of preunderstanding and the emphasis of motif research upon presupposition, i.e., what is prior to that which we assume. Grundtvig asserted that in order for people to hear the gospel they must first have a latent understanding of faith, hope, love, and truth. Without that preunderstanding, he said, it is not possible for people to know the Christian meanings of words such as "faith," "hope," "love," and "truth." The Danish Folk School, of which Grundtvig is the founder, is seen as a way to rejuvenate folk-life which is a foundation for our preunderstanding — a way to develop a sensitivity to the life which the gospel presupposes. There is here a bringing together of creation and redemption; something Lutherans historically have had great difficulty doing.

For Grundtvig the gospel presupposes a latent context of understanding, a life which the gospel can illumine and restore. What is presupposed here is life, not our understanding of it.

One of the most famous expressions of Grundtvig is "menske forst og kristen saa" [first of all human beings, then Christians]. In this lies a view of human life, human community, and creation which clearly reflects a foundational ingredient in the thought of Irenaeus. Life and death are the parameters, not nature or matter as over against grace or

185

spirit. Irenaeus sees human life — in solitude, in community, in history, a part of creation — to be in the hands of God.

There are possibilities here for building bridges to if not sharing common ground with people of other faiths, particularly with the Jews. Grundtvig affirmed with the Jews the exhortation to be "mensch," to be truly human, and he left a legacy.[10]

Richard Stone, an American ambassador to Denmark, reflecting on what the Danes did in October of 1943, asked what it was in the Danish geography, culture, and morality that made it the only occupied country in Europe to protect and in fact save the Jewish population. Part of the answer to that question lies in the legacy of N. F. S. Grundtvig. Jews were first of all human beings, secondly, Jews; folk-life was a given.

This strand of Lutheran life and thought integrates to a remarkable degree the sometimes disparate theological categories of anthropology, cosmology, epistemology, and ecclesiology. Interfaith dialogue urges Lutherans to seek patterns of meaning that are as deep and profound as the magnitude of the new questions being asked — a formidable theological assignment. If Lutherans are to meet the challenge, they will have to lift up in new ways the first and the third articles of the Apostles' Creed rather than focusing in nearly exclusive fashion on the second article. Joseph Sittler puts it this way:

> The grace of joy and creativity, the possibility of life-understanding and life-enhancement thus experienced, the sense of self-transcending engagement with the allure and power and mystery of the world refuses to be identified as absolutely separate from the grace and joy and new possibility given to human life in that Christically focused grace, greater than all, which is the forgiveness of sin. Precisely here is disclosed the theological and pastoral necessity to speak of the grace of the Triune God in a way that breaks out of the Protestant disposition to enclose the total reality of grace within the focal point of the second article of the doctrine — of Christ and redemption.[11]

10. A major study on this issue entitled *Grundtvig and the Jews* by Axel Torm has not yet been translated into English.

11. See Joseph Sittler's *Essays on Nature and Grace* (Philadelphia: Fortress Press, 1972), p. 115.

Conclusion

Yves Congar, the great Dominican ecumenical theologian, recently was asked this question: What do you think of Islam? "The theological status of Islam," he said, "is an immense problem that I haven't really studied."[12] If Lutherans were asked a comparable question about the challenge of religious pluralism, the answer would be about the same. Lutherans have just started to clarify their thinking about interfaith dialogue; the dialogue itself has barely begun.

---

12. See *Conversations with Yves Congar*, ed. Bernard Lauret (Philadelphia: Fortress Press, 1988), p. 34.

CHAPTER TWELVE

Interreligious Dialogue: A Wesleyan Holiness Perspective

FLOYD T. CUNNINGHAM

THOSE in the Wesleyan holiness tradition have done little to facilitate interreligious dialogue. I must begin with that confession. What this paper describes are hypothetical applications of the resources of Wesleyan theology that, largely speaking, have gone unused. One of the reasons I perceive for this lack of interest in interreligious dialogue is an assumption that no one is "saved" apart from both Christian conversion and present assurance of it. If that is the presupposition held, there is little need to discuss interfaith issues and, rather, great urgency to evangelize by bold and brash proclamations of the gospel. Another reason for the lack of participation in interfaith dialogue which I perceive is a lingering sectarianism unconcerned with broad issues and distrustful of ecumenism. A third is that the holiness tradition, like many American traditions, would rather be accomplishing something rather than reflecting upon its mission. But, as I hope to show to those inside as well outside the tradition, there are resources for interreligious dialogue in Wesleyanism which transcend these presuppositions and characteristics.

Theologians in the holiness movement consider themselves among the legitimate heirs of John Wesley. As such they accept the cardinal doctrines of Christianity as understood and taught by him, including his basic understandings of sin, justification by faith, the new birth, and Christian perfection. They consider the recovery and expression of his doctrine of sanctification the distinctive "reason-to-be" of the movement. Traditionally, holiness theologians have stressed the "crisic" and "entire" nature of the doctrine, but since the 1960s more emphasis than before has been placed upon both the content and goal of entire sanctification — perfect love and Christlikeness.[1]

Holiness theology is filled with an optimism of grace that at its best elicits rather than thwarts compassion and empathy to those outside the reaches of the established church. Grace abounds in and through those faithful to God. In the nineteenth century this optimism attached itself to "Christ the transformer of culture" social reforms, including, early in the century, abolition and, later, prohibition. By the early twentieth century leaders in the holiness movement were also active in urban rescue missions, homes for unwed mothers, and orphanages. The Salvation Army expressed this in a direct way by centering its attention on the urban poor.[2] However, changes in both the religious and social scene by the 1920s led to a more reactionary stance among holiness advocates. There came a "fundamentalist leavening," evident in the rise of premillennialism and assumptions about biblical inerrancy which were not inherently a part of the tradition.[3] At the same

1. Thomas A. Langford, *Practical Divinity: Theology in the Wesleyan Tradition* (Nashville: Abingdon, 1983), chap. 6; John A. Knight, *The Holiness Pilgrimage: Reflections on the Life of Holiness* (Kansas City: Beacon Hill, 1973), pp. 59-63. On recent ecumenical connections see Donald W. Dayton, "The Holiness Witness in the Ecumenical Church," *Wesleyan Theological Journal* 23 (spring-fall 1988): 92-106. Note the non-Methodist roots of some holiness churches, such as the Church of God (Anderson, Indiana). See John W. V. Smith, *The Quest for Holiness and Unity: A Centennial History of the Church of God (Anderson, Indiana)* (Anderson, Ind.: Warner Press, 1980), pp. 33-37.

2. Donald W. Dayton, *Discovering an Evangelical Heritage* (New York: Harper and Row, 1976), chaps. 2, 7, 8; Norris Magnuson, *Salvation in the Slums: Evangelical Social Work, 1865-1920* (Metuchen, N.J.: Scarecrow, 1977), chaps. 2, 6, 9. Yet note must be taken of Leonard Sweet's suggestion that "power" for service characterized more the elements of the holiness movement influenced by Northern evangelism, and "purity" those influenced by Southern; in "A Nation Born Again: The Union Prayer Meeting Revival and Cultural Relativism," in *In the Great Tradition: Essays on Pluralism, Voluntarism, and Revivalism in Honor of Winthrop S. Hudson*, ed. Joseph D. Ban and Paul R. Dekar (Valley Forge, Pa.: Judson, 1982), pp. 207-8.

3. Paul Bassett, "The Fundamentalist Leavening of the Holiness Movement, 1914-1940," *Wesleyan Theological Journal* 13 (spring 1978): 665-91; Bassett, "The Theological Identity of the North American Holiness Movement," in *The Variety of American Evangelicalism*, ed. Donald W. Dayton and Robert K. Johnson (Knoxville: University of Tennessee Press, 1991), pp. 72-108. Compare the simple "prefundamentalist"

time the holiness churches came to associate "holiness" more with legalistic extremes than with expressions of love and Christlikeness. This sectarian period saw little need for dialogue with nearly anyone, and certainly not members of different religions. It was a kind of "Christ against culture" motif which sent missionaries by the dozens out to convert the "heathen."[4] By midcentury, however, the holiness people began to feel more comfortable with other evangelicals through affiliations in the National Association of Evangelicals (NAE) and the Evangelical Foreign Missions Association. The 1950s was a decade of accommodation for the movement, as it emerged at least partly from sectarianism, with affinities being felt toward American culture, conservative politics, and dominant values. This included embracing a strongly anticommunist rhetoric as one rationale for world evangelism. There seemed to be few who separated American from Christian values during this "Christ of culture" era.[5]

A Wesleyan renaissance in the 1960s began to distinguish between Wesleyan and American holiness movement roots. The reclaiming and following of Wesley as chief theologian by such scholars as Mildred Bangs Wynkoop became theologically "correct" among many of the academically elite, embarrassed, as they were, by baptism with the Holy Spirit language and what they perceived to be the pneumatocentricity of American holiness theology. There was a movement toward accord, rather, with Methodist scholars who also promoted Wesleyan studies. But with the recovery of Wesley came also a renewed understanding

---

statement on Holy Scriptures in one of the constituent groups which became a part of the Church of the Nazarene: "His inspired Word, and the only rule of faith and practice." *Constitution of the Association of Pentecostal Churches of America* (Providence: Beulah Christian, 1897), p. 10.

4. Timothy L. Smith, *Called unto Holiness; The Story of the Nazarenes: The Formative Years* (Kansas City: Nazarene, 1962), pp. 216-20, 293-97; W. T. Purkiser, *Called unto Holiness*, vol. 2: *The Second Twenty-Five Years, 1933-58* (Kansas City: Nazarene, 1983), chap. 8.

5. See for example Russell V. DeLong, *We Can If We Will: The Challenge of World Evangelism* (Kansas City: Nazarene, 1947), which mentions nothing of a distinctive holiness mission and advocates cooperation; and James DeF. Murch, *Cooperation without Compromise: A History of the National Association of Evangelicals* (Grand Rapids: Wm. B. Eerdmans Publishing Co., 1956), pp. 105-8, which links the goals of the NAE to U.S. foreign policy, especially in combating communism. See also Ronald B. Kirkemo, *For Zion's Sake: A History of Pasadena/Point Loma College* (San Diego: Point Loma Press, 1992), chap. 10, "From Subculture to Mainstream."

of grace, and especially prevenient grace. The ramifications of this for interreligious dialogue, however, were slow in coming.[6]

It is still the case that when a call for "holiness" is made it has different tones among holiness people themselves: fidelity to strict rules for some; cultural and political "fundamentalism" for others; compassion, mercy, and social reform for still another segment. What resources for interreligious dialogue can emerge from a tradition which has expressed its own distinctive doctrine in such different ways across time?[7]

At their best the holiness churches may offer to interfaith dialogue the nuances they carry of Wesleyan theology: first, a dynamic understanding of Christ's prevenient grace, which reaches and is active within all human beings; second, an understanding that human beings may enjoy now full assurance of present salvation from sin, guilt, fear, and shame; third, a way of and emphasis upon discipleship.

Before discussing each of these emphases more completely, it is important to mention certain presuppositions in holiness theology. It is both classically trinitarian and christocentric. The creative God im-

6. Leo George Cox, *John Wesley's Concept of Perfection* (Kansas City: Beacon Hill, 1964), pp. 19-26, 129-34; Mildred Bangs Wynkoop, "A Hermeneutical Approach to John Wesley," *Wesleyan Theological Journal* 6 (spring 1971): 13-22; Wynkoop, "John Wesley — Mentor or Guru?" *Wesleyan Theological Journal* 10 (spring 1975): 5-14; Wynkoop, "Theological Roots of the Wesleyan Understanding of the Holy Spirit," *Wesleyan Theological Journal* 14 (spring 1979): 77-98; Rob L. Staples, "Present Frontiers of Wesleyan Theology," *Wesleyan Theological Journal* 12 (spring 1977): 5-15; Staples, "The Current Wesleyan Debate on the Baptism with the Holy Spirit" (privately printed and distributed); Donald W. Dayton, "The Doctrine of the Baptism of the Holy Spirit: Its Emergence and Significance," *Wesleyan Theological Journal* 13 (spring 1978): 114-26; Harold E. Raser, *Phoebe Palmer: Her Life and Thought* (Lewiston, N.Y.: Edwin Mellen, 1987), chap. 5, "Phoebe Palmer and the Doctrine of Christian Perfection: Continuities and Discontinuities."

7. J. Kenneth Grider, *Entire Sanctification: The Distinctive Doctrine of Wesleyanism* (Kansas City: Beacon Hill, 1980), esp. chap. 5, "The Holiness Movement and Spirit Baptism"; Timothy L. Smith, "Righteousness and Hope: Christian Holiness and the Millennial Vision in America, 1800-1900," *American Quarterly* 31 (spring 1979): 21-45; Timothy L. Smith, "The Holy Spirit in the Hymns of the Wesleys," *Wesleyan Theological Journal* 16 (fall 1981): 20-47; Timothy L. Smith, "John Wesley and the Second Blessing," *Wesleyan Theological Journal* 21 (spring-fall 1986): 137-59; David O. Moberg, *The Great Reversal: Evangelism and Social Concern*, rev. ed. (Philadelphia: Lippincott, 1977), pp. 11, 30-31; George M. Marsden, *Fundamentalism and American Culture: The Shaping of Twentieth-Century Evangelicalism, 1870-1925* (New York: Oxford University Press, 1980), pp. 85-93.

printed the divine nature with all that was made, and the creative Word of God from the beginning was Christ. The Spirit of God moves around the world, and that Spirit of God is the Spirit of Christ, proceeding from both the Father and the Son. The nature of God is adequately, though not solely, revealed in the person of Christ. The will of God is to establish redemptive relationships with human beings, such that Wesleyans must speak not so much of imputed "states" of grace, but of dynamic relationships with the Almighty, which come through Jesus Christ.[8]

A. Prevenient Grace

Much has been written about the Wesleyan understanding of prevenient grace. It is grace which goes "before." It is a universal benefit of the atonement of Christ given to all men and women, extending backward in time, to the Hebrew patriarchs, as well as forward, to present-day Hindus or Buddhists with no knowledge of Jesus. Grace is for Wesleyans universal in scope and effect. It seems to me that Wesleyanism fits best with the "inclusivist" school of thought regarding God's grace at work in other religions. Yet grace is not mystically "christocentric" in the sense of Teilhard de Chardin or Raimundo Panikkar, but historically rooted in the incarnation and atonement of Jesus Christ. Another component of the Wesleyan understanding of prevenient grace is that it is not quite the same as "common" grace, as some Calvinists teach, reflecting the remains of God's image in human beings, while aimed mainly at restraining evil; but that it is teleological, attempting to lead all men and women into the experience of salvation and into the sanctifying presence of God. Prevenient grace gives men and women power to say no to sin even before any conscious entrance

---

8. See A. H. Mathias Zahniser, "The Trinity: Paradigm for Mission in the Spirit," *Missiology* 17 (January 1989): 69-82. For "classical" treatments of Wesleyan theology from the holiness standpoint, see H. Orton Wiley, *Christian Theology*, 3 vols. (Kansas City: Beacon Hill, 1940-43), and J. Kenneth Grider, *A Wesleyan-Holiness Theology* (Kansas City: Beacon Hill, 1994). For "relational" restatements of holiness theology see Mildred Bangs Wynkoop, *A Theology of Love: The Dynamic of Wesleyanism* (Kansas City: Beacon Hill, 1972), and H. Ray Dunning, *Grace, Faith, and Holiness: A Wesleyan Systematic Theology* (Kansas City: Beacon Hill, 1988).

into the way of salvation. But, more than that, it provides the context or ground in which faith arises. There is no merit or "work" in faith, since it is a gift of grace. Wesley says that through the Spirit alone "the law of God is now made known to them that know not God."[9] Faith comes not in or through self-striving, but at the end of it, at the points of desperation with self-effort. Prevenient grace offers the opportunity to rely wholly upon God for salvation rather than upon oneself, as well as the enabling power for moral decisions. This grace never coerces. The choice of the individual is crucial. He or she may as easily choose what is not moral, and as easily say no to the offered salvation as yes.

In Wesleyanism there is a continuity of grace — it is all of Christ, leads all to Christ, and beckons all toward Christlikeness. Prevenient grace is the beginning stage of that soteriologically motivated and chris-tocentric flow. The next stage is "convincing" or convicting grace, by which the individual knows himself or herself to be a sinner. Without that self-knowledge there can be no onward progress toward God. By grace and the work of the Holy Spirit men and women come to know their true spiritual conditions. They are enabled to know whether or not they enjoy peace with God. Prevenient grace provides this light. It shines through certain societal and religious conventions, as well as through individual consciences. The religions of the world are instru-ments of this light, since men and women come to know their moral failures or triumphs through them. Within them is an imprint and witness to the Truth, which, though not recognized as such, is Christ. Where this imprint and witness in other religions is may be judged by Christians on the basis of biblical revelation. That God is making God-self and God's will known through social and religious means is the basis for moral accountability in the world. In Wesleyan theology no one is culpable for either the generic sin of humanity, or for sins which

9. John Wesley, "The Original Nature, Property, and Use of the Law," in *The Works of John Wesley*, ed. Albert C. Outler, bicentennial ed., vol. 2 (Nashville: Abing-don, 1985), pp. 7-10, 15. See also Wesley, "The Witness of Our Own Salvation," in *The Works of John Wesley*, ed. Albert C. Outler, bicentennial ed., vol. 1 (Nashville: Abingdon, 1984), p. 302. Lycurgus M. Starkey, Jr., *The Work of the Holy Spirit: A Study in Wesleyan Theology* (New York: Abingdon, 1962), pp. 41-45, 116-23, 130-33, 150-55; Floyd Cunningham, "A Wesleyan Reflection on the World Mission," *Asia Journal of Theology* 5 (April 1991): 104-10, 114-15. For a comparison of Wesley and Calvin on these points see Geoffrey Wainwright, *Wesley and Calvin: Sources of Theology, Liturgy, and Spirituality* (Melbourne: Uniting Church Press, 1987), esp. pp. 16-20.

could not have been avoided. But in every case the power to choose rightly is not based on unaided moral strength, which is nil, but upon Christ's Spirit hiddenly strengthening the will within.[10]

This is to say that moral power extends to those for whom the name and presence of Christ remains unknown. That is a part of the universal benefit of the atonement in classical Wesleyan-Arminian theology.[11] Does this grace empower a person to always say yes to the promptings of the Spirit? That would be too contrary to the sinfulness of humanity. Is there provision enough in the mercy of God through Christ to extend grace to such that have never known and will never know of Christ? The answer to that would depend upon the sincerity and repentance of the individual and ultimately upon God, but Wesleyans understand that God gives grace to all, and that if any respond in faith to whatever measure or form of grace is given, there is salvation.[12]

What does this theology of prevenient grace have to offer inter-religious dialogue? It recognizes the work of Christ in all people and, consequently, in all societies and religions. Wesley wrote that "even the heathens did not remain in total darkness. . . . Rays of light have in all ages and nations gleamed through the shade." He went on: "And however these were obscured or disguised by the addition of num-berless fables, yet something of truth was still mingled with them, and these streaks of light prevented utter darkness." Of course not all is of God in individuals, societies, or religions. Grace is able to be re-jected. Wesleyans would disagree with the belief of those such as Paul

---

10. Wesley, "The Circumcision of the Heart," in *Works* (Outler), 1:403; Wesley, "On Working Out Our Own Salvation," in *The Works of John Wesley*, ed. Albert C. Outler, bicentennial ed., vol. 3 (Nashville: Abingdon, 1986), p. 203; John Telford, ed., *The Letters of John Wesley* (London: Epworth, 1931), 5:322; Wiley, 2:344-57; Cox, pp. 28-46; J. Kenneth Grider, *Repentance unto Life: What It Means to Repent* (Kansas City: Beacon Hill, 1965), pp. 40-44, and Grider, *A Wesleyan-Holiness Theology*, pp. 242-47, 351-55.

11. James Arminius, *Writings*, trans. James Nichols (reprint, Grand Rapids: Baker, 1956), 1:317-21; William B. Pope, *A Compendium of Christian Theology* (London: Wesleyan Conference Office, 1877), 2:58-61; John Miley, *Systematic Theology* (New York: Methodist Book Connection, 1894), 2:505-24.

12. Wesley, "Predestination Calmly Considered," in *Works*, 3rd ed. (reprint, Kansas City: Beacon Hill, 1979), 10:229-30; a view close to Clark Pinnock, *A Wideness in God's Mercy: The Finality of Jesus Christ in a World of Religions* (Grand Rapids: Zondervan, 1992), pp. 157-68.

Knitter and Diana Eck that there are many paths to the one God, each equally adequate within one's culture. To Wesley, the light of prevenient grace was far short of divine revelation and assurance of salvation.[13]

But wherever there are assents to God's goodness, beauty, and truth, one may attribute these to the grace of God. Christians should therefore be delighted to discover through dialogue and study how God has manifested Godself around the world across time. They may perceive a mixture of grace and sin, assent and rejection, in both the Christian religion and other religions. They may perceive a manifestation of the ideals and values of Christ and the kingdom spread around the world. And they may sense how the Spirit has been at work, wooing, persuading, and beckoning closer to truth those who are yearning and searching for it.

However, is yearning and searching for salvation an equivalent for salvation itself? Generally Wesleyans would answer that prevenient grace is saving grace only until it has been consciously and deliberately rejected. From both biblical and experiential evidence it is obvious that people everywhere sin — they reject the light they have, they break their own consciences' warnings. But the question of salvation is answerable only by God. Prevenient grace defines theologically the basis by which it can be said that God has always and everywhere found a way into the hearts and lives of men and women. It is not simply something "imputed," but is rather something of God spiritually close.

---

13. Wesley, "Walking by Sight and Walking by Faith," in *The Works of John Wesley,* ed. Albert C. Outler, bicentennial ed., vol. 4 (Nashville: Abingdon, 1987), pp. 51-52. See especially Randy L. Maddox, "Wesley and the Question of Truth or Salvation through Other Religions," *Wesleyan Theological Journal* 27 (spring-fall 1992): 7-29. See also S. J. Samartha, "The Holy Spirit and People of Various Faiths, Cultures, and Ideologies," in *The Holy Spirit,* ed. Don Kirkpatrick (Nashville: Tidings, 1974), pp. 20-39. Compare Diana L. Eck, *Encountering God: A Spiritual Journey from Bozeman to Banaras* (Boston: Beacon, 1993), pp. 181-99. For divergent answers within Methodism to the question of pluralism, see not only Eck but Huston Smith's response to her in *Christian Century* 111 (March 9, 1994): 252-53; and compare Jerry Walls, *The Problem of Pluralism: Recovering United Methodist Identity* (Wilmore, Ky.: Good News, 1986), esp. chap. 3, to David L. Watson, *God Does Not Foreclose: The Universal Promise of Salvation* (Nashville: Abingdon, 1990), chap. 5.

B. Assurance

Thus there is room to hope that through the christological and redeeming reach of God's prevenient grace, some may transcend their own sin and the limits of their religion and society to come to faith in God. But there is more than this to be hoped for: men and women may enjoy assurance or knowledge of present salvation. This assurance is a seal or guarantee within oneself of present salvation. It is a spiritual assurance from God based on a present relationship with God. The holiness movement speaks often of the Spirit's role in justification and sanctification and it understands the Spirit's movement, witness, and work to be the Spirit of Christ. The Spirit is manifested to, and is experienced by, all persons, even those outside the Christian tradition, who cannot identify this Spirit with Christ. Yet the Spirit's ministry is to lead to Christ. The ways by which a person possesses assurance, in Wesleyan thought, are both inward and outward. There is an inward, subjective "feeling" of God's salvation and abiding presence; and there are also outward fruits of holiness and righteousness which should be evident to all. Outward marks prevent reducing assurance to pure subjectivism and emotionalism; and inward assurance prevents reliance on legalistic morality as the sign of salvation. This also suggests the balance Wesleyans try to maintain between faith and works.[14]

Often those within the holiness tradition have confused this assurance with salvation itself, and Wesley's own views seemed to vacillate and change across the years. Many, even Wesley himself at times, exclude from the ranks they consider "saved" those without such assurance. This was Wesley's early view on the matter, that all "true Christians" enjoy assurance. He could not, early in his ministry, and close upon his own Aldersgate experience, conceive of someone being justified without knowing it. Yet even then he made exceptions for the "heathen."[15] In later years, reflecting upon his own pre-Aldersgate days, he could not conceive that he, or others in similar states, living faithfully and sincerely as servants of God, would be lost — even if

14. John Wesley, "The Witness of the Spirit" and "The Witness of Our Own Spirit," in *Works* (Outler), 1:267-313; Starkey, chap. 4, "The Witness of the Spirit." Compare Eck, pp. 132-36; Pinnock, pp. 44-47, 49-80.

15. Albert C. Outler, ed., *John Wesley* (New York: Oxford University Press, 1964), p. 137.

such lacked the assurance of being "found." Rather, as Wesley in later years noted, assurance should be considered a privilege, that men and women may know themselves to be sons and daughters of God, and love God as such, rather than relating to God out of fear, only as servants would their master. In the mercy of God, "servants" who were "walking by sight" rather than by faith, without assurance of salvation, and without enjoying the certain knowledge of the love of God to them, are yet "saved." They serve God dutifully to the fullest extent of their resources and God's grace. Within the context of grace, Wesleyans hinge much upon the autonomy of individuals to respond to or to reject the gospel of God. Wesley's thought regarding Socrates, for instance, was that he was virtuous and, agreeing with Justin Martyr, a "Christian before Christ." But Socrates had no hope of his salvation, which is to say, no assurance of it. But, said Wesley, there can be an awareness of the saving grasp of God's love among those who know themselves to be God's children through redemption in Christ.[16]

But even among the non-Christians such fruits of the Spirit as "love, joy, peace, patience, kindness, goodness, faithfulness, gentleness, and self-control" should be evidence enough of the Spirit of Christ at work (and should not be considered as human righteousness). Likewise as "obvious" are the acts of immorality: "idolatry, witchcraft, hatred, discord, jealousy, fits of rage, selfish ambition, dissension, factions, envy, drunkenness, orgies." These marks of living by the "flesh" and not by the Spirit cut across the boundaries of religions. If these are marks of the Spirit's work, then they are transcultural, since the same Spirit is at work in all men and women. It is not difficult to see that *some* men

16. Wesley, *A Plain Account of Christian Perfection* (reprint, Kansas City: Beacon Hill, 1966), pp. 30-31, including Wesley's annotations; Wesley, *Works*, 3rd ed. (reprint; Kansas City: Beacon Hill, 1979), 1:98-104, recounting Aldersgate; Wesley, "The Spirit of Bondage and of Adoption," in *Works* (Outler), 1:249-50; Wesley, "The Case of Reason Impartially Considered," in *Works* (Outler), 2:596; Wesley, "On Faith," in *Works* (Outler), 3:497; and Wesley, "Walking by Sight and Walking by Faith," in *Works* (Outler), 4:49-59. I am following the lines of David Cubie, "Placing Aldersgate in John Wesley's Order of Salvation," *Wesleyan Theological Journal* 24 (1989): 32-53, in describing Wesley's stages. See also Maddox, pp. 15, 26-27 (nn. 56, 64); and compare Kenneth J. Collins, "Twentieth-Century Interpretations of John Wesley's Aldersgate Experience: Coherence or Confusion?" *Wesleyan Theological Journal* 24 (1989): 18-31, and Collins, "Other Thoughts on Aldersgate: Has the Conversionist Paradigm Collapsed?" *Methodist History* 30 (October 1991): 13-20.

and women of other faiths, just as *some* Christians, are living in God's Spirit. If so, it is grace upon grace.[17]

What are the implications of this for interfaith dialogue? First, Wesleyan theology, as well as Calvinist theology, acknowledges that a distinction may be maintained between salvation and assurance or knowledge of salvation. Salvation may be found among those who are accepted by God on the basis of Christ's atonement and yet have no explicit knowledge of it. That is one of the bases on which Wesleyans baptize infants. But it is broader than that. At some point there is either acceptance of God's acceptance, or rejection of God. The marks of this acceptance, however, would be similar. Such ones' accepting of God would be sincere, devoted, and charitable as well as filled with faith, hope, and love. Wesley called them "honest heathens" and contrasted theirs with the fate of unbelievers. Their knowledge of the love of God might be limited, lacking as it would faith in the revelation of God in the loving-kindness of Jesus, and they may serve a God considered to be both remote and stern. Yet such servanthood may produce from the gracious Spirit working within righteousness, holiness, and even Christlikeness.[18]

Many examples of such faith are represented in the Bible. It characterized the faith of the Old Testament patriarchs. They hoped for what they did not see, and lacked assurance of their faith's completion, having no direct knowledge of Christ. Yet New Testament as well as subsequent Christian writers considered them "righteous."[19]

---

17. Welsey, "To John Smith," in *The Works of John Wesley*, ed. Frank Baker, bicentennial ed., vol. 26 (Oxford: Clarendon Press, 1982), p. 199, cited by Maddox, p. 27 n. 63. See Pinnock, pp. 86-106; and Lesslie Newbigin, *The Gospel in a Pluralist Society* (Grand Rapids: Wm. B. Eerdmans Publishing Co., 1989), chap. 14.

18. Wesley, "On the Trinity," in *Works* (Outler), 2:386, cited by Maddox, p. 27 n. 63. Also see Pinnock, pp. 96-106; John V. Taylor, *The Go-between God: The Holy Spirit and the Christian Mission* (New York: Oxford University Press, 1972), chap. 9; Michael Lodahl, "The Witness of the Spirit: Questions for Clarification for Wesley's Doctrine of Assurance," *Wesleyan Theological Journal* 23 (spring-fall 1988): 188-92, 196; Rob L. Staples, *Outward Sign and Inward Grace: The Place of Sacraments in Wesleyan Spirituality* (Kansas City: Beacon Hill, 1991), pp. 177-82.

19. Among biblical passages see Matthew 8:11; Romans 4:3, 11-25; James 2:20-24; among early Christian writings, I Clement, chaps. 9 and 10. Irenaeus particularly wrote against Marcion's attempt to exclude Abraham from salvation in *Against Heresies*, bk. 4, chap. 8.

The same righteousness could be said of Cornelius. The predominant holiness movement view of Cornelius (though not that of John Wesley) has been that he was "saved" before the visit of Peter to him. What he lacked was the baptism with the Holy Spirit, meaning, in holiness ways of thinking, entire sanctification. Cornelius also lacked assurance of salvation, which also came to him with the baptism with the Holy Spirit. Many holiness movement exegetes have viewed the story of Cornelius in this way because it has seemed to provide an occasion for a clear "second blessing" teaching, as does the similar Spirit baptism of the Ephesian disciples of John the Baptist. In both cases these followers were already saved under the old dispensation of grace, and were living in expectation of something better yet to come. Wesley himself understood that these, like the disciples before Pentecost, were not evangelically converted until their baptism with the Spirit. Nevertheless, to Wesley they were already saved under the previous dispensation of grace before their "Pentecost." Even though historically they were living in the age of the Spirit, until the gospel was both preached to and received by them, they were living under the dispensation of the Father. These believers were saved under the old dispensation through the atonement of Christ, even though they lacked explicit knowledge of it. The implication is, given this paradigm, that there are those today living under the dispensations of the Father, Son, or Holy Spirit; and that there are those being saved within the grace, light, and expectations of faith and righteousness of that dispensation under which they live. The dispensation of the Father anticipates that of the Son, and that of the Son the dispensation of the Spirit, but each offers salvation.[20]

Though holiness movement defenders of the "second blessing" interpretation of what happened to Cornelius and the Ephesian disciples were not thinking of the missiological implications of this, clearly

---

20. Among those supporting the idea that Cornelius was already converted before Peter arrived: Charles Ewing Brown, *The Meaning of Sanctification* (Anderson, Ind.: Warner, 1945), pp. 109-10; J. Kenneth Grider, "Spirit-Baptism the Means of Entire Sanctification," *Wesleyan Theological Journal* 14 (fall 1979): 35-42, and Grider, *Entire Sanctification*, pp. 48-52; Lawrence W. Wood, *Pentecostal Grace* (Wilmore, Ky.: Francis Asbury, 1980), p. 91. For a description of the idea of dispensations within Wesleyanism see Knight, pp. 65-81, and his citations to John Fletcher, *Works* (reprint, Salem, Ohio: Schmul, 1974), including 1:565-66, 575, 579; 3:173-81.

there are some important ones. Luke's point in recording these incidents was to prove that Gentiles are fully incorporated into the scope of God's plan of salvation through Christ. However, the situations of Cornelius and the Ephesian believers were unique. They already possessed a relationship to God based on their living in the fullness of the salvation offered to them. Both Cornelius and the Ephesians worshiped the God of the Hebrews, and knew it. They were devout and sincere. They, so far as can be seen, lived in anticipation of the gospel, and when it was fully proclaimed gladly received it and became followers of Christ. Perhaps it is equally important to note that their "baptism with the Holy Spirit" gave them assurance of a salvation which they already possessed while at the same time sanctifying them (whether initially or entirely is not the missiological point). These along with other incidents convinced the early church of the universal appeal and power of the gospel.

Perhaps the state of the Moslems is comparable. They have as much knowledge of God as had Cornelius. They worship the God of Abraham, Isaac, and Jacob. As did Cornelius, many live lives of sincere and utter devotion to God, serving God out of fear, even out of love. Charitable acts follow. Perhaps these devout Moslems are saved in the same way that Cornelius or the patriarchs were saved, living under the dispensation of the Father, through the atonement of Christ, by means of the light and strength given them by the Holy Spirit. Do they also live in expectation or hope? When Christ is truly proclaimed, they might recognize continuity, not disparity, between their faith and the gospel, and might be both "baptized with the Holy Spirit" and receive assurance, if they needed it, of their salvation. At least that is what Christians might like to believe. Of course, realistically, the true proclamation of the gospel is hindered by political entrapments and other hindrances, many of them made by Christians' actions. But these are not boundaries to the saving arm of God.[21]

21. Cf. Phil Parshall, *New Paths in Muslim Evangelism: Evangelical Approaches to Contextualization* (Grand Rapids: Baker, 1980), chap. 6, "Theological Bridges to Salvation," and Hans Kung's responses to Islam in *Christianity and the World Religions: Paths to Dialogue with Islam, Hinduism, and Buddhism* (Garden City, N.Y.: Doubleday, 1986), pp. 22-24, 63-66, 85-87, 92-96, 109, 118-30. Also see Lyle Vander Werff, "The Names of Christ in Worship," in *Muslims and Christians on the Emmaus Road*, ed. J. Dudley Woodberry (Monrovia, Calif.: MARC, 1989), pp. 175-94.

Can there be assurance of salvation apart from Christian faith? It would be better, Wilfred Cantwell Smith instructs, to ask Hindus, Buddhists, and Moslems this than to speculate. But to think of it along Wesleyan lines, the sanctifying Spirit is present throughout the world within every man and woman, working to establish a saving relationship. While Wesleyans understand that this presence produces more abundant fruit among those going onward on their spiritual journey to Christlikeness, nascent fruits of the Spirit might be evident in any person who is obedient to Christ's Spirit. May one be obedient to a nameless, voiceless spirit within? Or to a differently named God? May one establish redemptive relationship with a God whose person and even personalness are hidden or unrevealed? The likelihood of all this seems remote through Christian eyes, but who can say how God might act? God might give some form of assurance related to Wesley's criteria of both inward and outward signs. The outward signs, or fruits of the Spirit, it seems to me, would be transcultural, and would include elements of Christlikeness. One may even be like Christ without ever knowing Christ by name; but how much better to have before one the image to follow.[22]

C. Christianization

While the holiness movement has been vitally interested in leading men and women into the experience of salvation, it has not been content with this. It has urged converts onward to entire sanctification and Christlikeness. Sometimes this call has overemphasized legalistic conformity and the crisic experience itself, to the neglect of the processes which both precede and follow crises, and also has neglected the moral

22. Close to this view is Hans Kung, "The Freedom of Religions," in *Attitudes toward Other Religions: Some Christian Interpretations,* ed. Owen C. Thomas (New York: Harper, 1969), pp. 213-17, and Karl Rahner, "Anonymous Christianity and the Missionary Task of the Church," in *Theological Investigations,* trans. David Bourke, vol. 12 (New York: Seabury, 1974), pp. 161-78 (esp. p. 165). Compare Wilfred Cantwell Smith, "The Christian in a Religiously Plural World," in *Christianity and Other Religions: Selected Readings,* ed. John Hick and Brian Hebblethwaite (Glasgow: Collins, 1980), pp. 102-3, 106-7. Also see Raimundo Panikkar, *The Unknown Christ of Hinduism,* rev. ed. (Maryknoll, N.Y.: Orbis, 1981), pp. 48-61.

content of the experience. But in general the call to holiness of heart and life is the same as that made by Christians at many times across history, a call toward complete discipleship, toward present salvation from sin, and toward both maturity of character and Christlikeness. The goal is to make true Christians of converts.

Looked at in this way, those in the holiness movement should be attuned to the present calls issued from various quarters in Christianity which advocate a kind of "paradigm shift" away from soteriological questions about the "lost" which cannot really be answered and toward an emphasis on discipleship or, to put it another way, living as Christians in this world. The problem apparent to many was apparent to early advocates of holiness, that Christian "conversion" has become morally meaningless. The zeal for making as many converts and planting as many churches as possible has always been an essential part of the Christian mission, insofar as holiness churches are concerned; but it has been considered only one part of it. The overarching mission is to see moral transformation, Christlikeness reproduced in converts, and the kingdom of Christ come to fulfillment. Too often evangelical conversion has required no transformation of character, and relatively few changes in belief, except about the necessity of "accepting" Christ for one's own salvation. Once a personal "decision" is made for Christ, persons are left quite as they were, with, perhaps, as much materialism and unconcern for others as they had before. Values go unchallenged; egoism remains. Among some, "discipleship" is a matter of Bible reading, habitual prayer times, church attendance, tithing, and the like — none of which requires transformation of character to be accomplished. For this reason, little seems to be achieved by Christians in the great moral arenas of life. There is no critique of materialism or capitalism; no evident attachment of Christian faith to how one responds to world hunger, illiteracy, poverty, and overpopulation. There is no call for a change in suburban and affluent lifestyle. Holiness advocates, admittedly, have not been great exceptions to this. Across the years they have accommodated themselves to living comfortably and well, with little discernible difference between themselves and other citizens. But this is a renunciation of the holiness message and contribution to Christendom.[23]

---

23. Among writers with holiness movement roots making such criticisms of modern evangelicalism are Howard A. Snyder, *The Problem of Wineskins: Church*

It was not always so. Former generations linked sanctification to simple and distinct ways of life. The "free" in Free Methodism was freedom from worldliness creeping into the Methodist Episcopal Church in the form of pew rentals, musical instruments, costly apparel, and — not in the least — tolerance of slavery. The worldliness of the church and its members was a loud and consistent cry of late-nineteenth-century holiness advocates. They identified with those seeming to be neglected by denominations rising in social status. They denounced alcohol because they saw its effects on poverty-laden families and on society as a whole. They gave women the right to preach the gospel as ordained ministers, believing, along with other reformers, that women, once given the right to vote and other prominent roles in society, would bring greater social purity.[24]

Even the later legalistic emphases banning theater, movie and circus attendance, smoking, mixed swimming, jewelry, makeup, and "bobbed" hair were to holiness people marks of purity; at best they were symbols of choices made renouncing the sinful world for the sake of remaking it. These symbols of holiness marked discipleship to them, distinguishing them from the "world." As is the tendency in all religious movements, the symbols became substitutes for the reality to which they pointed, purity of heart. The outward signs tended to sup-

---

Structure in a Technological Society (Downers Grove, Ill.: InterVarsity Press, 1975); Jon Johnston, *Will Evangelicalism Survive Its Own Popularity?* (Grand Rapids: Zondervan, 1980); Ronald J. Sider, *Rich Christians in an Age of Hunger: A Biblical Study,* rev. ed. (Downers Grove, Ill.: InterVarsity, 1984). Note also Richard S. Taylor's comments on the "feebleness" of modern repentance in *Exploring Christian Holiness,* vol. 3: *The Theological Formulation* (Kansas City: Beacon Hill, 1985), pp. 136-38. Note the statement of Stephen Neill that "Protestant missionaries have gone out with the earnest desire to win souls for Christ, but with very little idea of what is to happen to the souls when they have been won," in *Concise Dictionary of the Christian World Mission,* ed. Stephen Neill, Gerald Anderson, and John Goodwin (Nashville: Abingdon, 1971), p. 109. Also see Mortimer Arias, "The Kingdom of God," *Wesleyan Theological Journal* 23 (spring-fall 1988): 33-45.

24. Phineas Bresee, "Holiness and Civic Righteousness," in *Sermons on Isaiah* (Kansas City: Nazarene, 1926), pp. 79-87; Paul Boyer, *Urban Masses and Moral Order in America, 1820-1920* (Cambridge: Harvard University Press, 1978), pp. 195-204; Janette Hassey, *No Time for Silence: Evangelical Women in Public Ministry around the Turn of the Century* (Grand Rapids: Zondervan, 1986), pp. 97-105, 125-34; Rebecca Laird, *Ordained Women in the Church of the Nazarene: The First Generation* (Kansas City: Nazarene, 1993).

plant the more gracious and positive marks of the Spirit, including love, kindness, compassion, and joy.[25]

But at heart the holiness movement represents a call to live with full and serious commitment to the ethics of the kingdom, with optimism that kingdom life can be lived here and now. Though compassion has not always characterized the behavior or attitudes of champions of holiness, it is essential to the doctrine. Social benevolence characterized John Wesley's concern for the poor of his day, and America's early holiness advocates generally held positive views toward social reformation. However, both fundamentalism and the institutional pressures of organizing boards and establishing colleges crowded out much interest after the 1920s. But by the 1960s revivals of urban work and compassionate ministries were evident and growing among holiness bodies.[26]

The holiness movement has not been content with either emotional experiences void of ethical content or bare initiation experiences into Christianity. The churches in the holiness movement traditionally have called believers on to perfection, which demands an on-

25. Purkiser, chap. 8, "The Struggle over Standards"; Kirkemo, pp. 87-88, 103-4, 172-73, 384-85. See B. W. Miller and G. F. Owen, *Behold He Cometh: Inspirational Messages on the Second Coming* (Kansas City: Nazarene, 1924), and Basil Miller and U. E. Harding, *Cunningly Devised Fables: Modernism Exposed and Refuted* (n.p., n.d.), for bombastic responses to American culture in the 1920s. The best attempt to link conservative mores to both social ethics and the teachings of Wesley is that of the Free Methodist writer Mary A. Tenney, *Blueprint for a Christian World: An Analysis of the Wesleyan Way* (Winona Lake, Ind.: Light and Life Press, 1953). In the 1950s some on the rightward fringes wanted to see specific rules which would prohibit women's jewelry, makeup, and the like, and television. When the holiness denominations did not do so, some left to form their own denominations, including the Bible Missionary Church and the Church of the Bible Covenant. This left the holiness churches freer to move closer to American norms while still prohibiting smoking, alcohol, dancing, and movies. See A. O. Hendricks to Glenn Griffith, March 20, 1956, Nazarene Archives, Kansas City, Missouri; Spencer Johnson, "Twenty-One Reasons Why I Am Leaving the Church of the Nazarene" (pamphlet, n.d.).

26. Timothy L. Smith, *Called unto Holiness*, pp. 269-71, 289-97, 322-27, 349-50; Charles E. Jones, *Perfectionist Persuasion: The Holiness Movement and American Methodism, 1867-1936* (Metuchen, N.J.: Scarecrow, 1974), pp. 133-42. Compare Neil B. Wiseman, ed., *To the City with Love: A Sourcebook of Nazarene Urban Ministries* (Kansas City: Beacon Hill, 1976); Paul Moore and Joe Musser, *Shepherd of Times Square* (Nashville: Thomas Nelson, 1979); R. Franklin Cook and Steve Weber, *The Crisis: How the Hunger and Disaster Fund Is Helping* (Kansas City: Nazarene, 1987).

going transformation of values and character. Salvation is not merely defined as a future state of bliss, but rather as a present redemptive relationship to God. The journey in holiness is one of grace, with stages toward greater Christlikeness and the greater demonstration of perfect love.

Holiness demands that this love compel both respect for the dignity of others and deeds of compassion. Human beings must never serve as means toward some end, no matter how seemingly noble; it demands that actions, even evangelistic ones, be free of ulterior motives. It does not win by coercion, tricks, or gimmicks. Compassion is not a means of evangelism. It is an end in itself, a fruit of the hallowing Spirit. Those of the holiness movement believe that the Sermon on the Mount presents a realizable ethic for this time and place. It is an optimism that the kingdom is within as well as beyond the scope of this world, and that the kingdom is coming to completion, slowly through the providence and grace of God, and through the obedient responses of men and women of faith to God's intent.[27]

Wesleyanism is basically optimistic that sanctifying grace is sufficient enough for men and women to overcome both egocentricity and ethnocentricity, and to love others with pure motives and intents. At least that is the ideal. Love entails respect for the identity and being of the other. It refuses to allow status systems or hierarchies to dictate relationships. It seeks to relate to others with empathy, but not condescension.

What does this have to offer interfaith dialogue? It affirms the integrity of both partners in dialogue. It sees dialogue as taking place between equals. It does not hide an ulterior goal behind the stated ones. Even more, it links common religious goals which transcend those separating religions. Living now by kingdom of God standards is an image of world peace to which all faiths aspire. Christianity maintains that personal transformation of character is a necessary part of the kingdom, that inward value reorientations and outward lifestyle ad-

27. Leon O. Hynson, *To Reform the Nation: Theological Foundations of Wesley's Ethics* (Grand Rapids: Zondervan, 1984), chap. 5; Theodore W. Jennings, Jr., *Good News to the Poor: John Wesley's Evangelical Economics* (Nashville: Abingdon, 1990), chap. 7, "The Theological Basis of Wesley's Ethic"; Stephen S. Kim, "A Wesleyan Vision of Mission and Evangelism for the Twenty-first Century," *Journal of the Academy for Evangelism in Theological Education* 6 (1990-91): 42, 45, 50-52.

justments must characterize those living by the kingdom of God, and yet that these values cannot be identified with any one political agenda. It begins, first, by asking that Christians live as Christians, according to their own religion's values, which are rooted, content-wise, in the person of Christ. The kingdom does not come by coercion or to coerce, by violence or to initiate violence: it is a peaceable kingdom ushered in by peaceable means through kingdom-oriented and transformed men and women.[28]

Ones who are truly disciples of Christ have given up self-centered and ethnocentered ambitions and dreams. Their goals are broader — to topple the walls which separate classes, races, religions, and nations. If making Christlike citizens of the kingdom is the mission of God, then this transcends goals which aim only at personal salvation. The emphasis on personal salvation may sometimes tend to be self-centered and self-pleasing, and not to lead to renouncing self for the sake of others. Furthermore, the emphasis on personal salvation fits nicely with the narcissism and "me-centeredness" of the later part of the twentieth century. However, it does not fit with calls within many religions for holiness, which are calls for self-renunciation and self-denial. That is, measures of holiness as best understood by Christians are not so that "I" may be saved, but so that the kingdom might come. It is a holistic concern. Without this teleological component made clear, Christian and other holiness movements succumb to quietism and mysticism.[29]

For the Christian the way of holiness is the way of Christ. It is a way of concern for the welfare of society more than the salvation of self. Precisely what holiness is not is a self-centered obsession; it is the

28. Much in consonance with John H. Yoder, *The Politics of Jesus* (Grand Rapids: Wm. B. Eerdmans Publishing Co., 1972), and Stanley Hauerwas, *The Peaceable Kingdom: A Primer in Christian Ethics* (Notre Dame, Ind.: University of Notre Dame Press, 1983), pp. 111-15. See also Timothy L. Smith, "The Holy Spirit and Peace," in *Perspectives on Peacemaking: Biblical Options in the Nuclear Age*, ed. John A. Bernbaum (Ventura, Calif.: Regal, 1984), pp. 89-105.

29. Richard Quebedeaux, *The Wordly Evangelicals* (San Francisco: Harper and Row, 1980). See also Dallas Willard, *The Spirit of the Disciplines: Understanding How God Changes Lives* (New York: Harper, 1988), preface, pp. 220-50, 258-65. Among recent calls for a shift away from soteriological and toward discipleship models of the Christian mission, see Newbigin, pp. 121-27, 176-80; Watson, pp. 21-35, 109-14, 130-31; and David J. Bosch, *Transforming Mission: Paradigm Shifts in Theology of Mission* (Maryknoll, N.Y.: Orbis, 1991), chaps. 2, 12.

abandonment of concern for self. Although those in the holiness movement are as easily prone as anyone to being self-obsessed, the heart of the message is one of selflessness and radical discipleship. It is not really world-renouncing in the sense of some other "holiness" movements in other religions, but world-reforming, with teleologic aims, those of implementing Christ's ethics and kingdom. To the Christian such grounds are christocentric, revealed in and through Christ. Yet it would not be surprising to find impulses in other religions or individuals toward similar aims which should be affirmed and joined forces with, if the same Spirit of Christ is at work in all.[30]

The import of the "great commission," it is clear, is to make disciples. Baptizing and teaching are means toward this aim. In the context of Matthew it is clear that this mandate is one of bringing men and women into kingdom-relatedness and not only into a "conversion" experience. If the mandate of the church is to call men and women to a high quality of discipleship, it must never be content with narrowly defined soteriological goals, and must press men and women onward to new thresholds of commitment. However muted, this has been the message of Wesleyanism, and is its contribution to the religious dialogues of the world.

---

30. Compare Mircea Eliade, *The Sacred and the Profane: The Nature of Religion,* trans. Willard R. Trask (New York: Harcourt, Brace and World, 1959), pp. 179-88, 195-201; William Johnston, *The Inner Eye of Love: Mysticism and Religion* (San Francisco: Harper and Row, 1978), chaps. 14, 16, 18. Bruce Nicholls, "New Theological Approaches in Muslim Evangelism," in *The Gospel and Islam: A Compendium,* ed. Don M. McCurry, abridged ed. (Monrovia, Calif.: MARC, 1979), pp. 119-25, emphasizes the kingdom of God as key to the proclamation of the gospel to Moslems.

CHAPTER THIRTEEN

Elements of a Conversation

S. MARK HEIM

As in any living encounter, much took place at this consultation that was not captured in the written presentations. Since both ecumenical theology and interfaith relations depend on dialogue, this book would be incomplete without a sampling of the discussion that surrounded the papers it contains. There is no attempt to provide a verbatim account, but only to represent issues and perspectives that enriched the sessions.

Our meeting was inaugurated with "job descriptions" from five persons who outlined what they felt were crucial contemporary needs for Christians responding to religious pluralism. Two spoke from the primary context of interfaith relations. Mtangulizi Sanyika, a layperson deeply involved in Christian-Muslim relations, commended a focus on practice, the concrete behavior of people in various traditions. He also suggested careful attention to the African American experience, a context that has its unique manifestations within both Islam and Christianity and therefore gives Muslim-Christian relations a special character. Sanyika pointed to several key areas. First, he strongly encouraged biblical study as a key resource. The Bible is a record of interreligious and multicultural encounters; it is full of "people having experiences with other people of other religions." And these were not always experiences of conflict. Particularly, Christians need to intensively reexamine the story of Abraham, Sarah, Hagar, Isaac, and Ishmael with both Judaism and Islam in mind, for both the unity and the conflict of the "Abrahamic faiths" are rooted in this story and the different versions of it internalized in each tradition. Finally, he encouraged Christians to give special attention to identifying prayers which are theologically appropriate for Christians to offer in common with those from various faiths, so that people in our churches can be equipped and confident to undertake concrete acts of worship with others.

Harold Vogelaar, a seminary professor with extensive experience in the Middle East and in Muslim-Christian dialogue, outlined a series of theological topics which are key elements in Christian understanding of religions. How are we to understand the biblical themes of covenant and election in relation to God's covenant with the whole creation? Does our understanding of the biblical covenant include a shared concern for peace, justice, and care of the earth? Does God's covenant with Adam and Eve or with Noah provide helpful perspectives on how people of differing faith traditions might relate with integrity and mutual respect? Perhaps the most fundamental issue for Christians is our conception of mission. Vogelaar suggests that we return to the whole life and ministry of Jesus as our model for mission, and look toward biblical images like "leaven" or "firstfruits" as descriptive of the role of Christians. Further, we need study that "links the mission of the church with the work of the Holy Spirit" as God's living and pervasive presence in the world. Another critical question is whether we understand interfaith dialogue as peripheral to the gospel or essential to it. Is it a mere tool to be used when needed or is there an indissoluble link between Christian mission and dialogue?

Dorothy Rose, executive director of the Interreligious Council of Central New York, reinforces this last point. She noted that when she saw a prospectus for the consultation that mentioned the need for a theological articulation of interfaith dialogue as an "activity in continuity with apostolic faith," she said "hallelujah." This described exactly what she sees as the critical need. Of course we need papers, books, videos, and curricula that teach us about various religions. But in her view if we do not internalize outreach to those in other faiths as part of our identity — right along with worship, prayer, scriptural study, service to neighbor, or any other essential part of the Christian life — then we cannot expect any dramatic change.

Rose notes that in her organization she works daily with those who have already decided that a vital relationship between Christians and adherents of other faiths is important. She reviewed some of the personal reasons that are sometimes behind these decisions. But she said she was struck that among these reasons there was little or no sense of any intrinsically Christian motivation for this encounter with the "other." The absence of such a theological foundation has been felt in recent years as some Christian councils were transformed into interfaith organizations, or new interfaith organizations were founded. In most cases these changes took place without any clear theological rationale from the Christian participants. She pointed particularly to the difficulty surrounding the recent (1994) decision of the National Association of Ecumenical Staff to drop the membership requirement that one be "a Christian worker." There is no doubt in her mind "that sincere and deeply held Christian theological convictions militated against opening up the Association to those of other living religions." If Christians are to sustain both their authentic faith commitments and their active participation in such organizations, they will need to articulate theological convictions no less deeply held that ground that participation.

Clark Lobenstine, Executive Director of the Washington, D.C., Interfaith Council, picked up some of Sanyika's comments, particularly the emphasis on concrete religious practice. The burning need that Lobenstine sees is to apply theology to issues in the daily lives of people in pluralistic situations. Christians need to cooperate actively in formulating guidelines for interfaith marriages, resources for interfaith prayer and worship, principles regarding evangelism and proselytism, materials to help those in local congregations understand the rites and rituals of their neighbors. Ecumenical clergy groups are a particularly significant arena for this work to be focused in a local community.

Lobenstine put special stress on the role of seminaries. Students preparing for ministry should study the theological basis and resources for interfaith relations. It is also essential that the discussion not remain at the level of generalities, but that specific Jewish-Christian or Muslim-Christian issues — and others — be addressed. The challenge he sees is for such concerns to become not simply additional electives, but a part of the fundamental biblical, theological, and pastoral work. Nor can this remain an entirely internal Christian dialogue: we need to invite representatives of other traditions to participate in our reflection.

Finally, Michael Rivas, of the United Methodist General Board of Global Ministries, said Christians are unlikely soon to come to consensus on the most faithful response to religious diversity. Understanding of our different approaches as Christians is as important as understanding the other religions. We need to clarify and catalogue the various theological assumptions from which different groups in our communions approach other faiths. Rivas also suggests that in addition to our history we should explore our communions' contemporary actions. It is common for our churches to form alliances and coalitions with other religious and secular groups for a variety of purposes. There is a "working theology" here, implicit theological assumptions that merit further elaboration.

Rivas added another consideration: Many of the conflicts among Christians over interfaith issues may be in significant measure rooted in barriers of race and class. Even our choice of groups as possible partners for dialogue or for respectful study can be influenced by these factors more than theological conviction. Santeria may attract millions of adherents, and yet Christians hesitate to study it with the same seriousness as Buddhism, for instance. "Are these barriers really theological, or are they more cultural and ideological in nature?"

*   *   *

Discussion following the presentation of papers by Donovan, Finger, Solivan, and Rock focused particularly on Christology and the specificity of Christian commitment. Both Finger and Solivan stressed that in their communions (Mennonite, Pentecostal) a Christian way of life was the primary emphasis, rather than doctrine. Finger stressed that for Mennonites this had fostered a nonimperialistic form of Christian witness, based on the teachings of Jesus in the Gospels. Solivan indicated that Pentecostals respond to ecumenism and interfaith dialogue with a very practical observation. The Christian denominations most deeply involved in both appear to Pentecostals to be painfully lacking in church growth and in transforming spiritual power for individuals.

Must Christians "suspend" universal claims for Christ to authentically participate in interfaith relations? All agreed that Christians should not mitigate their own commitment to Christ, as the basis on which they thought and acted. Solivan noted that Muslim friends had sometimes reflected on conversation with Christians as follows: "How quickly you Christians give up your Jesus — what else do you have to speak from?" However, some did advocate suspending or bracketing the conviction that Christ is the source of salvation for all.

211

This inevitably led further into discussion of Christology itself. Rock stressed that Christ is the irreducible basis on which Christians do their thinking, but our understanding of that basis — Christology — "has been changing since it began." *Which* convictions about Jesus are appropriate? Can Christians find more positive guidance for inter-faith relations by focusing on the historical Jesus or incarnational chris-tological doctrines? For instance, it was noted that little had been said so far about the kingdom of God in Jesus' message. Would not a Chris-tian approach that did not draw so much attention to Jesus' person but focused on the purposes he served provide more common ground? Others disagreed. It is true, Rock indicated, that Christians sometimes confused the kingdom of God with the church — a confusion that Re-formed theology sharply challenged. But Finger observed that in the nineteenth century "the kingdom of God" was abstracted from Jesus and — defined in Western cultural and political terms — became as imperialistic as any christological claims.

One participant pointed out that in the consultation many pre-senters had found their most exciting models for interfaith relations in such "conservative" sources as Scripture and patristic theology. Another noted that in his experience some of the "best-thought-out" theologies of interfaith relations come from some of the most theologi-cally conservative positions." As an example, he pointed to Pope John Paul II, who uses traditional christological principles to arrive at some of the most open statements on religious pluralism. "High" or "low" Christologies, doctrine or practice: these polarities are largely foreign to Christian tradition itself. Opting for one side of such dualities offers little prospect of solving our problems.

Disagreement focused on the extent of change in Christian faith that honest consideration of religious diversity requires. Some argued that without substantive reconstruction of Christian beliefs, the church becomes increasingly irrelevant to people living in pluralistic environ-ments. Solivan expressed reservations about this, noting that such demands for change were a very modern idea. Does the entire church have to alter its faith for the sake of dialogue? Are there other important priorities that have equal or greater claim, such as evangelism or lib-eration? All seemed to agree that biblical and theological illiteracy within Christian communities was a significant obstacle to progress. On the one hand people reject "new" ideas that in fact are rooted in our sources. On the other, they are often unaware of occasions of religious division — such as the variant readings of the story of Abraham by Jews, Christians, and Muslims — because they do not even know the story as it is handed on in their tradition.

*   *   *

After presentation of papers by James Deotis Roberts, Michael Oleksa, Nehemiah Thompson, and Fred Norris, discussion resumed, with the focus turning to the matter of mission highlighted by Oleksa and Norris. One of the first questions raised was whether interfaith dialogue and mission are not in inevitable contradiction. What is the aim of mission? Norris responded that mission is grounded in the belief that the best of religion is to be found in Christ. The Christian's calling is to witness to this, though the response of others to that witness is between them and God. Others suggested that mission itself is premised on the assumption that God's truth and light is already present in various cultures and religions: on what other basis could one make an appeal for Christian truth?

Solivan said that in many cases it was missionaries who moved the church to consider issues of interfaith dialogue, just as many missionaries were pioneers in the study of other religions. Paul Meyendorff, who presented Oleksa's paper, stressed that the Christian position needs to be nonrelativist. God, creation, incarnation, Trinity — these things are held to be real. The most effective partners in dialogue, in any tradition, are those who have personally tasted the reality of the objects of their faith. But he pointed out that within such an outlook there are many different models of mission. He instanced an Orthodox example, Herman of Alaska, who lived twenty years on a Siberian island with native people without any direct attempt at conversion. Norris agreed, arguing that in the early centuries of the church mission was not done in a "Constantinian" mode but from a position of marginality. Moreover, that world was also one of tremendous religious diversity.

Another participant indicated that the question of mission and conversion is even more complex than first appears. There is a tension in religion between individuals and communities. This participant was aware of people who were born into one tradition and are now living

213

in another. But not all would describe themselves as "converts" from one to the other: They would say they never truly experienced the fullness of their natal tradition, or personally appropriated it. This individual freedom merits respect, she said, and yet in many religious groups the idea of detaching oneself from the community is out of the question. James Deotis Roberts noted that in his black Baptist tradition these issues of religious freedom — crucial to Baptists historically — are a primary basis for interfaith connection. The rights of other religious communities to freedom and respect are strongly defended, but so too is the "soul liberty" of individuals to follow their faith convictions. In his denomination, strong evangelical personal witness goes hand in hand with powerful social justice concerns. In interfaith relations, the emphasis tends to be on questions of ethics and social justice.

Norris pointed out that in our contemporary environment an affirmation of "pluralism" could quickly degenerate into a consumerist individualism where people shopped for religious enhancements for their lives but avoided responsibilities and connection. Meyendorff pointed out the importance in this connection of the early church's view of personhood as relational. The image of God is not in any individual but in the relations of humans to each other: in Genesis this is spoken of in terms of male-female relation; in the New Testament the community of the church, the body of Christ, is the relational image of God.

*   *   *

Following summaries of the papers from Peter Slater, Mozella Mitchell, Dan Martensen, and Floyd Cunningham (presented by Paul Bassett), discussion turned spontaneously toward issues of theological anthropology. Our common human nature is frequently proposed as the best foundation for interfaith dialogue. For instance, Rock and Martensen expressed interest in the Protestant notion of *simul justus et peccator*. If Christians recognize that they remain sinners at the same time they are saved by God, this can lead to a humbler attitude toward other faiths. Rock suggested that if all human beings are fallen, then any virtue or Christlikeness that is encountered among those of other traditions must signal the presence of divine grace. Mitchell suggested that the distinctive mix of "sacred" and "secular" in black churches reflected a similar appreciation of the mixed quality of Christian life. She also noted that "anthropological poverty" is a phrase used both by black and Third World theologians to designate the destruction of peoples' culture, the stigmatization by others as less than fully human. Therefore a common struggle with those whose humanity is denied is seen as the primary focus for interreligious work.

Martensen's motto from the nineteenth-century Danish theologian N. F. S. Grundtvig, "first human, and only then Christian," attracted a good deal of comment. Many saw it as an excellent avenue to dialogue. One participant pointed out that in Buddhist-Christian dialogue this is a natural focus, since Buddhists often see Christian views of original sin and fallenness as much more fundamental beliefs than those about God or Christ. However, though Christians share certain perspectives on humanity, they are not of one mind on this anthropological approach. Cunningham's paper had pointed out that the holiness movement, which developed in North America as a largely negative reaction to the American Christianity around it, was hardly likely to regard other religions more positively than it did existing Christian communions. Bassett noted that the holiness movement, as its name indicated, affirmed graced human nature's capacity for perfection, rejecting the notion that Christians, though saved, must remain at the same time active sinners. Finger added that Anabaptists were also critical of *simul justus et peccator*, which they thought too readily condoned Christian participation in oppressive or unjust structures rather than demanding behavior that reflected the gospel.

These contrasting approaches mean that when Christians speak of seeking common ground with other religions in our shared human nature they do not all agree on the definition of what is common. However, they do tend to agree that it can at times be experientially discovered, whether this is a common experience of our sinful inclinations or of the otherwise inexplicable transformations of divine grace. Here as in many other aspects of the discussion, participants found that the theological diversity among Christians was replicated in the approaches to religious pluralism.

*   *   *

The consultation was fortunate to have two Muslim observers. Dr. Adile Ozdemir was on an extended visit to the United States from Izmir,

Turkey. Dr. Ibrahim Abu-Rabi' is a professor at the Duncan Black Mac-Donald Center for Islamic Studies at Hartford Seminary in Connecticut. At a session for open discussion, they were invited to share their reflections on what they had heard.

Dr. Ozdemir, who has been a significant participant in Muslim-Christian dialogue in Turkey, made a number of gracious comments about the maturity and self-criticism he saw in the intra-Christian conversations at this consultation. This is a type of conversation he said he would like to see happen in a similar way within his own tradition. He also indicated the fundamental importance of unity — not only the unity of Islam but the unity of humanity — in the Qur'an and Islamic thought. He observed that he had been expecting to hear sharper and more definitive statements of the differences between the various Christian denominations. In light of what he had heard, the distinctions seemed difficult to articulate.

In fourteen years of interreligious dialogue Ozdemir had met and known Christians of many different orientations. He suggested that regardless of denomination, some attitudes are never helpful for dialogue. One, which he encountered more often in "conservative" Christians, was an inner feeling of superiority, coupled with an insistence on viewing Islam and Christianity through categories that were fixed in an earlier historical period. Another, which he encountered in "liberal" Christians, was a relativizing of theological questions, an insistence — conscious or not — on a thoroughly secular basis for dialogue in which no truly religious arguments come up. He encouraged the participants in the consultation to keep both these dangers in mind, as they sought both genuine openness and genuine integrity as Christians.

Dr. Abu-Rabi' also noted the striking diversity of Christian views he had heard, as well as the diversity of persons offering them: black, Asian, Hispanic, white, men and women. He said he had learned a good deal about the problems that face contemporary Christians around questions of authority, Scripture, history, and tradition. In many ways Islam and Christianity face these same problems together. Traditional Christian society has been severely disrupted by modernity, and the Islamic world faces the same secular challenge. In this there is an opportunity for cooperation.

But he said he was disappointed he had not heard more in the consultation about ideological issues. Though there was frequent mention of social justice, there was little attention to the way in which the world is in fact divided politically and economically. These divisions are integrally mixed up in any interreligious discussion. The relations of Islam and Christianity are tied up with the relations of Western and Islamic nations. With the fall of communism, for instance, he fears that for some Westerners Arabs or Muslims are becoming a new universal enemy. There are great dangers in thinking in "essentialist" terms of Christians or Muslims as monolithic communities. Both groups include rich and poor, men and women, diverse ethnic, political, and cultural traditions. To take Lebanon as one example, Abu-Rabi' pointed out that the possible pairings of the many Muslim and Christian groups are dizzying.

In the lively discussion that followed many picked up on Abu-Rabi''s comments about cultural and political issues. For the most part this focused on Muslims in the United States. In response to questions, Abu-Rabi' was frank to acknowledge that there was more freedom for diversity and exploration in Muslim thought in the United States than in most Islamic countries, and this might give Muslims here a special role. The United States is also unique in bringing together Muslims from groups which do not get along well together in other parts of the world. He pointed out, however, that in many cases the lack of healthy internal dialogue in much of the Islamic world was significantly influenced by the legacy of Western political involvement in those lands and even current policies. There is a "brain drain" of Muslim intellectuals toward the United States and other Western countries. Interestingly, he pointed out, many of these people become more serious and devout Muslims in their new environment than they might have been in their countries of origin. In his view, a ferment is under way which will produce an Islamicized American way of life, similar to different existing forms of Islam. African Americans are perhaps the most important community for this development, Abu-Rabi' suggested, both because of the long history of African Islam and because African Americans feel more strongly than recent Muslim arrivals that this is their culture.

Ozdemir said that in Turkey people had accepted a fundamental transition from a traditional to a modernized society. In his view the overwhelming majority adopt assumptions about politics, human rights, reason, and science which are also common in the West. In many ways this cultural marriage has been a success. But one way in which it has failed is that it has lost a religious vision, a religious vigor. Islam itself has become secularized. In opposition, a revivalist spirit has strengthened. This spirit seeks to see a living and visible religious presence in society. And it also wants to exercise a discrimination toward what comes from the West, picking and choosing between positive and negative elements without assimilating everything. He lives in the midst of this encounter. Ozdemir believes that "fundamentalism" is a misleading characterization of the revivalist side of this tension. There are abuses at both ends of the spectrum, but Turkey's example is crucial in the attempt to find a way forward.

Mtangulizi Sanyika picked up the issue of Islam in the United States and agreed that the African American community was a key element, because there are few African American family networks which do not now have Muslim members. Interfaith has become a personalized matter for African Americans: the Muslim is my sister or my brother first and not some generic stereotype. It is important for Christians to recognize the variety of Islamic experiences in this country. You can't extrapolate from Saudi Arabia to a Lebanese or Indonesian or African American Muslim. As we engage in conversation we also must recognize that the tools of the Enlightenment that we automatically bring have not been absolutized in the same way for most Muslims. Christians may be better advised that their own distinctive faith is a better starting point for respectful dialogue, if the focus rests on religious experience more than traditional dogma.

Peter Slater responded to Abu-Rabi''s comment about ideology by commending the thought of Martin Luther King, Jr. Here was a major Christian figure who addressed the way in which theology can be used either to reinforce social divisions or to liberate people from them. He was much criticized for bringing "ideology" into the church, but he fought racial and economic oppression on a fundamentally theological basis. The honor that is now given to King is often focused on his leadership of a social movement, but little serious attention is given to the theology behind that movement. King was influenced by Mahatma Gandhi's doctrine of *satyagraha* — truth force — which, in turn, had been influenced by C. F. Andrews's interpretation of the Sermon on the Mount. Mary Ann Donovan added some instances from Roman Catholic experience in Central America and suggested that Christians in the United States are often inhibited about bringing ideology and theology together because of qualms about the separation of church and state. We are clear that there are negative ways of combining faith and ideological commitments. How do we do it responsibly?

Fred Norris indicated that he felt an Enlightenment "ideology" had largely determined the way that theology and church history were taught. He was struck that in his own education in topflight institutions he had learned virtually nothing about the history of Islam or of interfaith relations. Even the best of our teachers and resources offer little help. To take his own arena of seminary teaching, he says we have little idea what a seminary would be like which was deeply committed to its own traditions and to interfaith dialogue.

Another participant remarked that he had heard a good deal of rhetoric about modernity and the Enlightenment, largely as a common foe of religions. He offered a different perspective, from one who works in Buddhist-Christian and also Confucian-Christian dialogue. Our conversation has been dominated by Muslim-Christian or Jewish-Christian dialogue. But there are more than a billion Chinese — the largest single group of humanity — and East Asia may well be the dominant economic force of the next century. In our consultation we have no one from that specific context. "Ideology" looks different in that part of the world. His dialogue partners for the most part think that modernity is the neatest thing since sliced bread. They are hungry for it, assimilating it and synthesizing their own religious traditions with it. Gandhi said that the only form in which God can come to the starving man is bread. An ideology won't feed him. From the East Asian perspective, what is interesting is the transformative, the effective power of modern methods. There is an important form of dialogue which takes place precisely on the "secular" ground of modernity.

These exchanges provoked some of the liveliest discussion of the consultation, which continued long after the end of this session!

* * *

The consultation closed with a panel of five persons who each offered a perspective on the conversation they had heard and the directions it set.

Debra Moody, the executive director of the Ohio Council of Churches, spoke of two themes she believed were particularly helpful

219

for Christians facing religious pluralism. The first clustered around the theme of "human first, then Christian" from Dan Martensen's paper. The idea of prevenient grace (stressed by Wesleyan authors), the emphasis on the realization of the kingdom of God (as opposed to confession of identical doctrine), and the emphasis on God's manifestation in the entire cosmos (in Michael Oleksa's paper) all point to convictions inherent in Christian faith which affirm the universality of God's presence and action. This provides a theological basis on which to build common human efforts.

A second theme was Christian ecumenical experience itself. Both bilateral conversations in which denominations move toward full unity and multilateral movements like the Churches of Christ Uniting (COCU) demonstrate what unity in diversity may actually look like. These experiences are crucial training for the mentality and techniques that we need in interfaith relations. We need to increasingly translate ecumenical principles into the interreligious realm.

If these were positive elements of the conversation, Moody also pointed to some crucial gaps. The consultation could offer few multicultural models of instances in which the church was adequately meeting the challenge of pluralism. Likewise, the way in which issues of racism and sexism cut across both our "external" interfaith relations and our "internal" ecclesial life has been mentioned but requires much more intensive dialogue. The consultation was also thin in examples of how these concerns might be concretely engaged by local congregations — at the level of community interaction and not just in terms of what individuals think about other faiths. Last of all, Moody called for special attention to "an interfaith theology of the Holy Spirit" which would take some of the themes in Sam Solivan's paper and pursue their pluralistic implications.

John Boonstra, executive minister, Washington Association of Churches, elaborated on the importance of ecumenism as a theological resource for response to religious pluralism. Christian ecumenism flourishes only when it becomes a lived reality in daily life. It is living together in the midst of differences that creates friendship and unity. There is a tension between "institutional" and "movement" ecumenism. The first seeks understanding and reconciliation among the traditions, structures, and practices of Christian communions. The second is composed of people from different denominations caught up in suffering or struggle together within historical transformations that transcend any single group. Within Christian ecumenical circles, this tension leads to a fundamental reconsideration of what we mean by church or "people of God."

Boonstra suggests that Christian ecumenism is training for what Matthew Fox calls "deep ecumenism," a movement that will "unleash the wisdom of all world religions." Ecumenism as it has existed so far provides us visions of how to live in a pluralistic world. But ecumenism cannot fulfill its intention as long as these visions stop short of the entire world and fail to incorporate cultures and religions on an equal footing, honoring "the mystery of God and the mystic in all of us." Theologies of equality will have to be formed out of common participation in the one struggle with global systems of inequality. It is here that the consultation has made only a very limited contribution.

Barbara Brown Zikmund, president of Hartford Seminary, responded from a somewhat different perspective. Interreligious relation plays a crucial role in the distinctive integrity of Christian faith and witness. In encountering other traditions, we grasp greater commonalities within the Christian family, we strengthen and articulate our own faith better, and we pass it on more effectively within our community as well as witness it more wisely to the world. We are also enabled by interfaith cooperation to carry out our Christian mandate to serve God and neighbor more faithfully.

The consultation led her to see several areas of theological work that deserve further attention. The first regards balancing integrity and openness in our faith. Can we conceive the core of apostolic faith in a way that leaves room for new insight from other traditions? Must Christians affirm that what is unique about Christ is of greater value than what is not? What would it mean to confess Christianity with greater emphasis on what is exemplary in Christ but not what is unique? The second question has to do with the place of mystery in our confession and witness. Can we leave more room for silence in our theology, without falling into relativism? Third, how can we uphold the faith that God's action in Christ is of cosmological significance without forcing other traditions into our mold? Fourth, are there limits to acceptable diversity? Is it legitimate to condemn practices or beliefs of a religious tradition from outside that tradition? Faith without tolerance violates the second commandment, "making a 'graven image' of *our* truth." Tolerance without faith violates the first commandment.

Elmo Familiaran, of the American Bible Society, stressed that the papers and discussion demonstrated the profound particularity of our Christian traditions. These particularities are in tension with each other, and yet they express a common commitment. And in all of the presentations he heard an honest confession that the Christian tradition has often been distorted and deformed. Three common themes stood out. One was constant return to the ethic of Jesus as a model for Christian practice in our pluralistic world. The second theme was the freedom of God, through the universal ministry of the Spirit. And the third was the pain of the divisiveness that exists among Christians in the midst of the current challenge.

These elements provide a thin outline of a way forward. We need a frank acknowledgment of the shared pain in our churches, our common lack of a confident and coherent response to religious diversity. This is the motive and foundation for ecumenical cooperation, a cooperation that will focus on love of neighbor and the extension of *koinonia* or Christian community to a vision of peace and harmony in the whole human family. The greatest contribution of a growing Christian unity will be to overcome fear of the future, and fear of our religious neighbors.

Elizabeth Mellen, from the Graymoor Ecumenical and Inter-religious Institute, spoke from the perspective of one involved in traditional Faith and Order ecumenical work. She pointed out that anyone familiar with those earlier conversations would see tremendous continuity with the discussion at this consultation. Different theological perspectives on authority or the church or baptism or ministry showed up here, in a new light. Therefore we learned anew to understand the texture of each other's traditions. The composition of the consultation — bringing together persons from Faith and Order, Interfaith Relations, and Ecumenical Networks — brought a healthy transcendence of the frequent ecumenical division between a "Faith and Order" theological emphasis and "Life and Work" social action emphasis.

She saw several important themes. One was the importance of experiences of marginalization. In different ways, African American Christians, Mennonites, Pentecostals, Orthodox, and others have known the struggle of minorities stigmatized within larger societies.

Varied though Christian communions' experiences of marginalization might be — racial, economic, or theological — they showed up as important points of reference for each communion's approach to religious diversity. Muslim observers reminded us that we cannot deal with religious pluralism if we do not frankly address political and economic issues which are frequently bound up in religious differences. In Christian ecumenical relations reference is frequently made to "nontheological factors" like institutional self-interest, cultural chauvinism, and racial prejudice which pose barriers to unity. In the interfaith area we need honesty and repentance about similar realities. The consultation also was helpful in highlighting sources of resistance to interfaith relations in our traditions, points that need to be addressed to evaluate the extent to which they are intrinsic to our Christian identity and the extent to which they can be reinterpreted.

Contributors

Floyd C. Cunningham (Church of the Nazarene)
Academic Dean and Professor of History and Religion
Asia-Pacific Nazarene Theological Seminary, Rizal, Philippines

Mary Ann Donovan, S.C. (Roman Catholic Church)
Professor of Historical Theology and Spirituality
Jesuit School of Theology, Berkeley, California

Thomas N. Finger (The Mennonite Church)
Professor of Systematic and Spiritual Theology
Eastern Mennonite Seminary

S. Mark Heim (American Baptist Churches in the USA)
Professor of Christian Theology
Andover Newton Theological School

Daniel F. Martensen (Evangelical Lutheran Church in America)
Director, Department for Ecumenical Affairs
Evangelical Lutheran Church in America

Mozella G. Mitchell (African Methodist Episcopal Zion Church)
Professor of Religious Studies
University of South Florida

Frederick W. Norris (Christian Church)
Dean E. Walker Professor of Church History and Professor of World
    Mission/Evangelism
Emmanuel School of Religion

Michael Oleksa (Orthodox Church in America)
Priest
St. Nicholas Church, Juneau, Alaska

Jay T. Rock (Presbyterian Church USA)
Co-director for Interfaith Relations
National Council of Churches of Christ in the USA

Peter Slater (Episcopal Church)
Professor Emeritus
Trinity College, Toronto, Canada

Samuel Solivan (Assembly of God)
Associate Professor of Christian Theology
Andover Newton Theological School

Nehemiah Thompson (United Methodist Church)
General Commission on Christian Unity and Interreligious Concerns
United Methodist Church

Participants (Panelists and Moderators)

John Boonstra (United Church of Christ)
Executive Minister
Washington Association of Churches

William D. Carpe (Christian Church — Disciples of Christ)
Pastor
Ludlow Christian Church, Ludlow, Kentucky

Elmo Familiaran (American Baptist Churches in the USA)
Director, Missionary Recruitment
International Ministries, American Baptist Churches in the USA

Deidre J. Good (Episcopal Church)
Professor of New Testament
General Theological Seminary

Clark Lobenstine (Presbyterian Church USA)
Executive Director
InterFaith Conference of Metropolitan Washington

Elizabeth H. Mellen (Episcopal Church)
Associate Director
Graymoor Ecumenical and Interreligious Institute

Paul Meyendorff (Orthodox Church in America)
Alexander Schmemann Professor of Liturgical Theology
St. Vladimir's Orthodox Theological Seminary

Lauree Hersch Meyer (Church of the Brethren)
Associate Professor of Theology
Colgate Rochester Divinity School/Bexley Hall/Crozer Theological
    Seminary

Debra Moody (African Methodist Episcopal Zion Church)
Executive Director
Ohio Council of Churches

Michael Rivas (United Methodist Church)
Deputy General Secretary, General Board of Global Ministries
United Methodist Church

James Deotis Roberts (American Baptist Churches in the USA)
Distinguished Professor of Philosophical Theology
Eastern Baptist Theological Seminary

Dorothy Rose (Episcopal Church)
Chief Executive Officer
InterReligious Council of Central New York

Mutangulizi Sanyika (Presbyterian Church USA)
Sojourner Truth Church, Roslyn, California

Harold Vogelaar (Evangelical Lutheran Church in America)
Scholar in Residence
Lutheran School of Theology, Chicago

Barbara Brown Zikmund (United Church of Christ)
President and Professor of American Religious History
Hartford Seminary

DATE DUE